DK EYEWITNESS

T0001263

TOP **10**
NEW YORK CITY

Top 10 New York City Highlights

The Top 10 of Everything

CONTENTS

New York City Area by Area

Within each Top 10 list in this book, no hierarchy of quality or popularity is implied. All 10 are, in the editor's opinion, of roughly equal merit.
  Throughout this book, floors are referred to in accordance with American usage; i.e., the "first floor" is at ground level.

Title page, front cover and spine
The stunning Manhattan Bridge
Back cover, clockwise from top left *Colorful buildings on Gay Street; Yellow cabs driving through Times Square; the High Line; Manhattan skyline; Central Park in winter*

Streetsmart

The rapid rate at which the world is changing is constantly keeping the DK Eyewitness team on our toes. While we've worked hard to ensure that this edition of New York City is accurate and up-to-date, we know that opening hours alter, standards shift, prices fluctuate, places close and new ones pop up in their stead. So, if you notice we've got something wrong or left something out, we want to hear about it. Please get in touch at **travelguides@dk.com**

Welcome to
New York City

High-kicking Broadway show tunes. World-class museums. Shopping on Fifth Avenue. Some of the tallest skyscrapers on the planet. Superlative cuisine. It's no surprise that New York is one of the most visited cities in the world. With DK Eyewitness Top 10 New York City, it's yours to explore.

New York, New York. As the saying goes, it's the city so nice, they named it twice. We agree: where else in the country can you cruise down the mighty **Hudson River**, climb to the crown of **Lady Liberty**, peruse phenomenal art and sculpture at the **Metropolitan Museum of Art**, stroll the shaded walkways of **Central Park**, and sip cocktails while gazing out at the most famous skyline in the world?

Few cities equal New York's diverse culinary offerings. It's not a question of finding a cuisine, but rather of choosing from the plethora of options, from boisterous Italian trattorias to old-world delis with towering pastrami sandwiches. The outstanding museums and iconic sights are equally varied, from the looming **Empire State Building** to the **Museum of Modern Art**, with one of the world's largest collections of contemporary art. The theater scene is also incomparable, from splashy Broadway shows with a cast of hundreds to tiny underground stages. Spend one evening on the buzzing streets of New York City and you will understand why it's called the city that never sleeps. Evenings start late, and go on even later, with bars and clubs in the Meatpacking District and the **Lower East Side** spilling over with revelers.

Whether you're coming for a weekend or a week, our Top 10 guide brings together the best of everything the city has to offer, from trendy **Tribeca** to the elegant **Upper East Side**. The guide has useful tips throughout, from seeking out what's free to getting off the beaten path, plus 15 easy-to-follow itineraries, designed to tie together a clutch of sights in a short space of time. Add inspiring photography and detailed maps, and you've got the essential pocket-sized travel companion. **Enjoy the book, and enjoy New York City**.

Clockwise from top: **Fulton Street Subway Station, Financial District, Statue of Liberty, Grand Central Terminal, Times Square, Chrysler Building, Bethesda Terrace Arcade in Central Park**

Exploring New York City

New York City is densely packed with sights and sounds. Whether you are visiting for a weekend or a week, it helps to strategize your sightseeing to maximize your time here. Here are ideas for two and four days of exploring the city.

Two Days in New York City

Day **❶**
MORNING

Enjoy the view from the **Statue of Liberty** *(see pp18–19)*, then saunter through **Lower Manhattan** *(see pp78–83)*, snapping photos of **Brooklyn Bridge** *(see p85)*. Have lunch in **Seaport District NYC** *(see p89)*.

AFTERNOON

Stroll through **Central Park** *(see pp30–31)* before perusing the **Metropolitan Museum of Art** *(see pp32–5)*.

Day **❷**
MORNING

Enjoy panoramic skyline views from atop the **Empire State Building** *(see pp12–13)*, followed by a walk up **Fifth Avenue** *(see pp14–15)*, making stops at its famous department stores.

AFTERNOON

Tour the **American Museum of Natural History** *(see pp40–43)*, before topping off your visit at **Times Square and the Theater District** *(see pp26–29)*.

Four Days in New York City

Day **❶**
MORNING

Get the lay of the land from atop the **Empire State Building** *(see pp12–13)*. Afterwards, window-shop along **Fifth Avenue** *(see pp14–15)*. Pass the **New York Public Library** *(see p128)*, then pop into **Grand Central Terminal** *(see p127)* before stopping by the **Rockefeller Center** *(see pp16–17)*.

AFTERNOON

Start your afternoon with contemporary art at **MoMA** *(see pp36–39)* followed by the world-class

Skyscrapers in Lower Manhattan tower over the streets below.

collections of the **Metropolitan Museum of Art** *(see pp32–5)*. Once you've had your fill of art, take a walk through **Central Park** *(see pp30–31)*.

Day **❷**
MORNING

Take the ferry (book ahead) to greet the morning on **Ellis Island** *(see pp20–23)*, followed by views from the crown of the **Statue of Liberty** *(see pp18–19)*.

AFTERNOON

Upon returning to Manhattan, walk through **Battery Park** *(see p81)* to the **National September 11 Memorial and Museum** *(see p80)*. Afterwards, head through Lower Manhattan, passing **City Hall Park** *(see p87)* and the **Brooklyn Bridge** *(see p85)*. Walk across the bridge to explore **Brooklyn Heights** *(see p155)*, and stay there for dinner and cocktails.

Day **❸**
MORNING

Arrive early at the **American Museum of Natural History** *(see pp40–43)* for a morning of exploration, plus a visit to the **Rose Center for Earth and Space**.

The facade of Grand Central Terminal is topped by a 13-ft- (4-m-) high clock.

City Hall Park is a peaceful spot next to City Hall and the Municipal Building.

AFTERNOON

Walk through the **Upper West Side** (see pp142–7) to the **Lincoln Center** (see p142), then head to **Times Square and the Theater District** (see pp26–29). Nab tickets to a Broadway show at the **TKTS booth** (see p73).

Day ❹
MORNING

Explore the elevated park, the **High Line** (see p121). Refuel at the **Chelsea Market** (see p122) with artisanal cheeses and fresh baked goods.

AFTERNOON

Explore **Greenwich Village** (see pp108–13), passing **Washington Square Park** (see pp108–9) on the way to **SoHo and Tribeca** (see pp102–7) for local cuisine and cocktails.

Top 10 New York City Highlights

Aerial view of Manhattan and the Hudson River

🔟 New York City Highlights

With its skyscrapers, great museums, and bright Broadway lights, New York is a city of superlatives. There are countless sights that have to be seen, but a handful are truly definitive of the city. The following chapter illustrates the very best of these.

1 Empire State Building

This Art Deco skyscraper is one of the most widely recognized symbols of the city. It offers unforgettable panoramas *(see pp12–13)*.

2 Fifth Avenue

Fashionable shops and world-class architecture define this avenue, one of New York's best-known addresses *(see pp14–15)*.

3 Rockefeller Center

An urban wonder, with gardens, restaurants, stores, over 100 artworks, offices, and a skating rink *(see pp16–17)*.

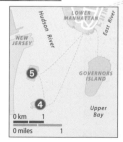

4 Statue of Liberty

The lady holding the torch is the symbol of freedom for millions seeking a new life in the US *(see pp18–19)*.

5 Ellis Island

Carefully restored buildings bring to life the experience of the immigrants who have moved to New York over the years *(see pp20–23)*.

6 Times Square and the Theater District

Bright lights illuminate Broadway and Times Square, where more than 40 famous theaters play host to a changing parade of hit shows *(see pp26–9)*.

7 Central Park

The area of green gives respite from the city's concrete. It took 16 years and over 500,000 trees to complete *(see pp30–31)*.

8 Metropolitan Museum of Art

It would take weeks to see all the treasures of this museum. It houses one of the greatest collections of the Western world and spans 5,000 years of culture *(see pp32–5)*.

The Museum of Modern Art

9 Museum of Modern Art (MoMA)

This vast museum hosts one of the world's most comprehensive collections of modern art. Its outdoor sculpture gallery is particularly popular *(see pp36–9)*.

10 American Museum of Natural History

Long famous for its dinosaurs, the museum moved into the space age with the dramatic Rose Center for Earth and Space *(see pp40–43)*.

TOP 10 ⭐ Empire State Building

The Empire State Building is the most famous skyscraper in New York. More than 120 million visitors have gazed down on the city from the observatories since it opened in 1931. Planned in the prosperous 1920s by the architectural firm of Shreve, Lamb, and Harmon, this Art Deco classic was completed during the Depression and was largely vacant for several years, giving rise to the nickname "Empty State Building." It has been featured in countless movies, most famously *King Kong*.

1 The Building

A mooring mast for airships, now the base of a TV tower, was built to ensure the 102-story, 1,454-ft (443-m) building would be taller than the Chrysler Building.

2 Lobby Mural

The main lobby houses a 36-ft (11-m) Art Deco relief **(left)** that showcases the Empire State Building image in steel, aluminum, and gold leaf with dramatic impact.

3 Elevators

While riding to the 80th floor, visitors can see an animated dramatization, depicting the construction of the building, on the elevator ceiling.

4 Main Deck

Breathtaking views from the 86th floor's open-air observatory, 1,050 ft (320 m) above the city, attract more than 4 million visitors yearly.

5 Top Deck

Visibility on a clear day **(below)** from the 102nd-floor deck is up to 80 miles (130 km). You must reserve tickets in advance (the Top Deck is an additional $33).

NEED TO KNOW

MAP K3 ▪ 350 5th Ave, at 34th St
▪ www.esbnyc.com

Open 10am–10pm Mon–Thu, 9am–10pm Fri–Sun

Main Deck: adm adults $44, seniors (62+) $42, children (6–12) $38, express ticket $80 for all

Top Deck: adm add $33; military in uniform and kids under 6 free; multimedia guide with all tickets

▪ There are a number of restaurants and shops on the ground level.

▪ Note that no bags over carry-on size are allowed.

9 Second Floor Exhibits

Nine interactive exhibits chronicle the history of the building – from its construction to its iconic status in pop culture today.

6 Spire

The spire is lit to honor holidays, seasons, events, causes, and the many ethnic groups of New York: red, white, and blue for national holidays; green for St. Patrick's Day **(above)**; and blue and white for Hanukkah.

10 Visitors' Center

This air-conditioned, spacious center, with self-serve kiosks and virtual concierges, is where visitors can purchase or print tickets, orient themselves, and clear security.

Empire State Building

7 Empire State Run-up

Each February, following a tradition dating to 1978, hundreds of runners **(above)** race up the 1,576 steps from the lobby to the 86th floor.

8 Valentine's Day

Weddings have been an Empire State Building tradition since 1994. Every year, one or two lucky couples are selected to get married on the one day that the ceremony is conducted here.

BUILDING THE EMPIRE STATE

William F. Lamb designed the building, following a brief to "make it big." It took only 410 days to build the 102-story, 365,000-ton limestone and granite skyscraper, with an average of four and a half stories added every week. However, in one outstanding ten-day period, the 3,500-strong construction team completed ten stories. Due to the building's relatively shallow foundations, 60,000 tons of steel beams were used to support the tower.

TOP10 ⭐ Fifth Avenue

Fifth Avenue is New York's best-known boulevard and home to three of its most famous buildings. In the late 1800s, it was lined with mansions belonging to prominent families, but as retailers moved north in the 1900s, society fled uptown. One remaining former mansion is the Cartier building, reputedly acquired from banker Morton F. Plant in 1917 in exchange for a string of pearls. Although commercial enterprises now share the avenue, it has remained a hub for luxury goods.

1 Grand Army Plaza

This ornamented plaza is presided over by the 1907 Plaza Hotel and Augustus Saint-Gaudens' gilded statue of General William T. Sherman, one of the most famous military leaders in US history.

2 Bergdorf Goodman

Founded in 1899 as a small ladies' tailoring and fur shop, New York's most elite department store **(left)** has been here since 1928 *(see p70)*. It sells contemporary designer clothing.

3 General Motors Building

Edward Durrell Stone's 1968 marble skyscraper is of interest not just for its architecture but for the iconic glass-cube entrance to the Apple Store *(see p130)*, which lurks below the sidewalk here.

4 Tiffany & Co.

Truman Capote's 1958 novella *Breakfast at Tiffany's* made this the most famous jewelry store in New York. The window displays are works of art, as are the items for sale within.

5 Trump Tower

A six-story open interior space, the atrium in Trump Tower **(left)** is graced by hanging gardens and a spectacular 80-ft (24-m) water wall.

6 St. Patrick's Cathedral

In 1878 James Renwick, Jr. designed the city's grandest Catholic church *(see p128)* in French Gothic style **(above)**. Highlights include the bronze doors, the high altar, the Lady Chapel, and the rose window.

8 Cartier

Look up to admire what remains of the fine 1905 Beaux Arts mansion housing this famous luxury jeweler. At Christmas, the whole building is wrapped in a giant red ribbon **(left)**.

9 Saks Fifth Avenue

One of New York's most attractive stores, Saks *(see p70)* is famous for the seasonal decor on the main floor of its 1924 building, and its exclusive fashions for men and women.

MILLIONNAIRE'S ROW

From its inception in the early 19th century, Fifth Avenue has been the territory of New York's well-heeled society, with homes costing as much as $20,000 after the Civil War. As commercial and retail ventures, albeit exclusive ones, encroached at the end of the 19th century, they moved their mansions further north. Mrs Astor set the trend by moving up to 65th Street after her nephew, William Waldorf Astor, built the Waldorf Hotel next to her former home.

7 New York Public Library

The epitome of Beaux Arts elegance, this 1911 landmark *(see p128)* features marble halls and a vast paneled reading room that glows with light from its arched windows **(above)**.

10 Fifth Avenue Presbyterian Church

This church has a history of social change: its congregation started the first free schools which expanded into the New York Public School System.

NEED TO KNOW

MAP H3–K3

The heart of Fifth Avenue is from the Empire State Building on 34th St, to the Grand Army Plaza, 59th St, a walk of over 1 mile (1.6 km)

Bergdorf Goodman: 754 5th Ave, at 57th St

General Motors Building: 767 5th Ave

Tiffany & Co.: 727 5th Ave

Trump Tower: 721–725 5th Ave

St. Patrick's Cathedral: 5th Ave, between 50th & 51st Sts

New York Public Library: 5th Ave, at 42nd St

Cartier: 653 5th Ave

Saks Fifth Avenue: 611 5th Ave, at 50th St

Fifth Avenue Presbyterian Church: 7 West 55th St

■ Free tours of the New York Public Library: 11am & 2pm Mon–Sat (except Jul & Aug).

■ For mass at St. Patrick's Cathedral, check website for timings *(www.saint patrickscathedral.org)*.

TOP 10 ⭐ Rockefeller Center

Begun in the 1930s, this city within a city and National Historic Landmark was the first commercial project to integrate gardens, dining, and shopping with office space. Rockefeller Center is the hub of Midtown Manhattan, busy day and night. The number of buildings has grown to 19, though the newer buildings do not match the Art Deco elegance of the original 14 structures.

3 Comcast Building

The centerpiece of Rockefeller Center or "30 Rock" is a slim, 70-story limestone tower **(right)**. The building, with gradual setbacks as it rises, houses the studios of the NBC television network.

1 Channel Gardens

Named after the English Channel because they separate the French and British buildings, the gardens **(above)** change with the calendar and are lined with glowing angels at Christmas.

4 Lower Plaza

A skating rink in winter and outdoor café in summer, the Lower Plaza is always popular. It is surrounded by flags that represent the members of the UN.

2 Prometheus Statue

An 18-ft (5.5-m) gold-leafed bronze statue **(above)** by Paul Manship presides over the Lower Plaza. The pedestal represents Earth and the ring represents the heavens.

⑦ Atlas Statue
Sculpted by Lee Lawrie, this 14,000-lb (6,350-kg), 15-ft (4.5-m) figure **(left)** is perched on a 9-ft (3-m) pedestal. One of 15 works by Lawrie at the Rockefeller Center, Atlas stands at the entrance to the International Building.

⑤ Today Show Studio
This morning TV show can be viewed live every weekday from the sidewalk. Outdoor concerts by well-known musicians often take place in the plaza.

⑥ Shopping Concourse
A variety of stores are found in the underground concourse of the Comcast Building, including a branch of the Lady M Cake Boutique.

⑧ NBC Studios
The Shop at NBC Studios **(below)** sells unique souvenirs related to NBC shows. Studio tours are usually available but were paused in 2020; check the website for the latest.

JOHN D. ROCKEFELLER, JR.

Eminent philanthropist and billionaire John D. Rockefeller, Jr. (1874–1960) was son and heir to Ohio oil magnate John Davison Rockefeller's fortunes. John D., as Rockefeller, Jr. was known, strongly believed his inheritance should be used for the public good. Among his philanthropic donations were contributions to the building funds of the Cloisters (see p37) and the United Nations Headquarters (see p128).

⑨ Radio City Music Hall
Tours of this Art Deco masterpiece and former movie palace offer a chance to admire the decor, the stage, and the Wurlitzer organ (see p63).

⑩ Top of the Rock
Visitors can enjoy breathtaking, 360-degree views **(below)** – and space to move about – on the observation deck's three levels.

NEED TO KNOW

MAP J3 ■ Rockefeller Center extends from 5th to 6th Aves, between 48th & 51st Sts ■ www.rockefellercenter.com

Today Show Studio: Rockefeller Plaza at 49th St; 7–11am Mon–Fri, 7–9am Sat, 8–9am Sun

NBC Studios: 30 Rockefeller Plaza; The Shop at NBC Studios 10am–7pm Mon–Sat, www.theshopatnbcstudios.com; backstage tours normally every 20 mins 8:20am–2:20pm Mon–Thu (to 5pm Fri & to 6pm select Sat & Sun) but suspended in 2020, www.thetouratnbcstudios.com

Top of the Rock: 30 Rockefeller Plaza; 9am–11pm daily (last entry 10:10pm); adm adults $40, seniors (62+) $38, kids (6–12) $34; www.rockefellercenter.com/attractions/top-of-the-rock-observation-deck

■ From 5th Avenue, walk via the Channel Gardens to the Lower Plaza.
■ Pick up a self-guided tour leaflet from the the Comcast Building lobby.

TOP 10 ⭐ Statue of Liberty

New York's most famous statue, officially titled "Liberty Enlightening the World," has been a harbinger of freedom for millions since 1886. The statue, a gift from France to mark the US's 100th birthday, was designed by the Frenchman Frédéric-Auguste Bartholdi, who devoted 21 years to the project. The unveiling on July 3, 1986 after the $100-million centennial restoration, was the occasion for one of the largest firework displays ever seen in the US.

1 Boat Ride
Ferries **(above)** carry a constant stream of visitors from Manhattan and Jersey City to the Statue of Liberty and on to Ellis Island. They offer stunning views en route.

2 Castle Clinton National Monument
Built as a fort in 1808, it now serves as a boarding point for Statue of Liberty and Ellis Island ferry passengers, and exhibits panoramas of New York history. The fort was built 300 ft (91 m) offshore, but landfill gradually joined it to Battery Park.

3 Crown
Legend says that Bartholdi's mother was the model for Liberty, but the face was actually based on his early drawings for a never commissioned statue in Egypt. The rays of her crown represent the seven seas and continents.

4 Close-up View of the Statue
A close-up view reveals the awesome size of the Statue of Liberty **(right)**. Dominating New York harbor, she stands 305 ft (93 m) tall and weighs 200 tons. Her right arm carrying the symbolic torch is 42 ft (13 m) long while her index finger measures 8 ft (2.4 m) and dwarfs most people.

5 Battery Park
With statues and monuments honoring everyone from New York's first Jewish immigrants to the US Coast Guard, the park **(left)** is also a great spot for sea-gazing.

> **GATEWAY TO THE NEW WORLD**
>
> The Statue of Liberty has symbolized the beginning of a new way of life for millions of immigrants fleeing poverty and hardship. She is an enduring symbol of the freedom and hope offered by the US and the subject of Emma Lazarus's poem *The New Colossus*: "… Give me your tired, your poor, Your huddled masses yearning to breathe free… Send these, the homeless, tempest-tost to me, I lift my lamp beside the golden door".

6 Statue of Liberty Museum

Opened in 2019, this museum documents the history of the statue using photos, prints, videos, and oral histories. The museum's Immersive Theater presents a dramatic short film explaining the statue's architecture and her origin story.

7 Frame

Gustave Eiffel, best known for his Paris tower, created the inner framework. The copper sheeting shell, weighing 31 tons, is hung on bars from a massive central iron pylon that anchors the statue to the base.

NEED TO KNOW

Take the 1 train to South Ferry, 4 or 5 train to Bowling Green, or the R and W train to Whitehall St to get to Battery Park by subway.
■ Ferries leave from Castle Clinton, Battery Park, every 20–30 mins 8:30am–4:30pm daily (winter: 9am–3:30pm)
■ www.nps.gov/stli

■ An early departure or an advance, timed booking is advised to avoid long lines.

■ For the best photos, sit on the right of the boat going out and on the left coming back.

8 Torch and Book

The new, gold-leaf-coated torch was added in 1986. The original is on display in the museum **(right)**. The book in Liberty's left hand is inscribed July 4, 1776, in Roman numerals.

9 Views

The observation decks in the pedestal and crown of the Liberty Statue offer spectacular views. The crown reopened in 2009 following closure after September 11, 2001. Advance reservation is required.

10 Pedestal

Prestigious American architect Richard Morris Hunt was chosen to design the 89-ft (27-m) pedestal. It sits within the 11-pointed, star-shaped walls **(above)** of Fort Wood, a fortress erected just before the War of 1812.

TOP 10 ⭐ Ellis Island

Ellis Island is the symbol of America's immigrant heritage. From 1892 to 1954, it was the arrival point for over 12 million people searching for a better life. Their descendants, more than 100 million people, comprise almost 40 per cent of today's US population. First and second class passengers were processed for immigration on board ship, but the poor traveling in steerage class were ferried to the crowded island for medical and legal checks. As many as 5,000 passed through in a day. The museum not only retraces their experience here, but provides a picture of the wider immigrant experience in America.

1 Arrival Area
Crowds of steerage passengers entered through the original gateway having been ferried from their arrival vessels. Instructions were given by interpreters in a babel of languages as they lined up for immigration.

2 Great Hall
In this hall **(below)**, immigrants awaited examinations that would determine whether they would be granted entry. Those needing special inspection were marked with chalk.

Aerial view of Ellis Island

3 Dormitory
Immigrants who were detained for further examinations slept here in separate quarters for men and women. Although the process was nerve-racking, only two per cent of those seeking refuge were sent back.

4 Railroad Ticket Office
Those traveling beyond New York were ferried to railroad terminals in New Jersey to continue their onward journeys. Agents could sell as many as 25 tickets per minute.

NEW JERSEY'S ELLIS ISLAND

Although a federal property, a long-fought battle over territorial jurisdiction of Ellis Island was settled in 1998. Originally a 3-acre (1-ha) site, Ellis Island's landmass was increased with landfill to more than 27 acres (11 ha) in the 1900s. A US Supreme Court ruling in 1998 adjudged the added landfill to be in the territory of New Jersey, and the original portion to be in New York State's jurisdiction.

6 The Peopling of America

Four hundred years of immigration history are displayed in more than 30 galleries. Exhibits such as *The Peopling of America* have heirlooms, posters, maps, and photos donated by immigrants' families.

5 Medical Examining Line

The most dreaded inspectors were the "eye men" **(above)**, looking for trachoma, a disease that lead to blindness and certain deportation.

7 Baggage Room

In this room, inspection officers checked the baskets, boxes, and trunks **(right)** that held the immigrants' meager belongings, which at that point constituted all their worldly possessions.

8 American Family Immigration History Center

Using computer and multimedia technology, visitors can access passenger arrival records **(below)** of the millions of people who entered New York between 1892 and 1957.

NEED TO KNOW

For a map, see Lower Manhattan to Midtown inset on p10 ■ 212 363 3200 ■ www.nps.gov/elis

Open Jun–Aug: 9:30am–5pm daily; Sep–May: 9:30am–3:30pm daily

Ferry rides to Statue of Liberty and Ellis Island: adults $24, seniors $18, children (4–12) $12; statue crown & pedestal access add 30 cents; children under 4 free; www.statuecruises.com

- ■ Try to catch an early ferry from Battery Park to avoid the crowds.
- ■ The ferry ticket includes audio tours.
- ■ The island's cafeteria and picnic areas are great spots for lunch.
- ■ Stop at the information desk for tickets to a free 30-minute film.

9 American Immigration Wall of Honor

To honor their forebears, Americans pay to have their names inscribed on this list. Including the families of John F. Kennedy and Barbra Streisand, the wall contains over 775,000 names.

10 Oral History Collection

First-hand recollections of immigrants who passed through the station are preserved at the Ellis Island Oral History Program. Around 900 of these fascinating interviews are accessible at the Bob Hope Memorial Library, located on the third floor of the Immigration Museum.

Milestones in Immigration History

1 1624
The first Dutch founded New Amsterdam in Leni Lenape territory. The town thrived as a trading center, attracting settlers from many other nations. By 1643, the 500-strong population spoke 18 different languages.

Peter Stuyvesant forced to leave

2 1664
The dislike of Dutch governor Peter Stuyvesant and unpopular tax demands by the Dutch West India Company meant little resistance to their ousting by the British, who renamed the city New York.

3 1790
For the first US Census, New York's population of 33,131 was the second largest in the Colonies. This consisted of mostly settlers of British and Dutch descent.

4 Mid-1800s
Ireland's 1845–8 Great Famine and economic hardship in Germany led many to seek new lives in New York, where the city's rapid growth as a seaport and manufacturing center opened many jobs.

5 1880–1910
Thousands of Russian and Polish Jews, Italians and Scandinavians arrived, fleeing persecution or hard economic times.

Polish immigrant

6 1892
When Castle Island, an immigrant depot set up in 1855, could no longer handle the inflow, Ellis Island took over. "Settlement Houses" were set up in the city to help those living in squalid tenements, and "Americanization" programs encouraged assimilation.

7 1924
Nearly 40 per cent of New York's population was foreign-born. US laws set national quotas on immigration; inhabitants of Great Britain's Caribbean colonies benefited from the British quota and arrived in large numbers.

8 1965
The Hart-Cellar Act ended discrimination based on national origin, beginning a new wave of immigration to the city.

Chinatown, Manhattan

9 1980s
One million mainly Asian and Latin American newcomers arrived. The Chinese population topped 300,000 (mostly in Chinatown), Korean and Dominican numbers also grew.

10 1990–present
Over 1.2 million newcomers entered, swelling the city's foreign-born population to over 40 per cent of the total population. One-third of the city's 3 million foreign-born residents arrived after 2000. The New York borough of Queens is classified as the most ethnically diverse in the US.

THE RESTORATION OF ELLIS ISLAND

Museum visitor

Laws enacted in 1924 defining immigration quotas drastically curtailed the numbers of foreigners coming into the US, and Ellis Island was no longer needed to serve as an immigration depot. It became a detention and deportation center for undesirable aliens, a training center for the US Coast Guard, and a hospital for wounded servicemen during World War II. In 1954, the US government closed the island. It remained abandoned until 1984, when a $156 million project replaced the copper roof domes, cleaned the mosaic tiles, and restored the interior, preserving any surviving original fixtures in the largest historic restoration in US history. The restoration included the establishment of the Ellis Island Immigration Museum *(see pp22–3)*, telling the immigrant story through more than 2,000 artifacts. It also has an interactive children's exhibit, plus an oral history archive that can be visited by appointment. Reopened in 1990, Ellis Island receives over 3 million visitors every year.

TOP 10 NATIONALITIES ENTERING ELLIS ISLAND

(Between 1892–7, 1901–31)

1 **Italy**: 2,502,310
2 **Austria and Hungary**: 2,275,852
3 **Russia**: 1,893,542
4 **Germany**: 633,148
5 **England**: 551,969
6 **Ireland**: 520,904
7 **Sweden**: 348,036
8 **Greece**: 245,058
9 **Norway**: 226,278
10 **Ottoman Empire**: 212,825

The entrance to the Ellis Island Immigration Museum

Following pages The Statue of Liberty and Jersey city skyline

TOP 10 ⭐ Times Square and Theater District

Known as the "Crossroads of the World," Times Square is New York's most famous intersection and center of the lively Theater District. It was called Longacre Square until 1904, when the *New York Times* built One Times Square, a 25-story tower, on the site. Its occupancy on New Year's Eve was marked with fireworks, a celebration that continues today. A giant crystal ball descends the building at midnight to herald the new year.

1 Nasdaq MarketSite

The video tower of this electronic stock market dominates the corner of Broadway and 43rd Street with a screen that regularly broadcasts financial news and live stock information **(below)**.

3 Broadway Lights

The city's longest street is known best for the section north of 42nd Street, dubbed the "Great White Way" for its array of bright lights **(right)** on marquees and billboards.

4 Times Square News Tickers

In 1928, the *New York Times* erected the world's first moving electronic sign to post breaking news. The "zipper" was removed in 2019, but ABC, Morgan Stanley, and Reuters all still have news tickers in the square.

2 ABC Times Square Studios

The show *Good Morning America* is taped at these Disney-owned studios (7–9am Mon–Fri). Large viewing windows **(below)** allow passers-by to catch a glimpse of the celebrity guests or watch the occasional live pop concert.

NEED TO KNOW

MAP J3 ■ Times Square is located where Broadway and 7th Ave intersect at 42nd St ■ www.timessquarenyc.org

Madame Tussauds, New York: 234 West 42nd St; 1 800 246 8872; open Jun–Aug: 9am–10pm daily (Jul & Aug: to midnight), Sep–May: 10am–8pm daily (to 10pm Fri & Sat); adm $43.99; www.madametussauds.com/new-york

■ Go to the TKTS booth in Times Square (*212 221 0013; www.tdf.org*) for discounted tickets to all kinds of Broadway shows.

■ Most stores in Times Square are open daily, from 10am to 9pm; H&M is usually open until 11pm. The NYPD Times Square Substation (*1479 Broadway*) is open 24 hours.

5 Flagship Stores

Among the huge stores in Times Square are Hershey's Chocolate World, a large H&M, Disney, and M&M's World with its two-story M&M chocolate wall.

6 4 Times Square

The environmentally friendly, 48-story skyscraper houses Nasdaq, several law firms and tech companies. It remains a sign of the resurgence of Times Square.

9 New 42nd Street

The renovation of the New Amsterdam Theatre in the 1990s uplifted 42nd Street. Today, New 42 Studios and several theaters line the block.

10 Madame Tussauds, New York

Barack Obama, Brad Pitt, and Madonna are among the wax inhabitants of this 42nd Street tenant. The museum has exterior glass elevators and a huge hand holding the illuminated sign **(right)**.

8 Duffy Square

The block was revitalized with the unveiling of the TKTS area in 2008, a dramatic wedge of red overlaid with a set of stairs to nowhere **(left)**. A statue of World War I hero Father Duffy stands beneath the steps.

THEATER DISTRICT

It was the move by the Metropolitan Opera House to Broadway in 1883 that drew lavish theaters and restaurants to this area. In the 1920s, movie palaces added the glamour of neon to Broadway. After World War II, the popularity of movies waned and sleaze replaced glitter. Since the 1990s, a redevelopment program has brought the public and bright lights back to this area.

7 Off-Broadway

Before the rest of 42nd Street was rejuvenated, the block between 9th and 10th Avenues was resurrected by Off-Broadway theater companies needing inexpensive homes. New plays are premiered at Playwrights Horizons, one of the area's better-known tenants **(right)**.

Theaters

1 Palace Theatre
MAP J3 ▪ 1564 Broadway

Sarah Bernhardt inaugurated the stage, and playing here became the ultimate assignment. It is currently undergoing extensive renovation and is expected to reopen in 2023.

2 Lyric Theatre
MAP K3 ▪ 214 West 42nd St

The Lyric and Apollo Theatres were combined to form this showcase for musicals in 1998, marking the arrival of corporate sponsorship for theaters.

3 Shubert Theatre
MAP J3 ▪ 225 West 44th St

Built in 1912–13 as a lavish site for musicals and headquarters for the Shubert Organization. The Booth, opposite, was built at this time.

4 New Amsterdam Theatre
MAP K3 ▪ 214 West 42nd St

This Art Nouveau beauty housed the famous *Ziegfeld Follies*. Restored by Disney in the 1990s, it is now home to hit Disney musical *Aladdin*.

5 New Victory Theater
MAP K3 ▪ 209 West 42nd St

Built for Oscar Hammerstein in 1900, this theater once showed X-rated films. It was restored in 1995 to present off-Broadway family entertainment.

Detail of the facade, Lyceum Theatre

6 Lyceum Theatre
MAP J3 ▪ 149 West 45th St

The oldest playhouse *(see p142)* boasts a vaulted ceiling, murals, and elaborate plasterwork. It is often used as an auxiliary for Lincoln Center.

7 Hudson Theatre
MAP J2 ▪ 141 West 44th St

A restrained facade belies the lavish interior, including an inner lobby with a Classical arcade and domes of Tiffany glass. After years as an event venue, it reopened as a theater in 2017.

8 Belasco Theatre
MAP J3 ▪ 111 West 44th St

This 1907 monument to impresario David Belasco, who supervised the unusual Georgian Revival design, was restored in 2010. The rooftop duplex, with the decor of a Gothic church, was his personal residence.

9 Lunt-Fontanne Theatre
MAP J3 ▪ 205 West 46th St

Originally the Globe (finished in 1910), part of the roof of this venue could be removed to create an open-air auditorium. It was rebuilt in 1958.

10 Winter Garden Theatre
MAP J3 ▪ 1634 Broadway

Previously the American Horse Exchange in 1885, this was acquired by the Shuberts in 1911 and remodeled in 1922. Popular musicals have included *Mamma Mia!* (2001–2013) and *Back to the Future: The Musical* (from 2023).

Interior of New Victory Theater

A BRIEF HISTORY OF NEW YORK CITY THEATER

Oscar Hammerstein

New York's first theater is thought to have been the New Theater, erected in 1732. The city's theatrical center steadily moved uptown to the Bowery, Astor Place, Union Square, and Herald Square, before finally settling around Longacre Square (now Times Square), after Oscar Hammerstein's Olympia Theater opened on Broadway in 1895. Some 85 theaters were built over the next three decades, many with grand Beaux Arts interiors by architects such as Herts & Tallant, who were responsible for designing cantilevered balconies that eliminated the need for columns. Impresarios like the Shuberts and the Chanins made theater-going more democratic by blurring the class distinction between orchestra and balcony, using a single entrance for all. As modern theaters replaced them, more than 40 of these beautiful theaters were demolished. Fortunately, the rest have now been designated as Historic Landmarks.

TOP 10 BROADWAY CLASSICS

1 **The Phantom of the Opera**

2 **Jersey Boys**

3 **Chicago**

4 **The Lion King**

5 **Mamma Mia!**

6 **Rent**

7 **Annie**

8 **Wicked**

9 **Hello, Dolly!**

10 **Hamilton**

The Ambassador Theatre, designed by Herbert J. Krapp in 1921, remains one of the Shubert Organization's most frequented theaters.

⭐ Central Park

New York's "backyard," an 843-acre (341-ha) swathe of green, provides recreation and beauty for around 38 million visitors a year. Designed by Frederick Law Olmsted and Calvert Vaux in 1858, the park took 16 years to create and involved the hauling in of vast amounts of stone and earth to form hills, lakes, and meadows, the planting of over 500,000 trees and shrubs, and the building of more than 30 bridges and arches.

1 Great Lawn
This 13-acre (5-ha) oval lawn **(above)** hosts free concerts by the Metropolitan Opera and New York Philharmonic in the summer. The concerts draw up to 100,000 people.

2 Belvedere Castle
This stone castle **(below)** offers peerless views in all directions. Inside is the Henry Luce Nature Observatory with exhibits covering the park's diverse wildlife.

3 Bethesda Terrace
Overlooking the Ramble and the Lake, the ornate terrace and its fountain **(above)** form the focal point of the park. On the adjacent tree-lined Mall is the Women's Rights Pioneers Monument, installed in 2020.

4 The Ramble
This wooded 37 acres (15 ha) is a bird-watcher's paradise. Central Park is on the Atlantic migration flyway. Over 270 species have been spotted here, including the purple grackle and many species of warblers.

CREATING CENTRAL PARK

Central Park was the first landscaping project of Frederick Law Olmsted. Rejecting the usual formal plantings, he created passages of contrasting scenery, the pastoral against the rugged. Areas for active and passive recreation were separated, and dense plantings shut out the city. The park brought him high praise and set a pattern for future landscapes. He went on to be America's most prolific designer of parks.

5 Reservoir

This 106-acre (43-ha) lake **(above)** is the largest of the park's five, which include Conservatory Water, where model boat races are often held.

9 Strawberry Fields

This peaceful garden area was created by Yoko Ono in memory of John Lennon (shot in 1980), who lived in the nearby Dakota apartments. Gifts for the memorial come from all over the world.

10 Conservatory Garden

This formal garden with fountains and beautiful displays of flowering trees and bulbs is at its best in spring, when everything is in bloom.

6 Charles A. Dana Discovery Center

At the northern end of the park, this center offers exhibits, tours, and free "catch-and-release" fishing pole rentals to be used at the nearby Harlem Meer.

8 Delacorte Theater

Home of the two "Shakespeare in the Park" summer productions. Get in line early for free tickets. The SummerStage music and dance series offers free entertainment too.

7 Hans Christian Andersen Statue

Children's storytelling sessions are held around the statue **(right)** in the summer. Other activities include nature workshops, a carousel, and a marionette theater.

NEED TO KNOW

MAP D3–H3 ■ From Central Park South to 110th St, and between 5th Ave and Central Park West ■ www.centralpark nyc.org

Open dawn–dusk

■ Refreshments are available at the Boathouse snack bar. The Loeb Boathouse restaurant serves gourmet meals.

■ Make your first stop the Dairy, a Victorian Gothic building housing the Visitor Center. Ask about the free nature workshops and guided walks.

■ Rent rowboats from the Boathouse, bikes from Bike Rent NYC, and ice skates from the Wollman Rink in the winter.

TOP 10 ★ Metropolitan Museum of Art

One of the world's great art museums, the Metropolitan (Met) spans 5,000 years of culture from across the globe. Each specialized gallery holds an abundance of treasures. Founded in 1870 with three European collections and 174 paintings, the Gothic Revival building has been expanded many times and the present holdings number over 2 million.

1 European Paintings
The 2,500 European paintings form one of the world's greatest collections. Highlights include the Vermeers, Rembrandts, and the many Impressionist and Post-Impressionist canvases.

2 Egyptian Art
One of the largest collections of Egyptian art outside Cairo includes masks, mummies, statues, jewelry, the Tomb of Perneb, and the spectacular Temple of Dendur **(right)**, built around 15 BCE and reassembled as it appeared on the banks of the Nile.

3 Michael C. Rockefeller Wing
Inca masks **(above)**, Pre-Columbian gold, ceramics from Mexico and Peru, and art from the court of Benin in Nigeria are the top picks among 1,600 objects covering 3,000 years.

4 American Wing
This collection includes Tiffany glass, paintings, sculptures **(right)**, and period rooms from the 17th to early 20th centuries.

5 Robert Lehman Collection
This extraordinary private collection includes Renaissance masters, Dutch, Spanish, and French artists, Post-Impressionists and Fauvists, plus ceramics and furniture.

6 Costume Institute

Women's fashions from ball gowns to miniskirts, and menswear from the French courts **(left)** to the present day are on display here. The glamorous Met Gala is hosted at this institute.

7 European Sculpture and Decorative Arts

This collection reflects the development of Western European design. It includes French and English period rooms, tapestries, and sculptures by Rodin and Degas **(right)**.

8 Roof Garden

From May to October the Iris and B. Gerald Cantor Roof Garden boasts outstanding annual displays of contemporary sculpture. It also offers an opportunity to enjoy a drink with a peerless view of Central Park and the surrounding skyline.

9 Asian Art

The West's most comprehensive collection features paintings, textiles, sculpture and ceramics.

10 Lila A. Wallace Wing

The Metropolitan has a growing collection of art, sculpture, and design from the 20th century, with works ranging from Picasso and Matisse to Émile-Jacques Ruhlmann and Jackson Pollock.

NEED TO KNOW

MAP F3 ■ 1000 5th Ave ■ 212 535 7710 ■ www.metmuseum.org

Open 10am–5pm Mon–Thu & Sun, 10am–9pm Fri & Sat (galleries cleared 15 mins before closing)

Adm adults $30, seniors $22, students $17; children under 12 and members free

■ If time is short, the European Paintings, Egyptian Art, and American Wing will give you a sense of this institution's greatness.

■ Less-crowded weekend evenings have bar service and live music.

Key to Floor Plan

- Ground Floor
- First Floor
- Second Floor

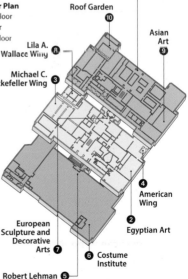

European Paintings **1**
Roof Garden **10**
Lila A. Wallace Wing **R**
Michael C. Rockefeller Wing **3**
Asian Art **9**
American Wing **4**
Egyptian Art **2**
European Sculpture and Decorative Arts **7**
Costume Institute **6**
Robert Lehman Collection **5**

Metropolitan Museum of Art Floor Plan

Paintings in the Met

 Self-Portrait
Rembrandt (1606–69) painted a self-portrait each decade of his whole career. In this moving study from 1660, when he was 54, he portrayed age very honestly.

2 View of Toledo
Darkening clouds set an eerie mood for one of El Greco's (1541–1614) most memorable paintings, depicting the capital city of the Spanish Empire until 1561.

3 Young Woman with a Water Pitcher
Painted between 1660 and 1667, this is a classic example of the subtle and sensitive use of light that has made Vermeer (1632–75) one of the most revered Dutch masters.

The Harvesters (1565), Bruegel

4 The Harvesters
This is Bruegel the Elder (c. 1525–69) at his best, an example of the use of detail that set him apart. It is one of five remaining panels depicting different times of the year.

5 Madame X
Part of the excellent American art collection, this canvas by John Singer Sargent (1856–1925) is of Virginie Amélie Avegno, who married a French banker and became a notorious Paris beauty in the 1880s.

6 Garden at Sainte-Adresse
This resort town on the English Channel where Monet spent the

Garden at Sainte-Adresse (1867), Monet

summer of 1867 is portrayed with sparkling color and intricate brushwork. The work combines illusion and reality, demonstrating why Monet (1840–1926) was considered to be one of the greatest of the Impressionists.

7 Gertrude Stein
This portrait, created when Picasso (1881–1973) was just 24 years old, shows the influence of African, Roman, and Iberian sculpture and a shift from the slender figures of his early years, foreshadowing his adoption of Cubism.

8 The Card Players
Better known for landscapes and still lifes, Cézanne (1839–1906) was intrigued by a scene of peasants intent on their card game. This ambitious project emphasizes the concentration of the participants.

9 Cypresses
Painted in 1889, soon after Van Gogh's (1853–90) voluntary confinement at an asylum in Saint-Rémy, this painting shows the swirling and heavy brushwork typical of his work from this period.

10 Cow's Skull: Red, White, and Blue
This work is by the Modernist Georgia O'Keeffe (1887–1986), who was based in New Mexico for the last 40 years of her life. The skull's weathered surfaces and jagged edges symbolize the eternal beauty of the desert.

THE CLOISTERS

Reliquary Shrine ("The Elizabeth Shrine")

As well as the medieval treasures in the main building, the Met oversees this spectacular branch, built in medieval architectural style, overlooking the Hudson River in Fort Tryon Park in northern Manhattan. Opened in 1938, it consists of elements from five medieval cloisters and other monastic sites in France. The collections are noted for Romanesque and Gothic sculptures and include manuscripts, tapestries, stained glass, enamels, ivories, and paintings. The gardens are serene. John D. Rockefeller Jr. *(see p17)*, who donated items to the collection, is largely responsible for funding the Cloisters *(see p46)*. To reach the complex, take the A train to 190th Street.

TOP 10
CLOISTERS SIGHTS

The medieval gardens of the Cloisters make for a peaceful escape from the city.

TOP10 ★ Museum of Modern Art (MoMA)

Founded in 1929, this modern art powerhouse contains one of the world's most comprehensive collections of late 19th and 20th-century art. Around 200,000 works of art by more than 26,000 artists, ranging from Post-Impressionist classics to an unrivalled collection of contemporary masterpieces, can be found here. As well as its extraordinary collection of paintings, the museum also exhibits examples of design, sculpture, drawings, performance art, and early examples of photography and film.

GALLERY GUIDE

MoMA's art displays rotate every six to nine months (with a few exceptions). This means that even the most famous paintings will not be on permanent display. If there's a work you want to see, check the website in advance. Floors are divided by historical period, but galleries are thematically based – you might wander through a room of Matisse into a gallery on early skyscraper design.

1 Sculpture Garden

The Sculpture Garden **(above)** features two asymmetrical fountain pools at the center of its art collection. Look out for the four *Backs* by Matisse, Picasso's *She-Goat*, and *The River* by Maillol.

2 Film Center

With more than 22,000 films and four million stills, the collection here offers a wide range of programs and exhibits. Film conservation is key to the MoMA film department's work and many directors have donated copies of their films to help fund it.

3 Creativity Lab

The Creativity Lab, on MoMA's second floor, offers hands-on activities designed to get under the skin of the artistic process (themes change every few months). Facilitators, many of them working artists, are on hand as guides. Everyone is welcome to join in.

4 First Floor Galleries

Everything on the first floor of MoMA is free, including two street-level galleries. The main gift and design store **(right)** can be found down the stairs. The Michelin-starred The Modern restaurant and the Garden Café are also located here. Outside you'll find the Sculpture Garden, a leafy retreat in the heart of the city.

5 Second Floor Galleries

Here you'll find a gift store, a casual cafe, and the contemporary galleries ("1970s–Present").

6 Third Floor Galleries

The large Steichen, Johnson, and Menschel galleries here show more contemporary work. Yoko Ono's installation *Peace Is Power* is on permanent display on this floor.

7 Fourth Floor Galleries

The fourth floor galleries (400–421) focus on MoMA's core collection, with work from the 1940s to 1970s. Henri Matisse's famous *Swimming Pool* is in gallery 406.

8 Fifth Floor Galleries

Preceding the fourth floor chronologically, galleries 500–523 display works from the 1880s to the 1940s, including Matisse's *Dance (I)*. Gallery 515 houses Monet's beloved *Water Lilies* **(right)**.

9 Sixth Floor

This floor hosts a series of temporary art exhibitions in the Cohen Center for Special Exhibitions. The Terrace Café here has a fabulous open-air space.

10 The Studio

On the fourth floor, The Studio is a two-story gallery for live and experimental performance, dance, and sound works. It's also a space for residencies and commissions by various artists.

NEED TO KNOW

MAP J3 ■ 11 West 53rd St between Fifth Ave & Ave of the Americas ■ 212 708 9400 ■ www.moma.org

Open 10:30am–5:30pm Sun–Fri, 10:30am–7pm Sat

Adm adults $25, seniors (65 and over) $18, students $14, children 16 and under free

■ Mornings are always busiest at MoMA; arrive later in the day to avoid the crowds. Booking timed entry tickets online in advance is also highly recommended.

■ If you have a smartphone, be sure to download the free Bloomberg Connects app. The app allows you to scan QR codes placed throughout the museum and access features related to specific artworks (Wi-Fi is free throughout MoMA).

Paintings in MoMA

Visitors exploring MoMA

1 Starry Night by Vincent Van Gogh

This magical reimagining of the view from Van Gogh's room in a Saint-Rémy asylum, painted in 1889 during his treatment for mental illness, is dominated by vivid blues and yellows.

2 Emerging Man by Gordon Parks

Parks' photograph shows a man's head emerging from a manhole on a Harlem street in the 1950s. A symbol of the African American struggle for Civil Rights, it was inspired by Ralph Ellison's novel, *Invisible Man*.

3 Broadway Boogie Woogie by Piet Mondrian

Mondrian completed this abstract work in 1943 after moving to New York. The series of yellow squares, punctuated by blue and red boxes, was inspired by the order of New York's grid plan clashing with the wild creativity of boogie-woogie blues music.

4 The Persistence of Memory by Salvador Dalí

Perhaps the most famous Surrealist work, Dalí's "melting clocks" are now globally familiar symbols of decay and impermanence. Painted in 1931, *The Persistence of Memory* incorporates the rugged cliffs of Dalí's Catalan homeland into his unsettling dreamscape.

5 Abstraction Blue by Georgia O'Keeffe

O'Keeffe made a decisive transition from naturalistic to abstract painting with this 1927 work, dominated by swirls and curves of blue and white. Some see it as a symbol of fertility.

6 Les Demoiselles d'Avignon by Pablo Picasso

Picasso's composition of five naked women marked a decisive break from his conventional perspective. Painted in 1907, it is regarded as a seminal piece of early Cubism.

7 Water Tower by Rachel Whiteread

This resin cast sculpture of a typical New York water tower was created by the British artist in 1998 and originally displayed on a SoHo rooftop. Today it stands in the Sculpture Garden.

8 American People Series #20: Die by Faith Ringgold

This graphic painting by the iconic African American artist evokes the

Civil Rights struggles of the 1960s. It features a group of distressed men, women, and children all covered with blood.

9 Self Portrait by Frida Kahlo

Painted in 1940, just after her painful divorce from artist Diego Rivera, Kahlo's *Self Portrait* depicts her in a man's suit with short hair. Critics suggest the painting symbolizes her newfound independence and, perhaps, Kahlo's bisexuality.

10 And Then We Saw the Daughter of the Minotaur by Leonora Carrington

This strange Surrealist work depicts a flower-faced figure, a minotaur, and two boys with hooded cloaks looking at a crystal ball. The mythical landscape suggest a fantastical, matriarchal universe.

THE MAKING OF THE MUSEUM

MoMA was primarily conceived by three remarkable women. Abby Aldrich Rockefeller (wife of John D. Rockefeller Jr.), Lillie P. Bliss, and Mary Quinn became friends through their love of modern art. However, New York's primary art museum, the Met *(see p32–5)*, refused to show contemporary artwork in the 1920s. Without J. D. Rockefeller's help (he apparently hated modern art), the three women set about raising the funds and hiring the staff for the first modest museum at 730 Fifth Avenue in 1929. Here they hosted seminal landmark shows such as the Picasso retrospective of 1939–40. The museum moved several times in Manhattan before settling on its current location in 1939, a building designed in the International Style by architects Philip L. Goodwin and Edward Durell Stone. American architect Philip Johnson completed the sculpture garden in 1953 while César Pelli, an Argentine-American

architect, oversaw the museum's third expansion in 1984. Japanese architect Yoshio Taniguchi then completed a major renovation in 2004 that nearly doubled exhibition space, while the latest revamp was completed in 2019 by Diller Scofidio + Renfro.

MoMA co-founder Abby Aldrich Rockefeller

TOP 10 STATISTICS

1 MoMA's collection includes almost 200,000 works of art.

2 MoMA's website features more than 98,000 artworks.

3 MoMA has six curatorial departments: Architecture and Design; Drawings and Prints; Film; Media and Performance; Painting and Sculpture; and Photography.

4 MoMA's library contains over 1,000 periodicals, and around 300,000 books.

5 The museum's flagship restaurant, The Modern, has two Michelin stars.

6 The Painting and Sculpture Study Center maintains files on over 3,600 paintings and sculptures.

7 Over four million people visit the museum annually.

8 MoMA membership rates begin at $65 per year.

9 The Film Center collection includes over 30,000 movies.

10 MoMA lists over 1,200 art-related publications on its website.

TOP10 ★ American Museum of Natural History

Few city children grow up without visiting the dinosaurs, the life-size dioramas of animal life, and natural wonders in this popular museum. Since its founding in 1869, the museum has grown to more than 40 exhibition halls, spanning 4 city blocks, with more than 34 million specimens and cultural artifacts, many unique in the world. The museum's Rose Center for Earth and Space is home to the Hayden Planetarium and its 429-seat Space Theater, which screens the latest space shows.

Dinosaurs and Fossils

The museum's collection of dinosaur fossils, spread across the fourth floor, is the world's largest. Giant dinosaur skeletons include the Barosaurus, the Titanosaur, and a nearly complete Tyrannosaurus rex **(right)**.

2 Mammals

Dramatic dioramas of life-size animals are divided by continent and shown in accurate natural habitats. The two main galleries are the Akeley Hall of African Mammals and the Hall of Asian Mammals.

3 Milstein Hall of Ocean Life

This hall explores the waters of the earth and their inhabitants. A 94-ft (29-m) life-size blue whale **(below)** presides over the hall.

4 Hall of Asian Peoples

Exquisite artifacts, artworks, clothing, and dioramas of daily life show cultural practices in China, Korea, India, Japan, and other parts of Asia.

5 Hall of African Peoples

Exhibits, such as masks, ceremonial costumes, tools, and musical instruments, displayed here illustrate the cultural heritage of peoples from across the African continent.

6 Northwest Coast Hall

The museum's most historic hall, known for its totem poles, re-opened in 2022 after a major renovation in consultation with ten Pacific Northwest Indigenous communities.

7 Spitzer Hall of Human Origins

This hall presents the "family tree" of human evolution with life-size tableaux of hominid ancestors.

8 Hall of Biodiversity

Opened in 1998 to inspire conservation, the hall features the Spectrum of Life **(left)**, a 100-ft- (30-m-) long exhibit with around 1,500 specimens that show the diversity of life on Earth, and an immersive rain forest diorama.

American Museum of Natural History Floor Plan

Key to Floor Plan

First Floor
Second Floor
Third Floor
Fourth Floor
Rose Center

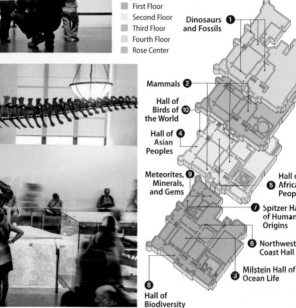

Dinosaurs and Fossils ❶

Mammals ❷

Hall of Birds of the World ❿

Hall of Asian Peoples ❹

Meteorites, Minerals, and Gems ❾

Hall of African Peoples ❺

Spitzer Hall of Human Origins ❼

Northwest Coast Hall ❻

Milstein Hall of Ocean Life ❸

Hall of Biodiversity ❽

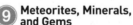

NEED TO KNOW

MAP F2 ■ 200 Central Park West, between 77th & 81st Sts ■ 212 769 5100 ■ www.amnh.org

Open 10am–5:30pm daily

Adm adults $23, students and seniors $18, children (2–12) $13, members free; General Adm + One (special exhibition, giant-screen film, or space show) $28/$22.50/$16.50; General Adm + All (special exhibitions, giant-screen film, & space show) $33/$27/$20

■ Eat at the lower-level food court, or at the café on the fourth floor.

■ Join a free tour at 15 minutes past the hour, 10:15am–3:15pm, daily.

9 Meteorites, Minerals, and Gems

The Ross Hall of Meteorites displays wonders such as the Cape York meteorite weighing 34 tons, while the new Mignone Halls of Gems and Minerals house stunning crystals, including the 563-carat sapphire Star of India **(right)**.

10 Hall of Birds of the World

The 12 dioramas on display here depict different regions around the world along with the birds that have adapted to those extraordinary habitats.

Rose Center for Earth and Space

Rose Center Floor Plan

8 Scales of the Universe Walkway

Big Bang Theater 9

10 Cosmic Pathway

Dynamic Earth Globe 6

Hall of Planet Earth 5

7 Earthquake Monitoring Station

Key to Floor Plan
- Lower Level
- First Floor
- Second Floor
- Third Floor

3 Ecosphere

4 Astro Bulletin

2 Hall of the Universe

1 The Building
Opened in 2000 to explore inner earth and the outer universe, the dramatic exhibit building is a huge glass cube enclosing a three-story, 87-ft- (27-m-) wide sphere containing the Hayden Planetarium.

2 Hall of the Universe
Exhibits, divided into the universe, galaxies, stars, and planets, show the discoveries of modern astrophysics. Digital scales measure your weight on Saturn, Jupiter, and the Sun.

Hall of the Universe

3 Ecosphere
A sealed glass sphere in the Hall of the Universe holds a complete, self-sustaining ecosystem of plants, algae and animals that recycle nutrients and obtain energy solely from sunlight. The exhibit explores the basis of life on Earth.

4 Astro Bulletin
This high-definition screen displays the latest imagery from telescope observations worldwide and current NASA missions.

5 Hall of Planet Earth
Geological samples from around the world and videos explain the various processes that formed the earth and continue to shape it.

Hall of Planet Earth

6 Dynamic Earth Globe
This globe, suspended above an amphitheater in the Hall of Planet Earth, uses a projection system to recreate views of a rotating earth as seen from space.

7 Earthquake Monitoring Station
Earthquakes are monitored on a screen as they unfold. Other video stations show scientists at work.

8 Scales of the Universe Walkway
Models show the relative sizes of cosmic, human, and microscopic objects, from galaxies and stars down to the smallest atom.

9 Big Bang Theater
Glass flooring around a circular opening lets visitors look down into a multisensory interpretation of the first movements of the universe.

10 Cosmic Pathway
The Big Bang exits to this sloping 360-ft (110-m) pathway with astronomical images tracing landmarks through 13 billion years of cosmic evolution.

THE HAYDEN PLANETARIUM

Entrance to the Rose Center for Earth and Space

The Hayden Planetarium (3rd floor), a remarkable advance in the study of astronomy and astrophysics, boasts a highly sophisticated Digital Dome System that is the most advanced high-resolution virtual reality simulator ever built. The space shows take place in a 429-seat Space Theater and are virtual flights through a scientifically accurate universe. It is advisable to order tickets for the space shows in advance, or to pick them up early in the day to secure a spot. Don't miss *Worlds Beyond Earth*, a spectacular space show that launches visitors into the night sky on an epic voyage through time and space.

**TOP 10
FEATURES**

1 **Milky Way Galaxy Model**

2 **Space shows** such as *Worlds Beyond Earth*

3 **In-depth study** of the galaxies

4 **Advanced** Zeiss star projector

5 **Up-to-date** planetary data supported by NASA

6 **Astronomy Live** programs

7 **Digital Universe Atlas** of the cosmos

8 **Continuous calculation** of star locations

9 **Digital Dome System** with a 67-ft- (20-m-) wide hemispheric dome

10 **Simulations** of current events

Worlds Beyond Earth **space show at the Hayden Planetarium**

The Top 10
of Everything

Interior of the Basilica of St. Patrick's
Old Cathedral, Lower Manhattan

Figures in History

1 Peter Stuyvesant

Sent from the Netherlands in 1647 to govern New Amsterdam, Peter Stuyvesant (1612–72) was so disliked by his subjects that they welcomed British occupation.

2 Alexander Hamilton

Revolutionary leader and first Secretary of the Treasury, Hamilton (1755–1804) introduced business-friendly policies that were instrumental in New York's emergence as the financial center of the US. He lost his life in a duel with political opponent Aaron Burr and is buried in Trinity Church graveyard.

Alexander Hamilton

3 Elizabeth Jennings Graham

A school teacher, Graham (1827–1901) challenged racial segregation in 1854 when she boarded a streetcar that prohibited Black passengers and was forcibly removed by the conductor and the police when she refused to leave. Graham successfully sued the Third Avenue Railroad Company, the conductor, and the streetcar driver. The landmark case was the first step toward ending transit segregation in the city.

Elizabeth Jennings Graham

4 Jacob Riis

Appalled by immigrant living conditions, Riis (1849–1914), a social reformer, writer, and photographer, used photos taken in tenements to illustrate his stories, shocking the middle class and motivating them to act. His 1888 article, "Flashes from the Slums," as well as his book, *How the Other Half Lives*, brought national attention.

5 John D. Rockefeller, Jr.

The largess of John D. Rockefeller, Jr. (1874–1960) helped support housing in Harlem, the Bronx, and Queens, created Fort Tryon Park and the Cloisters, and provided land for the United Nations. Construction of Rockefeller Center *(see pp16–17)* employed thousands at the height of the Depression, giving the city an enduring landmark.

6 Fiorello H. LaGuardia

Considered to have been the best mayor of the city, after his election in 1933 Fiorello H. LaGuardia (1882–1947) modernized and centralized a chaotic city government, eliminated waste, unified the transit system, and obtained federal funds to help the city. A man of the people, he is popularly remembered for his reading of comics on the radio during a city newspaper strike.

7 Robert Moses

As construction supervisor and parks commissioner from the 1930s to the 1950s, Robert Moses (1888–1981) vastly enlarged and upgraded the city's recreational areas, but he also covered the city with highways rather than develop a public transport system and was responsible for urban renewal projects that razed many neighborhoods in favor of high-rises.

8 Adam Clayton Powell, Jr.

Powell (1908–72) took over from his father as pastor of the Abyssinian Baptist Church in 1937. He also worked to persuade Harlem's store owners to employ people from the Black community. He went on to be the first person of African American descent elected to the city council, and later became New York City's first Black congressional representative, serving from 1945 to 1961.

9 Shirley Chisholm

In 1968, Chisholm (1924–2005) became the first Black woman to be elected to the United States Congress. She was posthumously awarded the Presidential Medal of Freedom by Barack Obama in 2015. Shirley Chisholm State Park in Brooklyn opened in 2019 in her honor.

10 Alexandria Ocasio-Cortez

In 2019, Alexandria Ocasio-Cortez (b. 1989) became the youngest woman ever to serve in the United States Congress when she was elected to represent New York's 14th Congressional district (areas of the Bronx and Queens). Popularly known as AOC, Cortez is considered to be a rising star in the Democratic Party.

Alexandria Ocasio-Cortez

TOP 10 DATES IN NEW YORK CITY'S HISTORY

Peter Minuit buys Manhattan

1 Pre-1626
The area that would eventually become New York is part of Lenapehoking, the Lenape/Delaware homeland.

2 1626
Peter Minuit buys Manhattan from the Lenape tribe. Beads and trinkets worth about 60 Dutch guilders at the time accomplished the deal.

3 1664
The British take Manhattan from the Dutch. New Amsterdam becomes New York.

4 1789
George Washington is inaugurated as first President and takes his oath of office in Federal Hall. New York serves as the first US capital.

5 1792
New York Stock Exchange is established, 24 traders sign an agreement beneath a tree on Wall Street, and the city becomes a financial center.

6 1886
The Statue of Liberty is unveiled, becoming the symbol of freedom for millions of immigrants, who form a "melting pot" of nationalities.

7 1898
The five boroughs unite to form New York, the world's second largest city.

8 1931
The Empire State Building establishes New York as the skyscraper capital of the world.

9 1952
The city becomes home to the headquarters of the United Nations.

10 2001
Terrorists use hijacked planes to destroy the World Trade Center.

TOP10 Museums

1 Metropolitan Museum of Art

It would take weeks to see all the treasures of this mammoth, ever-changing museum (see pp32–5), which includes a collection of more than 3,000 European paintings. The Greek, Roman, Cypriot, and Asian halls contain some exceptional artifacts, and the Joyce and Robert Menschel Hall for Modern Photography is also worth seeking out.

2 American Museum of Natural History

Exhibiting everything from dinosaurs to traditional Chinese costumes, this is the largest museum (see pp40–43) of its kind in the world. In addition to the planetarium show in the Rose Center, there are films screened in a giant IMAX theater.

3 Museum of Modern Art (MoMA)

The renovation of this museum in 2019 cost $400 million and added

Museum of Modern Art

40,000 sq ft (3,716 sq m) of gallery space, an experimental "platform", and a studio space. Affectionately shortened to MoMA (see pp36–9), this modern art powerhouse has one of the most comprehensive collections of late 19th and 20th- century art in the world.

4 Solomon R. Guggenheim Museum

The Guggenheim (see p137) has expanded its collection with several major donations, including Justin Thannhauser's Impressionist masters, Peggy Guggenheim's Cubist, Surrealist, and Abstract Expressionist works, a collection of American Minimalist and Conceptual art, and the most extensive collection of Kandinsky's works in the US.

5 Whitney Museum of American Art

The entire range of 20th- and 21st-century American art can be seen in the permanent collection in this striking Renzo Piano building, along with changing contemporary exhibitions. The museum (see p109) showcases works by renowned artists such as Warhol, Calder, O'Keeffe, and Hopper.

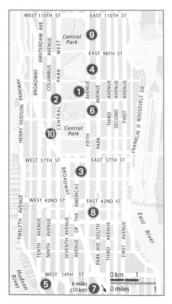

6 Frick Madison

The art collection *(see pp138–9)* of steel magnate Henry Clay Frick (1849–1919) will be on display in the Breuer Building until the end of 2023, when a massive renovation of the old Frick Mansion (1 East 70th St) is completed. Frick's collection of Old Masters, French furniture, sculptures, and rare Limoges enamels are exhibited in Breuer's modern galleries. Highlights include works by renowned artists Rembrandt, Vermeer, Hals, Holbein, Titian, and Bellini.

Museum of the City of New York

7 Brooklyn Museum

200 Eastern Pkwy, Brooklyn ■ Subway 2, 3 to Eastern Pkwy ■ Open 11am–6pm Wed–Sun; first Sat of month (Feb–Aug): free 5pm–10pm ■ Adm ■ www.brooklyn museum.org

Housed in a fine Beaux Arts building, this museum presents a wide range of special exhibitions alongside its permanent collections of Asian, Egyptian, African, and American art. The Elizabeth A. Sackler Center for Feminist Art is the first public space of its kind in the country.

8 Morgan Library and Museum

MAP K4 ■ 225 Madison Ave, at 36th St ■ Open 10:30am–5pm Tue–Thu & Sat–Sun, 10:30am–7pm Fri ■ Adm (free 5–7pm Fri) ■ www. themorgan.org

This Italian Renaissance-style palazzo was designed in 1902 to hold the collection of billionaire J. Pierpont Morgan – an extraordinary assemblage of rare manuscripts, bindings, books, ancient artifacts, and over 10,000 drawings and prints by the likes of Da Vinci and Dürer. Morgan's original opulent study and library are highlights. There are also galleries with changing exhibitions.

Egyptian exhibit, Brooklyn Museum

9 Museum of the City of New York

MAP D3 ■ 1220 5th Ave, at 103rd St ■ Open 10am–9pm Thu, 10am–5pm Fri–Mon ■ Adm ■ www.mcny.org

The toy collection is a highlight and rotating exhibitions explore fashion, architecture, entertainment, cultural identity and traditions, and social history. A film documenting the evolution of the city is featured.

10 American Folk Art Museum

The first New York museum built from the ground up has critiqued the country's cultural history since opening in 1961. The eight-level, innovative structure *(see p144)* shows off a collection of all-American paintings, sculptures, quilts, and furniture. Exhibitions here usually revolve, but the permanent collection is always on display.

American Folk Art Museum

📻 Art Galleries

Balloon Swan by Jeff Koons at the Gagosian gallery

1 Gagosian
MAP E4 ▪ 980 & 976 Madison Ave; 821 Park Ave; 555 & 541 W 24th St, 522 W 21st St ▪ Opening times vary, check website for details ▪ www.gagosian.com

Expect big names and equivalent price tags at this blue-ribbon gallery with six locations – three uptown and three Chelsea addresses *(see p124)* – each with the lofty spaces necessary for exhibiting large-scale art. Damien Hirst, Anselm Kiefer, Richard Serra, and Jeff Koons are among the contemporary artists represented.

2 Marlborough
MAP L2 ▪ 545 West 25th St ▪ Open 10am–6pm Mon–Sat ▪ www.marlborough newyork.com

This impressive gallery, representing the estates of artists including Larry Rivers, Red Grooms, and R. B. Kitaj, is located in Chelsea *(see p124)*. Marlborough has shown work by sculptors such as Anthony Caro and Jacques Lipchitz, as well as a host of contemporary painters.

3 David Zwirner
One of the biggest names in the art world, this gallery started out at a humble location in SoHo back in 1993, with Franz West as the first exhibitor. Since then, new galleries have opened in New York, London, and Hong Kong. From the very beginning, Zwirner focused on experimental shows by emerging artists such as Stan Douglas, Diana Thater, and Jason Rhoades. The gallery on 20th Street *(see p124)*, designed by Selldorf Architects in 2013, is an imposing contemporary space in exposed concrete and teak.

4 Pace Prints
MAP L2 ▪ 536 W 22nd St ▪ Open 10am–6pm Tue–Sat ▪ www.paceprints.com

Founded in 1968, Pace Prints, affiliated with the Pace Gallery *(see p124)*, exhibits fine art prints from the late 19th century to the mid-20th century. It is housed in the same building as the Pace African &

Oceanic Art gallery, which displays traditional art, such as masks and sculptured figures, from Africa, Oceania, and Asia. Much of the gallery's antique inventory is museum-quality.

5 Sperone Westwater
MAP N4 ▪ 257 Bowery ▪ Open 10am–6pm Tue–Sat (Jun–Sep: Mon–Fri) ▪ www.speronewestwater.com

This is an excellent place to see some of the most creative contemporary art being produced today. The gallery was set up in 1975 to showcase European artists who had little recognition in the US. In 2010 it moved to a building designed by Foster + Partners. Exhibitions have included works by Bruce Nauman and Donald Judd.

The Drawing Center

6 The Drawing Center
Formed in 1977 to promote the art of drawing, this non-profit center (see p105) has displayed the drawings of more than 2,500 emerging artists, including the early work of Shahzia Sikander and Kara Walker, as well as the work of the Old Masters. The center also hosts monthly events, including book signings and panel discussions.

7 apexart
MAP P3–4 ▪ 291 Church St ▪ Open 11am–6pm Tue–Sat ▪ www.apexart.org

Contemporary visual arts exhibitions, as well as public lectures, readings, children's workshops, and innovative performances are on offer at this not-for-profit organization, which aims to promote cultural and intellectual diversity. Over 17,000 visitors pass through its doors each year to see the latest works by artists such as Dave Hickey, Martha Rosler, and David Byrne.

8 Matthew Marks
This was one of the first commercial galleries to open in Chelsea, in a converted garage in 1994. Matthew Marks (see p124) specializes in displaying the work of big-name artists such as Ellsworth Kelly, Jasper Johns, Nan Goldin, and Brice Marden. Two other Chelsea locations show new works by photographers, painters, and sculptors.

9 Paula Cooper
Paula Cooper, the first gallery to open in SoHo in 1968, deserted the area in 1996 to move to Chelsea (see p124). There, the vast, creatively designed space filtering natural light through a cathedral ceiling is a superb setting for conceptual and minimalist art by Donald Judd, Sol LeWitt, Sophie Calle, and others.

10 Kasmin
The late Paul Kasmin was the son of an alternative London art dealer and his gallery continues the family tradition of taking chances on new artists (see p124) – it usually features these artists in group shows. More established names, including those of sculptors and photographers, regularly appear here in solo exhibitions.

Gallery shop, Kasmin

New York City Skyscrapers

1 Empire State Building
The Empire State Building (1930–31) was eclipsed as the tallest structure in New York for 28 years by the World Trade Center, which was destroyed in the 9/11 terrorist attack. It was overtaken again upon completion of One World Trade Center in 2014. With an 86th-floor observatory, the Empire State Building *(see pp12–13)* receives some 4 million visitors a year.

2 Chrysler Building
The gleaming, stainless-steel, tiered spire of the Chrysler Building (1928–30) adds grace to the city skyline. William Van Alen fashioned this Art Deco classic as a tribute to the automobile. The building *(see p127)* has a decorative frieze of stylized hubcaps and silver gargoyles, much like the winged radiator caps of a Chrysler automobile.

Woolworth Building

3 Woolworth Building
Prominent architect Cass Gilbert was responsible for this flamboyant 1913 Neo-Gothic building *(see p85)*, the tallest in the world for two decades after it was completed. The rich terra cotta ornamentation accentuates the structure's steel frame, which soars to a graceful crown 60 stories above Broadway. The small lobby inside the building boasts a luxurious marble interior using stone from Greece and Vermont.

4 Comcast Building
MAP J3 ▪ 30 Rockefeller Plaza, between 50th & 51st Sts ▪ Lobby open 7am–midnight daily
This dramatic 70-story skyscraper (1931–3), designed by Raymond Hood, and known as 30 Rock, has shallow setbacks that recede into the distance. Part of the greatness of Hood's design is the contrast between the building's height and the surrounding Rockefeller Center *(see pp16–17)*.

5 Flatiron Building
This 21-story, triangular-shaped building *(see p116)* has intrigued New Yorkers since it was built by Daniel Burnham in 1902; the shape was so unusual

Spire of the Chrysler Building

space. Inside is the Grill, a restaurant from celebrity chefs Mario Carbone and Rich Torrisi.

⑧ 601 Lexington Avenue
MAP J4 ■ 601 Lexington Ave ■ Plaza and lobby open during office hours

This was considered New York's first Postmodern skyscraper upon its completion as Citicorp Center in 1978. The triangular top never served its original purpose as a solar panel, but it did make the building instantly recognizable. An open base on four tall columns and a reflective aluminum-and-glass exterior give it an airy quality.

⑨ 56 Leonard
MAP P3 ■ 56 Leonard St, at Church St ■ Closed to public

The tallest building in Tribeca, 56 Leonard is a shimmering stack of cantilevered glass blocks dubbed the "Jenga Building". The condo was designed by Herzog & de Meuron and completed in 2016.

⑩ One World Trade Center

Marking the rebirth of Lower Manhattan after 9/11, One World Trade Center opened in 2014. The tallest building in the city (see p80), it stands at the symbolic height of 1,776 ft (541 m), reflecting the year of America's declaration of independence.

One World Trade Center

that people took bets on whether it would topple. The secret of this successful design was in the steel frame support, which was used instead of traditional heavy stone walls: a precursor of skyscrapers to come.

⑥ Lever House

Gordon Bunshaft's 24-story Lever House (see p131), completed in 1952, was revolutionary; it was New York's first skyscraper built in the form of a vertical slab of glass and steel. It began the eventual transformation of Park Avenue into an avenue of glass towers.

⑦ Seagram Building
MAP J4 ■ 375 Park Ave, between 52nd & 53rd Sts ■ Plaza and lobby open during office hours

The first New York building by Mies van der Rohe is this landmark "glass box" with slender bands of bronze amid walls of smoked glass rising from the open plaza. The glass-walled lobby by Philip Johnson helps blur the division between indoor and outdoor

Historic Buildings

Interior of St. Patrick's Cathedral

1 St. Paul's Chapel
Completed in 1766, this church *(see p86)* has a glorious Georgian interior lit by Waterford Crystal chandeliers. The pew where George Washington prayed after his inauguration as President has been preserved.

2 City Hall
This Georgian building (1803–12) with French Renaissance influences is one of New York's finest. The interior of the hall *(see p86)* features a rotunda circled by ten Corinthian columns, opening to twin spiral marble staircases.

City Hall

3 Trinity Church
This square-towered church *(see p79)*, built between 1839 and 1846 has bronze doors designed by Richard Morris Hunt. The spire was once the tallest structure in Manhattan but is now dwarfed by Wall Street towers. Alexander Hamilton *(see p46)* and Robert Fulton are buried here.

4 St. Patrick's Cathedral
James Renwick, Jr. designed America's largest Catholic cathedral (opened in 1879) in French Gothic style with twin 330-ft (100-m) towers. The interior of this magnificent cathedral *(see p128)* has side altars dedicated to saints and holy figures, chapels, and stained-glass windows.

5 Carnegie Hall
Industrialist Andrew Carnegie financed the city's first great concert hall, built in 1891. Major renovation in 1986 restored the interior bronze balconies and ornamental plaster, and a museum was added. The corridors of the hall *(see p129)* are lined with memorabilia of the great artists who have performed here.

6 Cathedral Church of St. John the Divine
The world's largest cathedral *(see p148)* was begun in 1892 and is still a work in progress. The part-Romanesque, part-Gothic building is impressive for its stonework, enormous nave, bay altar windows, and rose window. The seat of New York's episcopal archdiocese, the church is the scene of many avant-garde musical and theatrical events.

7 New York Stock Exchange

Opened in 1903, the facade of this 17-story edifice (see p79) is appropriately monumental for the building at the center of the US economy. The figures on the pediment represent the "sources of American prosperity." "Black Thursday," the start of the Great Depression, began here in 1929.

8 US Custom House

One of the city's best Neo-Classical buildings, this eight-story structure (see p79), built in 1907, features an elaborate mansard roof and fine sculptures, including four by Daniel Chester French. A 1937 nautical mural by Reginald Marsh adorns the huge, oval rotunda.

9 New York Public Library

This white marble, 1911 Beaux Arts edifice (see p128) is magnificent both inside and out. Imposing stairways, terraces, and fountains inspire awe, while reading rooms invite repose. Events and lectures are frequently held here.

10 Grand Central Terminal

This 1913 train station (see p127) is remarkable for its beauty; the main concourse is suffused with natural light and the vaulted ceiling is decorated with myriad twinkling constellations.

The main concourse of Grand Central Terminal

TOP 10 CHURCHES AND TEMPLES

Temple Emanu-El

1 Temple Emanu-El
MAP G4 ▪ 1 East 65th St
World's largest synagogue, built in 1929.

2 St. George Ukrainian Catholic Church
MAP M4 ▪ 30 East 7th St
A contemporary church built in Byzantine style.

3 St. Nicholas Russian Orthodox Cathedral
MAP E4 ▪ 15 East 97th St
Five onion domes mark this Russian Baroque church.

4 St. Sava Serbian Orthodox Cathedral
MAP L3 ▪ 16–20 West 26th St
Byzantine windows were added to this 1856 church.

5 St. Vartan Armenian Cathedral
MAP K4 ▪ 630 2nd Ave
The gold-leaf dome was inspired by the churches of Armenia.

6 St. Elizabeth of Hungary Church
MAP F4 ▪ 211 East 83rd St
This Neo-Gothic church has a painted vaulted ceiling.

7 Holy Trinity Cathedral
MAP G5 ▪ 319 East 74th St
Built in 1931 in Byzantine style as the seat of the Greek Orthodox diocese.

8 Zion St. Mark's Evangelical Lutheran Church
MAP F5 ▪ 339 East 84th St
Built in 1892, this church is a reminder of the Upper East's German past.

9 First Chinese Presbyterian Church
MAP P5 ▪ 61 Henry St
The stone sanctuary dates from 1819.

10 Islamic Cultural Center
MAP E4 ▪ 1711 3rd Ave, at 96th St
Ninety bulbs hang from the dome.

🔟 Off the Beaten Path

Aerial view of Governors Island

1 Governors Island
MAP R2 ■ New York Harbor ■ Open May–Oct: 7am–10pm Mon–Fri, 7am–11pm Sat & Sun; Nov–Apr: 7am–6pm daily ■ www.govisland.com

The ferry ride only takes 10 minutes to this former Coast Guard base in the middle of New York harbor. It features open-air sculpture exhibits, summer concerts, and festivals.

2 Socrates Sculpture Park
MAP F6 ■ 32-01 Vernon Bvd, Queens ■ Open 9am–sunset daily ■ www.socratessculpturepark.org

This vibrant sculpture park hosts lots of free events from summer solstice to Halloween.

3 Green-Wood Cemetery
500 25th St, Brooklyn ■ Open Apr–Sep: 7am–7pm daily; Oct–Mar: 8am–5pm daily ■ www.green-wood.com

Roam the final resting place of many New York personalities, from Jean-Michel Basquiat to Leonard Bernstein, at this landscaped cemetery.

4 Roosevelt Island and Tramway
MAP H5

Climb aboard the Roosevelt Island Tramway, one of the oldest aerial commuter tramways in the US, to this island in the East River, with everything from a 19th-century lighthouse to the quiet, riverfront Franklin D. Roosevelt Four Freedoms Park.

5 New York Earth Room
MAP N4 ■ 141 Wooster St ■ Opening hours vary, check online ■ www.diaart.org

The draw of this modern installation by Walter De Maria is the juxtaposition – in SoHo, amid the most expensive real estate in the world, is a massive room filled with nothing but dirt.

6 Wave Hill
4900 Independence Ave, Riverdale, Bronx ■ Open 10am–5:30pm Tue–Sun (Nov–mid-Mar: to 4:30pm) ■ Adm ■ www.wavehill.org

Walk in the footsteps of Mark Twain and Theodore Roosevelt, who once resided in the stately Wave Hill House, which presides over this historic garden and cultural center.

7 Alice Austen House
2 Hylan Blvd, Staten Island ■ Open Mar–Dec: noon–5pm Tue–Sat ■ Adm ■ www.aliceausten.org

See historic New York City through the photos of Alice Austen, one of the

Alice Austen House, Staten Island

nation's pioneering photographers, in this museum on the shores of the Narrows on Staten Island.

8 Museum of the Moving Image

It's a long way from Hollywood, but Queens has one of the finest movie museums in the nation – and it's free on Thursday afternoons (2pm to 6pm). The permanent exhibition includes historic cameras and vintage TVs (see p158), but the real draw is the museum's interactive exhibits; for example, you can dub in your own voice over famous movie scenes.

Museum of the Moving Image

9 Greenacre Park

MAP J4 ■ East 51st St, between 2nd and 3rd Aves ■ www.greenacre park.org

A waterfall in Midtown Manhattan? Your eyes do not deceive you. This often overlooked but lovely "vest-pocket" park features leafy corners, fragrant flowers and a tumbling 25-ft- (8-m-) high waterfall that sends off a refreshing spray of cooling water over passers by.

10 Red Hook

South Brooklyn ■ www.red hookwaterfront.com

Take in gorgeous vistas of the New York City skyline and a straight-on view of the iconic Statue of Liberty (Manhattan and New Jersey only get views of the back and side) from this waterfront neighborhood, dotted with homey spots like the Red Hook Lobster Pound and Steve's Authentic Key Lime Pie.

TOP 10 PARKS AND GARDENS

Madison Square Park in spring

1 Madison Square Park
MAP L3 ■ 5th Ave & Broadway, at 23rd St
A landscaped park, Madison Square has striking displays of public art.

2 The High Line
This elevated train-track-turned-stylish-park (see p121) has transformed the surrounding Meatpacking District.

3 Bryant Park
MAP K3 ■ 6th Ave, between 41st and 42nd Sts
A pocket of green with formal planting in Midtown, behind the New York Public Library.

4 Central Park
The grand dame (see pp32–3) of New York City's parks.

5 91st Street Community Garden
MAP E2 ■ Riverside Park, at 91st St
A lovely grove filled with flowers.

6 Hudson River Park
MAP N2 ■ From 59th St to Battery Park
The longest waterfront park in the US.

7 New York Botanical Garden
The city's premier botanical garden (see p155) with plants and flowers from all around the world.

8 The Cloisters' Gardens
An oasis of serene beauty (see p37), where over 250 kinds of plants grown in medieval Europe can be found.

9 Battery Park
MAP R3 ■ Southern tip of Manhattan
Waterfront park with views of New York Harbor and the Statue of Liberty.

10 John Jay Park
MAP F5 ■ East 77th St & FDR Drive
Past the playgrounds and pool is a seating area with East River views.

Children's Attractions

Chelsea Piers sports complex

1 Chelsea Piers
MAP L2 ■ 23rd St, at Hudson River ■ Open 5:30am–11pm Mon–Fri (to 10pm Fri), 8am–9pm Sat & Sun ■ Adm ■ www.chelseapiers.com

This family-friendly sports complex has a bowling alley, an ice-skating rink, golf driving ranges, batting cages, and playing fields.

2 Central Park
Popular activities at this park (see pp32–3) include carousel rides, boating, storytelling, and guided walks. In winter, the Wollman Rink and Harlem Meer Center (under renovation until 2024) both offer ice-skating (and skate rentals). The Belvedere Castle is also worth a visit.

3 Children's Museum of Manhattan
Educational fun with exhibits like Body Odyssey – exploring a giant crawl-through body – and a TV studio where kids produce their own shows. The museum (see p144) also has a play area for under-fours.

4 American Museum of Natural History
Introduce children to dioramas of wild animals in realistic natural habitats and fascinating dinosaur exhibits. The enormous meteorites and mineral rock specimens at this museum (see pp40–41) are also favorites. The Rose Center will intrigue older children and teens.

5 Brooklyn Children's Museum
This hands-on museum (see p159) has exhibitions on history, science, and the environment, as well as the diverse ethnicities and cultures found around Brooklyn. The bright, specially designed underground building houses over 30,000 artifacts, ranging from masks and musical instruments to rocks and fossils.

6 New Victory Theater
MAP J3 ■ 209 West 42nd St, between 7th & 8th Aves ■ Box office open noon–7pm Tue–Sat, 11am–5pm Sun ■ Adm ■ www.newvictory.org

New York's first major theater devoted to family entertainment. Pre-performance workshops with the theater's staff and cast offer interesting insights into how a theater works.

An exhibit at the American Museum of Natural History

7 Coney Island

Coney Island has undergone major redevelopments after years of neglect. Features of the island include Luna Park *(see p159)*, which has thrilling rides, the landmark Ferris wheel, a long sandy beach, and a beachside boardwalk with a carnival atmosphere with marine mosaics, gaming arcades, concession stands hawking prizes, and sideshows. It is a fabulous children's playground. Summer is the best time to visit, as most of the attractions are outdoors, but the crowds can get heavy on weekends.

Rides at Coney Island

8 New York Transit Museum

Discover the intricate world of New York City's subways, trains, buses, and bridge and tunnel systems at this lively museum *(see p159)* Exhibits include models, photographs, and maps, as well as aged turnstiles and a few interactive displays of fuel technologies. A gallery annex *(see p132)* is also at Grand Central Terminal.

9 Tall Ship Cruises

MAP Q4 ▪ Pier 16 at Seaport District NYC ▪ Cruises May–Oct: Wed–Sun ▪ Adm ▪ www.southstreet seaportmuseum.org

A boat ride in Manhattan harbor is always a thrill, and what better

way to go to sea than aboard the 1885 iron-hulled schooner *Pioneer* at Seaport District NYC? Visitors can choose between the two-hour daytime sails and the two-hour sunset cruises. Advance reservations are recommended.

10 New York Hall of Science

When little ones get fed up with sightseeing, bring them to this popular spot in Queens *(see p158)*. Kids are invited to create scientific models using a range of raw materials and interact with various hands-on exhibits. The museum also hosts a varied program of events, including free creative sessions for neurodiverse children and their families, and a series of adult-only social events. There's a 3D theater, showing educational movies, and a mini-golf course, too.

🔟 LGBTQ+ New York City

Stonewall Inn

It features exhibits across all mediums, ranging from photography and video to paintings and drawings.

① Stonewall Inn
MAP N3 ■ 53 Christopher St

A police raid on this bar on June 27, 1969 turned into a riot as LGBTQ+ patrons rose up against constant police harassment. In 2016 it became the first US National Monument dedicated to LGBTQ+ rights.

② Christopher Street
MAP N3

The profusion of bars and shops between 6th and 7th Avenues used to be the epicenter of gay Greenwich Village before the community moved on to Chelsea and Hell's Kitchen. The street still retains a sense of history.

③ Leslie-Lohman Museum of Art
MAP P3 ■ 26 Wooster St ■ 212 431 2609
■ Open noon–6pm Wed–Sun, noon–8pm Thu ■ www.leslielohman.org

This museum is one of the nation's oldest LGBTQ+ art museums.

④ Chelsea
MAP M2/L2 ■ 8th Ave, between West 14th & West 23rd Sts

This neighborhood is popular with the LGBTQ+ community. Gay revelers pack the bars and spill onto the sidewalks at the weekend, and a scene of some sort can be found in every café and club.

⑤ Lesbian, Gay, Bisexual, and Transgender Community Center
MAP M2 ■ 208 West 13th St
■ Open 10am–10pm Mon–Sat (to 8pm Sun) ■ www.gaycenter.org

Since 1983, The Center has served as a meeting space for local organizations, a leader in public education, health, and emotional counseling, and a destination for social events. It also documents LGBTQ+ history in its extensive library.

⑥ Performance Venues

Various venues in the city provide space for performers from the LGBTQ+ community. The Playhouse NYC (100 7th Ave South, www.playhousebar.com) hosts lively drag shows and competitions (on

Facade of the Leslie-Lohman Museum of Art

Wednesdays) as well as a show-tunes night on Sundays. Meanwhile, 3 Dollar Bill (260 Meserole St, Brooklyn, www.3dollarbillbk.com) organizes LGBTQ+ storytelling, drag shows, and femme speed dating.

⑦ Club Nights
Check listings publications for details
Many bars and clubs have party nights, like Thursdays at The Eagle, and Sundays at The Monster. The Cock is lively most nights. Be warned: because of rising rents and complaining neighbors, venues frequently change.

⑧ Lesbian Herstory Archives
484 14th St, Brooklyn ▪ Subway (F) 15th St, Prospect Park ▪ 718 768 3953 ▪ Open by appointment ▪ www.lesbianherstoryarchives.org
The world's largest and oldest lesbian archive, founded in 1973, is located in Park Slope, a popular lesbian neighborhood. The volunteer-run archive houses art, books, photos, periodicals, and films. It also holds events supporting lesbian writers and artists in all media.

⑨ New York Sports Club
MAP M3 ▪ 128 8th Ave, at West 16th St ▪ Open 6am–10pm Mon–Thu, 6am–9pm Fri, 7am–8pm Sat & Sun ▪ Adm
Fitness fans in Chelsea flock to this popular gym, which is one of several outlets of a local chain. Expect high-tech equipment, yoga, BFX, spin classes, and steam rooms.

⑩ Bluestockings Cooperative
MAP N5 ▪ 116 Suffolk St ▪ Open 1–7pm Mon, 11am–7pm Tue–Sun ▪ www.bluestockings.com
This Lower East Side haunt, named after an 18th-century feminist group, is a favorite among the LGBTQ+ community.. It's a solid source for LGBTQ+ literature and also hosts a full calendar of readings, performances, and book clubs.

TOP 10 EATING AND MEETING PLACES

Henrietta Hudson logo

1 Henrietta Hudson
MAP N3 ▪ 438 Hudson St
Warm, down-to-earth, lesbian bar in Greenwich Village.

2 Gym
MAP L2 ▪ 167 8th Ave
This friendly, casual site is home to New York City's first gay sports bar.

3 The Boiler Room
MAP N4 ▪ 86 East 4th St
Popular East Village gay dive bar, known for its Sunday tea dances.

4 Julius'
MAP M3 ▪ 159 West 10th St
The oldest gay bar in New York still boasts plenty of character and serves up tasty burgers.

5 Flaming Saddles
MAP H2 ▪ 793 9th Ave
A casual saloon-style gay bar complete with dancing bar staff.

6 Phoenix
MAP M5 ▪ 447 East 13th St
An East Village hangout with an old-school vibe. Unpretentious, with cheap drinks.

7 The Eagle
MAP L2 ▪ 554 West 28th St
In this place, it's all about Levi's, leather, and fetish.

8 REBAR Chelsea
MAP L2 ▪ 225 West 19th St
Popular bar and club with half-price drinks during Happy Hour (4–7pm).

9 Club Cumming
MAP N5 ▪ 505 East 6th St
Known for its wild parties, this club/bar is owned by actor Alan Cumming.

10 The Cubbyhole
MAP M2 ▪ 281 West 12th St
A cozy, unpretentious lesbian bar beloved for its old school jukebox and *Finding Nemo* decor.

🔟 Performing Arts Venues

A ballet dancer performs at David H. Koch Theater

1 David H. Koch Theater

Formerly known as the New York State Theater, this famous stage was built in 1964 to the specification of legendary choreographer George Balanchine, the founder of the New York City Ballet *(see p142)*, which dances here in winter and spring. The venue also hosts performances by international dance troupes.

2 Metropolitan Opera House

Lincoln Center's most elegant performance venue, the Metropolitan Opera *(see p142)* shows off glorious oversize murals by Marc Chagall inside great arched windows. The interior boasts exquisite starburst chandeliers that are raised to the ceiling before each performance. The Metropolitan hosts the American Ballet Theatre and many traveling groups, as well as its famous opera company.

3 David Geffen Hall

Renamed in honour of the entertainment mogul David Geffen, who donated $100 million to the Lincoln Center *(see p142)*, this hall is home to the New York Philharmonic, the oldest symphony orchestra in the US. A bust by Rodin of composer and once Philharmonic Music Director Gustav Mahler, on the west side of the building, is one of the finest pieces of sculpture in Lincoln Center.

4 Carnegie Hall

This historic concert hall *(see p129)* opened in 1891 with Tchaikovsky making his US debut on the podium. A campaign led by violinist Isaac Stern saved the hall from demolition after Lincoln Center *(see p142)* was completed in 1969, and it entered its second century with old-world style intact after being lavishly renovated.

5 Alice Tully Hall

This hall (see p142), with its stunning modern facade, was built in 1969 for the Chamber Music Society of Lincoln Center. Besides chamber and vocal concerts, it is used for shows by the Juilliard School students and faculty, many of which are free to the public.

6 New York City Center

MAP H3 ■ 131 West 55th St, between 6th & 7th Aves ■ 212 581 1212 ■ Adm ■ www.nycity center.org

The ornate, Moorish-style building with a dome of Spanish tiles was opened in 1923 as a Shriners Temple. Having been saved from developers by city mayor Fiorello H. LaGuardia (see p46), it survived after losing its companies to Lincoln Center, and is now a major venue for touring dance companies. The center was extensively renovated in 2011.

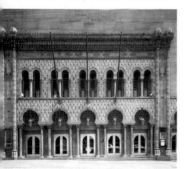

The ornate New York City Center

7 Joyce Theater

MAP L2 ■ 175 8th Ave, at 19th St ■ 212 242 0800 ■ Adm ■ www.joyce.org

This 1941 Art Deco movie theater was converted in 1982 to become an intimate home for dance. Small and medium-sized modern dance companies from around the world present an exciting range of work that can't be seen elsewhere in Manhattan. Question-and-answer sessions with the artists and performers follow some of the shows.

The neon lights of Radio City

8 Radio City Music Hall

MAP J3 ■ 1260 6th Ave, at 50th St ■ 212 247 4777 ■ Tours 9:30am–5pm daily ■ Adm ■ www.msg.com

This opulent, Art Deco hall opened in 1932 as part of the Rockefeller Center. Once a movie palace, it now hosts musical performances and special events. The Christmas show starring the Rockettes, a troupe of long-legged dancers, is a festive New York tradition.

9 Brooklyn Academy of Music (BAM)

30 Lafayette Ave, Brooklyn ■ Subway 2, 3, 4, 5, B, Q to Atlantic Ave ■ 718 636 4100 ■ Adm ■ www.bam.org

This Neo-Italianate 1908 building hosts the city's most avant-garde program of international music, theater, and dance, most notably the Next Wave Festival, a fixture since 1981.

10 Madison Square Garden

MAP K3 ■ 7th Ave, at 32nd St ■ 212 465 6741 ■ Tours 10:30am–2pm Mon, Tue, Thu, & Fri (12:15–3pm on game days) ■ Adm ■ www.msg.com

Home court for the New York Knicks basketball team and the New York Rangers hockey team, this 20,000-seat venue is also used for rock concerts (Billy Joel is a regular performer), ice shows, tennis, boxing, and dog shows.

TOP 10 Music Venues

Auditorium of the Beacon Theatre

1 Beacon Theatre
MAP G2 ▪ 2124 Broadway at West 74th St ▪ Open 1 hour before show ▪ Adm

Name the star and they've probably been on stage at Beacon Theatre, where the likes of Bob Dylan and B. B. King have performed. Shows range from pop and light rock to gospel.

2 Village Vanguard
MAP M3 ▪ 178 7th Ave South ▪ Open 7pm–midnight ▪ Adm

Since 1935, this club has featured a "who's who" of jazz. The early years were eclectic, also launching calypso singer Harry Belafonte.

3 Birdland
MAP J2 ▪ 315 West 44th St, between 8th & 9th Aves ▪ Hours vary ▪ Adm

Another legendary venue, although no longer in the location Charlie Parker performed at in 1949; it is now near Times Square. The Birdland Big Band plays on Fridays.

4 SOBs
MAP N3 ▪ 204 Varick St, at West Houston St ▪ Opening times vary ▪ Adm

The letters stand for Sounds of Brazil, but the music ranges from reggae to hip-hop via soul or jazz. The beat is contagious, and the dance floor gets crowded.

5 Music Hall of Williamsburg
MAP M7 ▪ 66 North 6th St, Williamsburg (Brooklyn) ▪ Shows at, 7pm, 8pm, or 9pm daily ▪ Adm

Set in a former mayonnaise factory, the Music Hall of Williamsburg boasts a big performance space with stellar acoustics and three bars. One of Brooklyn's top venues, the music hall is operated by the same group as Webster Hall, Brooklyn Steel, and Forest Hills Stadium in Queens.

6 The Iridium
MAP J3 ▪ 1650 Broadway, at West 51st St ▪ Open 7pm–midnight daily ▪ Adm

Opened in 1994, Iridium has funky decor, good food, and excellent established and new jazz groups. The great guitarist Les Paul used to play here from 1996 to 2009.

7 Dizzy's Club
MAP H2 ▪ 10 Columbus Circle ▪ Sets at 7:30 & 9:30pm Mon–Sat (also 11:15pm Tue–Sat), 5 & 7:30pm Sun ▪ Adm & cover charge

Part of Jazz at Lincoln Center, this club features top jazz groups. The cover charge is steep, but late-night sessions (from 11:15pm) are just $15 on the door (walk-ups only), plus one drink minimum.

8 Brooklyn Steel
319 Frost St (at Debevoise Ave), East Williamsburg ■ Opening times vary, check website for details ■ Adm ■ www.bowerypresents.com/venues/brooklyn-steel
Opened in 2017, this venue is housed in a repurposed steel manufacturing plant. It hosts a roster of local and international bands such as LCD Soundsystem and Arctic Monkeys.

9 Bowery Ballroom
MAP N4 ■ 6 Delancey St, between Bowery & Chrystie Sts ■ Opening times vary ■ Adm
The opening of the Bowery Ballroom in 1998 helped spearhead a Lower East Side renaissance. It boasts great acoustics and sightlines. Well-known touring acts, mid-scale indie rockers, and local bands feature.

10 Blue Note
MAP N3 ■ 131 West 3rd St, between MacDougal St & 6th Ave ■ Open 6pm–2am Sun–Thu, 6pm–4am Fri & Sat ■ Adm & cover charge
Tony Bennett, Natalie Cole, and Ray Charles have all played here. The emphasis is on jazz, but blues, Latin, R&B, soul, and big band also feature.

Blue Note jazz club

TOP 10 DANCE CLUBS

Busy dancefloor at Schimanski

1 Schimanski
MAP M7 ■ 54 North 11th St, Williamsburg
Cutting-edge club with an underground techno/dance music scene.

2 House of Yes
2 Wyckoff Ave, Bushwick
Lots of dance parties, plus theater and cabaret at this trendy spot in Brooklyn.

3 Rumpus Room
MAP N4 ■ 249 Eldridge St
Popular student hangout, thanks to dance parties throughout the week.

4 Eris Evolution
167 Graham Ave, Williamsburg
Art and performance space that hosts themed dance nights (especially 1980s).

5 Marquee
MAP L2 ■ 289 10th Ave
Tough to get in, but worth it. House and hip-hop.

6 bOb Bar
MAP N4 ■ 247 Eldridge St
Hip Lower East Side club showcasing all forms of dance music.

7 Beauty Bar
MAP M4 ■ 231 East 14th St
Part dive bar, part salon with nightly dance parties with throwback DJs playing 80s and 90s music.

8 Nowadays
■ 56-06 Cooper Ave, Queens
Huge bar with an atmospheric outdoor area and late-night DJs.

9 Le Bain
MAP M2 ■ 848 Washington St
Lively club and a rooftop bar on the top floor of The Standard, High Line.

10 Bar 13
MAP M4 ■ 35 East 13th St
Three floors, roof deck, and rocking DJs.

⭐10 Restaurants

The luxurious interior of Le Bernardin

1 Le Bernardin

Seafood doesn't come any better than at this quietly luxurious French restaurant *(see p133)* lauded for revolutionizing the way fish is served in New York City. Chef Eric Ripert seems to have no critics. Of course, perfection has its price and you'll pay dearly, but the meal will be memorable.

Dining room at Daniel

2 Daniel

Another New York luminary, Daniel Boulud has a Venetian Renaissance-inspired dining room *(see p141)* worthy of his talents. Seasonal menus with choices like black truffle-crusted cod are divine. Lunch tends to be a little cheaper than the other meals.

3 Eleven Madison Park

Indulge in a French-inspired feast – from suckling pig and tender duck to a dizzyingly delicious chocolate tart drizzled with caramel – at this grand Madison Avenue restaurant *(see p119)* helmed by famed restaurateur Will Guidara and chef Daniel Humm.

4 Gotham Restaurant

A perennial favorite. Former chef Alfred Portale was one of the first with "vertical food," delicious layers so artfully stacked you can hardly bear to disturb them. Now, the new American fare at this restaurant *(see p113)* is still elegant, and the lofty space is sophisticated and casual. The restaurant reopened in 2021 under new ownership.

5 Jean-Georges

Already a culinary star from his Jo Jo and Mercer Kitchen restaurants, in his namesake restaurant *(see p147)* Jean-Georges Vongerichten turns out food that is among the very best in New York, transformed by the French master's delicate sauces and creative combinations. Designer Adam Tihany has created a polished, almost austere, setting that does not upstage the talented chef.

Russ & Daughters Café
The celebrated Lower East Side Jewish store *(see p98)* opened this restaurant in 2014. It features an open kitchen and a soda fountain bar. The café serves favorites such as smoked and cured salmon, home-made salads, and a variety of cream cheeses. Try the classic bagel with lox, or smoked sturgeon and sable.

 Momofuku Noodle Bar
Wunderkind David Chang brings humor (and lots of pork products) to this inventive restaurant *(see p101)*. The steamed pork buns are legendary, and one can always count on some unusual seafood and market vegetables to appear.

⑧ Per Se
You need to call two months in advance to get a seat in Thomas Keller's expensive restaurant *(see p147)*. One of a handful of eateries to receive 4 stars from *The New York Times*, diners come for the food, service, and views of Central Park.

⑨ Babbo
Set in a converted carriage house, this restaurant *(see p113)* by Joe Bastianich serves inventive Italian fare. The menu includes seasonal produce, cheeses, game and seafood. Most of the *salumi*, *soppressata*, and *lardo* is made in-house.

Exterior of Gramercy Tavern

 Gramercy Tavern
Another Danny Meyer success offers perhaps New York's most unpretentious fine dining *(see p119)*. Chef Michael Anthony has maintained the high standard here.

TOP 10 CHEAP EATS

Shake Shack, a popular burger joint

1 Shake Shack
MAP L4 ▪ Southeast corner of Madison Square Park ▪ 212 889 6600
Sink your teeth into juicy burgers and crisp fries at the original Shake Shack.

2 Superiority Burger
MAP M5 ▪ 119 Ave A
Fabulous, reasonably priced vegetarian and vegan burgers, plus sandwiches, salads, and wraps.

3 Laoshan Shandong Fried Dumpling
MAP P4 ▪ 106 Mosco St ▪ 212 693 1060
Tasty fried pork dumplings at a bargain price of $5 for 15.

4 Nyonya
MAP P4 ▪ 199 Grand St ▪ 212 334 3669
Good, traditional Malaysian food.

5 NY Dosas
MAP N3 ▪ 50 Washington Square S Blvd ▪ 917 710 2092
This vegan-friendly food cart sells Sri Lankan-style dosas.

6 Flor de Mayo
MAP D2 ▪ 2651 Broadway ▪ 212 595 2525
A mix of Peruvian, Cuban, and Chinese cuisine; rotisserie chicken is a specialty.

7 Joe's Pizza
MAP N3 ▪ 7 Carmine St ▪ 347 312 4955
One of the best thin-crust pizzas in town.

8 Tasty Hand-Pulled Noodles
MAP P4 ▪ 1 Doyers St ▪ 212 791 1817
Excellent selection of Chinese noodles, served in soup or fried with a variety of toppings.

9 La Bonne Soupe
Midtown's best bet *(see p133)* for onion soup and other bistro specialties.

10 Corner Bistro
MAP M2 ▪ 331 West 4th St ▪ 212 242 9502
Giant burgers in the West Village.

Bars and Lounges

① King Cole Bar and Lounge

MAP H4 ■ St. Regis Hotel, 2 East 55th St, between 5th & Madison Aves ■ 212 753 4500

Maxfield Parrish's famous mural of Old King Cole, rich mahogany paneling, and sumptuous seating set the stage for New York's most famous hotel bar, where the Bloody Mary is believed to have first been created. Lush, luxurious, and very expensive.

② Dead Rabbit

MAP R4 ■ 30 Water St ■ 646 422 7906

Step back into the 1800s at this convivial bar in a 200-year-old building on the Lower Manhattan waterfront. Dimly lit and cozy, this is the perfect hybrid of cocktail lounge and old Irish tavern, with gleaming wooden bars, sawdust-strewn floors and complimentary spiked punch.

③ Gansevoort Rooftop

MAP M2 ■ Gansevoort Hotel, 18 9th Ave, at 13th St ■ 212 206 6700

Enjoy superb views of the New York skyline and the Hudson River from this rooftop bar at the trendy Gansevoort Hotel, located in the Meatpacking District. Although a little on the expensive side, this is a great spot to hang out in during the summer months.

④ Ear Inn

This pub *(see p106)* dates back to 1890, making it one of the city's oldest. Closed during Prohibition, it reopened with no formal name in the 1930s (it was known colloquially as the "Green Door"). In 1977, the new owners painted out part of the "B" in the "BAR" sign, and the "Ear" Inn was born. Expect a casual, friendly atmosphere inside.

⑤ Flûte

MAP H3 ■ 205 West 54th St, between 7th Ave & Broadway ■ 212 265 5169

Proudly stocking over 150 different types of champagne, several of which are available by the glass, this former speakeasy blends high-end opulence with a romantic atmosphere and friendly service. It was operated during Prohibition by notorious showgirl manager, Texas Guinan.

The bright, airy interior of the Gansevoort Rooftop

The bar at Employees Only

6 Employees Only
MAP N3 ▪ 510 Hudson St ▪ 212 242 3021

Sip impeccably mixed cocktails at this stylish bar and restaurant. A fortune teller greets guests at the entrance, while the retro interior features mahogany paneling and warm lighting throughout.

7 Salon de Ning
MAP H3 ▪ Peninsula Hotel, 700 5th Ave, at 55th St ▪ 212 956 2888

This swanky Asian-themed bar features breathtaking views of the Manhattan skyline from its 23rd-floor perch. The outdoor terrace is an unbeatable spot.

8 Bemelmans Bar
MAP F4 ▪ Carlyle Hotel, 35 E 76th St ▪ 212 744 1600

Step back in time with classic cocktails and live music at Bemelmans Bar, named after Ludwig Bemelmans, the creator of the popular Madeline children's books and artist responsible for the murals that adorn the walls. The stylish Art Deco theme is finished off with leather banquettes and a 24-carat gold leaf-covered ceiling.

9 Paul's Casablanca
This hip cocktail bar (see p106) with Moroccan decor is especially busy during Fashion Week. The DJs focus on a different genre every night, ranging from rock to hip hop. The Smiths are featured on Sundays.

10 Death & Co
MAP M5 ▪ 433 East 6th St ▪ www.deathandcompany.com/

Lauded East Village cocktail bar with a speakeasy theme (the wait staff wear bow ties and braces). Most of the artfully crafted cocktails run $19–23 (non-alcoholic cocktails are $15).

TOP 10 ROOFTOP BARS

1 Bar Blondeau
MAP M7 ▪ 80 Wythe Ave, Williamsburg ▪ www.wythehotel.com
This French-themed bar affords sensational views of Manhattan.

2 Metropolitan Museum Roof Garden Bar
MAP F3 ▪ 5th Ave and 82nd St ▪ www.metmuseum.org
Cocktails with views of Central Park.

3 Hotel Chantelle
MAP N5 ▪ 92 Ludlow St ▪ www.hotelchantelle.com
Parisian-style rooftop lounge with old-fashioned lampposts and greenery.

4 Gansevoort Rooftop
MAP M2 ▪ 18 9th Ave ▪ www.gansevoorthotelgroup.com
One of the top places to party in NYC.

5 Broken Shaker
Sip creative, perfectly blended cocktails here (see p118).

6 Jimmy
MAP P3 ▪ 15 Thompson St ▪ www.jimmysoho.com
A 360-degree vista of Manhattan.

7 Berry Park
4 Berry St, Brooklyn ▪ www.berryparkbk.com
Brooklyn rooftop with Manhattan views.

8 Empire Rooftop Bar & Lounge
MAP H7 ▪ 44 West 63rd St ▪ www.empirehotelnyc.com
Jazz, with views of the Upper West Side.

9 Loopy Doopy Rooftop Bar
MAP Q3 ▪ 102 North End Ave ▪ www.hilton.com
Seasonal bar with Statue of Liberty views.

10 230 Fifth Rooftop Bar
This popular bar (see p118) offers stunning views of the Empire State.

Rooftop terrace at 230 Fifth

TOP 10 New York City Stores

Macy's department store

1 Macy's

Iconic Macy's has long been a major part of New York life, with its spring flower show, Thanksgiving parade, and festive Christmas tree lighting celebrations. Its selection of goods instore is vast, featuring everything from food to futons, baby clothes to beauty items.

2 Bloomingdale's

MAP H4 ▪ 1000 Lexington Ave, at 59th St

After Macy's, this is New York's best-known department store, renowned for high fashion for men and women. The main floor, with cosmetics, jewelry, and accessories, can get very busy, but don't be discouraged; the upper floors are more manageable.

Shoes at Bloomingdale's

3 Bergdorf Goodman

MAP H3 ▪ 754 5th Ave, at 57th St

Opened in 1928, Bergdorf Goodman offers a range of well-known designer clothing for men, women, and children, as well as an upscale selection of home accessories. The store also features stylish seasonal window displays that are worth checking out.

4 Saks Fifth Avenue

MAP K3 ▪ 611 5th Ave, at 50th St

Saks has been operating its high-end department store at this location since 1924. Today it's primarily known for stocking luxury fashion from designers such as Alexander McQueen, Balenciaga, Burberry and Gucci, plus a wide-range of accessories.

5 Nordstrom

Opened in 2019 with a dramatic glass facade, Nordstrom's New York flagship luxury department store (see p130) spans seven floors and has clothing, shoes, accessories, and home goods as well as beauty salons, restaurants, cafés, and bars.

6 Brooklyn Flea

MAP M7 ▪ 80 Pearl St, Dumbo

Held on weekends and packed with hundreds of furniture, vintage clothing, art, and antique stalls, Brooklyn Flea has become the doyen of New York markets. It usually takes place outdoors (Apr–Dec) on Saturdays and Sundays in Dumbo. The folks behind Brooklyn Flea also run the open-air food market, Smorgasburg, which takes place every weekend (Apr–Oct) in Williamsburg and Prospect Park in Brooklyn.

Brooklyn Flea market, Dumbo

7 Marc Jacobs
MAP N4 ■ 127 Prince St

Local boy Marc Jacobs is the king of the New York fashion world, and fashionistas flock to this store for the latest must-have bags, shoes, and dresses. There are also stylishly designed watches, wallets, and sunglasses, and men's clothes.

8 Madison Avenue Designers
MAP F4–H4 ■ Giorgio Armani: 761 Madison Ave ■ Ralph Lauren: 867 Madison Ave

The epicenter of designer boutiques in New York used to be 57th Street between 5th and Madison Avenues, where shops like Burberry are still found. But as stores like Nike and Levi's have invaded this territory, the designers, from Giorgio Armani to Ralph Lauren, have moved to Madison Avenue.

9 SoHo Boutiques
MAP N3–N4 ■ Alexander McQueen: 71 Greene St ■ A.P.C.: 131 Mercer St ■ Miu Miu: 100 Prince St ■ Prada: 575 Broadway ■ Portico: 139 Spring St ■ Kirna Zabête: 477 Broome St

SoHo is home to trendy boutiques such as Alexander McQueen, A.P.C., Miu Miu, and Prada. The stores are between Thompson Street and Broadway and between Prince and Greene Streets, though any block in this area may yield a special find. This is also prime hunting ground for art at galleries such as Portico.

Miu Miu's SoHo boutique

10 Union Square and 6th Avenue
MAP L3 ■ Whole Foods Market: 4 Union Square South

Union Square is ringed by various stores and places to refuel, including a massive Whole Foods Market. Nearby, around 18th Street, is the shopping hub of 6th Avenue, lined with historic buildings now housing homeware and clothing stores.

🔟 New York City for Free

The Staten Island Ferry on the New York Harbor

① Staten Island Ferry
MAP R4

This ferry journey *(see p159)* is one of the greatest deals the city of New York has to offer. You will see sweeping views of New York Harbor, the Statue of Liberty, and the glittering Manhattan skyline on its journey between Lower Manhattan and Staten Island – all to be enjoyed without paying a cent.

② New York Philharmonic Concerts in the Parks
Jul–Aug ■ www.nyphil.org

Ease yourself into the night with some soaring classical music, played in the open air during the New York Philharmonic's annual summer concerts, which are staged in parks throughout all five of the boroughs of New York.

Philharmonic summer concert

③ Recording of TV Shows
The Late Show with Stephen Colbert: www.cbs.com/shows/the-late-show-with-stephen-colbert ■ *Rachael Ray*: www.rachaelrayshow.com

New York City is the land of TV talk shows, from *The Late Show with Stephen Colbert* to *Rachael Ray*. You can watch these shows being recorded for free as a member of the studio audience. Apply for tickets via the shows' websites.

④ Downtown Boathouse Kayaks
MAP P2 ■ Pier 26, Hudson River Greenway at North Moore ■ Opening hours vary, check website for details ■ www.downtownboathouse.org

The Hudson River is ideal for kayaking and the Downtown Boathouse offers complimentary use of kayaks at various locations on the river and Governors Island.

⑤ Chelsea Art Galleries
MAP L2 ■ Between 10th & 11th Aves, from West 18th to West 28th Sts

Saunter through Chelsea on a Thursday night, when many of the area's formidable galleries have free exhibition openings, along with complimentary nibbles and wine.

6 Open House New York
Runs over a weekend, October
- www.ohny.org

Open House New York opens up the city's most fascinating architectural structures, from churches to government buildings, to the public every October. Tours, talks, performances, and other special events also take place.

7 Brooklyn Brewery
79 North 11th St, Williamsburg, Brooklyn
- **Free tours every hour 1–6pm Sun**

There are free tours of the handsome Brooklyn Brewery in Williamsburg every hour on Sunday, when visitors can sample some of the great brews made here. Bottles are also available to purchase.

Brooklyn Brewery beer

8 New York Public Library
MAP K3

This stately library *(see p128)* hosts all manner of free events, from lectures and readings to career classes.

9 Free Museum Entry
Many museums offer free entry at least once a week: Guggenheim (Saturday 6pm to 8pm, www.guggenheim.org); Frick Madison (Thursday 4pm to 6pm, www.frick.org); Morgan Library & Museum (Friday 5pm to 7pm, www.themorgan.org); New York Historical Society (Friday 6pm to 8pm, www.nyhistory.org), and the Whitney (Friday 7pm to10pm, www.whitney.org).

10 Parks
New York City is home to a number of gorgeous green spaces that are ideal for whiling away a morning, afternoon, or entire day. The High Line *(see p121)* and Central Park *(see p136)* are both free and two of the best parks in the US. There's also Bryant Park *(see p57)*, Washington Square Park *(see p108)*, and Prospect Park *(see p156)* in Brooklyn.

TOP 10 BUDGET TIPS

Union Square Greenmarket

1 Farmers' Markets
Try the Union Square Greenmarket *(see p115)* for reasonably priced produce.

2 New York Pizza
Pizzerias around the city offer a slice of this New York staple for just $1.50.

3 TKTS Theater Tickets
MAP J3 ▪ 47th St & Broadway ▪ www.tdf.org
Same-day theater tickets are discounted.

4 Changing Money
Transaction fees are generally lower at ATMs than at currency exchanges.

5 Saving on Transit
Metropolitan Transportation Authority: www.mta.info
The 7-day MetroCard allows unlimited subway and bus rides for just $33. All MetroCards provide a free transfer between subways and buses as well as between two buses.

6 Restaurant Week
Jan & Jul ▪ www.nycgo.com/restaurant-week
Two-course lunches $30; three-course dinners $45–60.

7 Discount Passes to Sights
CityPass: www.citypass.com ▪ New York Pass: www.newyorkpass.com
CityPass ($129, nine days) covers 5 top sights; New York Pass covers over 115 ($142, one day). Longer periods available.

8 Sale Periods
Coats are on sale in November and February, bathing suits after July 4, and everything before and after Christmas.

9 Free Happy Hour Nibbles
Many bars include snacks with a drink.

10 Discount Stores and Malls
Thrift stores to 200 outlets at Woodbury Common (www.woodburybus.com; bus tickets from $42).

TOP 10 Festivals and Events

Fireworks display, 4th of July

1 St. Patrick's Day Parade
MAP H3 ■ **5th Ave** ■ **11am Mar 17** ■ **Check press for exact route**

People dress up in green for this big spectacle when marching bands, politicos, and civic groups march down 5th Avenue to proclaim their love of the Emerald Isle. Millions come to watch and the citywide celebrations last way into the night.

2 Easter Parade
MAP H3–J3 ■ **5th Ave** ■ **11am Easter Sunday**

Following a long-time tradition, 5th Avenue closes to traffic in Midtown, and New York families in their Sunday best stroll up the avenue, with ladies sporting amazing hats, both traditional and outrageous.

3 Juneteenth NY Festival
Various locations ■ **June 19** ■ **www.juneteenthny.com**

This national commemoration of the end of slavery in the US on June 19 1865 is now an official public holiday. It is celebrated all over New York City with concerts, food festivals, talks, and parties. Museums in the city often hold special events, too.

4 NYC Pride March
MAP L3–M3 ■ **25th St at 5th Ave to 16th St and 7th Ave** ■ **Last Sunday in June** ■ **www.nycpride.org**

New York Pride Week is one of the world's largest LGBTQ+ celebrations. Various parties, street fairs, and conferences all lead up to the main Pride March on Sunday, which involves over 100,000 participants and millions of spectators.

5 4th of July Fireworks
MAP R3 ■ **East River or Hudson River** ■ **9:30pm Jul 4**

Huge crowds come out to enjoy this pyrotechnic spectacular over the Hudson or East rivers. Macy's spends well over $9 million each year for this salute to the red, white, and blue.

6 West Indian Day Carnival
MAP R6 ■ **Eastern Parkway, Brooklyn** ■ **Subway C to Franklin Ave** ■ **Labor Day (1st Mon in Sep)**

Brooklyn's West Indian population celebrates its heritage with a parade of floats, colorful, feathered costumes, and Caribbean music. Street stands offer Caribbean specialties.

7 Feast of San Gennaro
MAP P4 ■ Mulberry St
■ 3rd week in Sep for 10 days

The patron saint of Naples is carried through the streets of Little Italy, and Mulberry Street is packed with music, game booths, and tons of tasty, traditional food. Sausage and pepper sandwiches are the trademark of this 10-day event.

8 Indigenous Peoples' Day
MAP B5–C5 ■ Randall's Island Park ■ Second Mon of Oct

An alternative to Columbus Day, this celebration of Native American culture involves Indigenous music and dancing, talks from activists, and food stalls on Randall's Island.

9 Macy's Thanksgiving Day Parade
MAP G2 ■ Central Park West, at 77th St along Broadway to 34th St ■ 9am Thanksgiving Day (4th Thu in Nov)

New Yorkers take to the streets and America watches on television as cartoon character balloons, marching bands, lavish TV and movie star-laden floats, and the dancing Rockettes announce the start of the Christmas season.

Macy's Parade

10 New Year's Eve Ball Drop
MAP K3 ■ Times Square ■ Midnight Dec 31

Huge crowds gather in Times Square to cheer as a giant Waterford Crystal ball is lowered at midnight to mark the new year. This annual ball drop has been taking place in the city since 1907 and is usually preceded by a variety of live entertainment. There's also a midnight run, with a costume parade and fireworks, in Central Park.

TOP 10 SPORTS EVENTS AND TEAMS

Athletes at the Millrose Games

1 Millrose Games
Feb ■ www.millrosegames.org
America's fastest runners compete in this indoor track meet.

2 New York Red Bulls & New York City FC
Mar–Oct ■ New York Red Bulls: www.newyorkredbulls.com ■ NYCFCC: www.nycfc.com
New York has two teams that compete in Major League Soccer (MLS).

3 New York Yankees & Mets
Apr–Sep ■ www.mlb.com
These perennial rivals dominate the summer baseball season in the city.

4 New York Liberty
May–Sep ■ https://liberty.wnba.com
Women's professional basketball.

5 Belmont Stakes
2nd Sat in Jun ■ www.belmontstakes.com
The last of racing's "triple crown" series of annual horse races.

6 US Open Tennis Championships
Aug–Sep ■ www.usopen.org
The last Grand Slam of the year.

7 New York Jets & NY Giants
Sep–Dec ■ New York Jets: www.newyorkjets.com ■ NY Giants: www.giants.com
New York's football teams both play in East Rutherford, New Jersey.

8 New York Rangers & NY Islanders
Sep–Apr ■ www.nhl.com
New York has two NHL hockey teams.

9 New York Knicks & Brooklyn Nets
Oct–Apr ■ www.nba.com
The city has two teams competing in the NBA (National Basketball Association).

10 New York Marathon
1st Sun in Nov ■ www.nyrr.org
This iconic race starts on Staten Island and finishes in Central Park.

New York City
Area by Area

Aerial view of Central Park

TOP10 Lower Manhattan

This is where old and new New York meet. The city was born here under Dutch rule and became the nation's first capital after the Revolutionary War (1775–83). At the intersection of Broad and Wall Streets are the Federal Hall National Memorial, marking where George Washington was sworn in as President, and the New York Stock Exchange, founded in 1817, whose influence is felt worldwide. In the 20th century, skyscrapers added drama to the skyline. The area's recovery after the destruction of the Twin Towers has been striking, and the National September 11 Memorial and Museum offers an opportunity to remember the events of September 2001. The 104-story One World Trade Center opened in 2014.

September 11 Museum

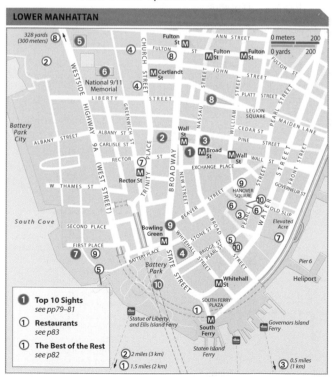

LOWER MANHATTAN

328 yards (300 meters)
0 meters 200
0 yards 200

WESTSIDE HIGHWAY
CHURCH STREET
National 9/11 Memorial
LIBERTY STREET
GREENWICH ST
Battery Park City
ALBANY STREET
ALBANY ST
CARLISLE ST
RECTOR ST
TRINITY PLACE
BROADWAY
W. THAMES ST
9A (WEST STREET)
South Cove
SECOND PLACE
FIRST PLACE
Bowling Green
BATTERY PLACE
STATE STREET
Battery Park
WHITEHALL STREET
SOUTH FERRY PLAZA
Statue of Liberty and Ellis Island Ferry
South Ferry
Staten Island Ferry

Fulton St
ANN STREET
FULTON ST
Cortlandt St
JOHN STREET
PLATT STREET
NASSAU STREET
WILLIAM STREET
LEGION SQUARE
CEDAR ST
PINE STREET
Wall St
Broad St
Wall St
EXCHANGE PLACE
BEAVER STREET
STONE ST
BRIDGE ST
PEARL STREET
HANOVER SQUARE
WATER STREET
GOVERNEUR ST
OLD SLIP
Elevated Acre
Pier 6
Heliport
Whitehall St
PEARL STREET
MAIDEN LANE
FRONT STREET

Governors Island Ferry

2 miles (3 km)
1.5 miles (2 km)
0.5 miles (1 km)

1 **Top 10 Sights**
  see pp79–81

1 **Restaurants**
  see p83

1 **The Best of the Rest**
  see p82

1 New York Stock Exchange

MAP R4 ■ **20 Broad St, at Wall St** ■ **Closed to public** ■ **www.nyse.com**

The present building opened in 1903, and behind its Neo-Classical facade is the financial heart of the US *(see p55)*. The New York Stock Exchange has grown from dealing with local businesses to a global enterprise. On the

Antique stock ticker tape

busiest days, billions of shares are traded for around 2,600 companies, although the action is much calmer now that everything is computerized. On its most active days, around 40 million trades are made on the exchange.

2 Trinity Church

MAP Q4 ■ **75 Broadway, at Wall St** ■ **Church & graveyard open 8:30am–6pm daily** ■ **Services 8am, 9am, 11:15am Sun, 9am & 12:05pm Mon–Fri** ■ **www.trinitywallstreet.org**

This much-admired Gothic building is the third church on this site serving one of the oldest Anglican parishes in the US, founded in 1697. The church has had notable additions since its completion in 1846, including the sac-risty, the chapel, and the Manhattan wing. The bronze doors were donated as a memorial to John Jacob Astor III. Trinity Church is known for its musical programs, with performances and concerts held by the renowned Choir of Trinity Wall Street. The cemetery outside contains the memorial to Alexander Hamilton.

3 Federal Hall National Memorial

MAP R4 ■ **26 Wall St, at Nassau St** ■ **Open 9am–5pm Mon–Fri** ■ **www. nps.gov/feha**

Although the bronze statue of George Washington on the steps marks the site where the nation's first president took his oath of office in 1789, the original building was replaced by this handsome, columned Greek Revival structure in 1842. It served as the US Custom House and as a branch of the Federal Reserve Bank before being turned into a museum in 1955, with exhibits on the Constitution and the Bill of Rights. Guided tours are available several times daily.

4 US Custom House

MAP R4 ■ **1 Bowling Green, between State & Whitehall Sts** ■ **Museum open 10am–5pm daily** ■ **www.americanindian.si.edu**

The galleries that encircle the grand rotunda were installed during a renovation of this classic building in 1994. It now houses the George Gustav Heye Center of the Smithsonian's National Museum of the American Indian, which displays changing exhibits of Indigenous life, including costumes and fine crafts. Completed in 1907 and in use until 1973, the Beaux Arts building is itself part of the attraction; the facade is adorned with elaborate statues by Daniel Chester French.

Stained-glass window, Trinity Church

One World Trade Center

5 One World Trade Center

MAP Q3 ■ 285 Fulton St (enter on West St, at Vesey St) ■ One World Observatory: open 9am–9pm daily (to 8pm Oct–Apr) ■ Adm ■ www. oneworldobservatory.com

The tallest skyscraper in the US (if the spire is included) measures 1776 ft (541 m) and was finally completed in 2012. This gleaming pinnacle of glass and steel has five high-speed elevators called Sky Pods that whisk you to the One World Observatory on floors 100, 101 and 102 in just 60 seconds. From here, visitors can see stunning views of the harbor, Staten Island, and Manhattan's rooftops.

6 National September 11 Memorial and Museum

MAP Q3 ■ 180 Greenwich St ■ Museum open 10am–5pm Wed–Mon ■ Adm (museum only) ■ www. 911memorial.org

Opened on September 11, 2011, on the 10th anniversary of the terrorist attacks, this memorial features the name of every person who died, inscribed in bronze panels around the two memorial pools that sit where the towers once stood. Artifacts, memorabilia, and photographs in the museum pay tribute to the victims. For admission to the museum, reserve a timed-entry ticket on the website before visiting. The memorial itself is free with open access.

7 Museum of Jewish Heritage

MAP R3 ■ 36 Battery Pl, Battery Park City ■ Open 10am–5pm Sun & Wed, 10am–8pm Thu, 10am–3pm Fri & Jewish holiday evenings (to 5pm mid-Mar–Oct) ■ Adm (free Thu 4–8pm) ■ www.mjhnyc.org

A memorable experience for all faiths is this chronicle of the 20th-century Jewish experience before, during, and after the Holocaust, told with a collection of over 2,000 photographs and hundreds of artifacts, as well as original documentary films.

8 Federal Reserve Bank

MAP Q4 ■ 33 Liberty St, between William & Nassau Sts ■ Check website for tour times ■ www.newyorkfed.org

Though gold is no longer transferred between nations, much of the gold reserves of the world remains stored in the vault below this imposing building. All bank notes from here have the letter B in the Federal Reserve seal.

Memorial pool at National September 11 Memorial and Museum

FEARLESS GIRL AND THE BULL

In 2017, Wall Street's famous *Charging Bull* was challenged by the *Fearless Girl* (**right**). Designed by Kristen Visbal, the bronze sculpture of a small girl defiantly staring down the beast became a feminist icon. In 2019, it was moved to a more accessible location in front of the New York Stock Exchange.

9 Charging Bull
MAP R4 ■ Broadway at Bowling Green Park

Sculptor Arturo di Modica secretly unloaded this bronze statue in front of the New York Stock Exchange late at night in December 1989. It was later removed and given a permanent spot on Broadway.

Castle Clinton, Battery Park

10 Battery Park
MAP R3–4 ■ Broadway and Battery Pl ■ Open daily

This park at New York harbor – built largely on 18th- and 19th-century landfill – is usually visited for Castle Clinton, the 1811 fort and embarkation point for Ellis Island and Statue of Liberty ferries. This welcome swath of green is of interest for its many monuments and statues.

A DAY EXPLORING
LOWER MANHATTAN

▶ MORNING

Begin at **Battery Park** for a view of the waterfront, and look into **Castle Clinton** *(see p20)*, an 1807 fort, to see dioramas of a changing New York. Then visit the Museum of the American Indian at the **US Custom House** *(see p79)*. Cross over to **Bowling Green**, the city's first park, then turn right onto Whitehall, and left on Pearl Street for the **Fraunces Tavern Museum** *(see p82)*, a restoration of the 1719 building where George Washington bade farewell to his troops.

Head up Broad Street to Wall Street and the **New York Stock Exchange** *(see p79)*, where there is chaos on the trading floor. Close by is the **Federal Hall National Memorial** *(see p79)*, where the country's first president took his oath of office. Wander north along Broadway then left down Liberty Street to take a break for lunch at **Eataly NYC Downtown** *(see p83)*, in 4 World Trade Center.

AFTERNOON

Retrace your steps on Liberty Street to Nassau Street to see **Chase Plaza** *(28 Liberty St)* and its famous sculptures. At the end of the plaza is the ornate **Federal Reserve Bank** and then Louise Nevelson Square, which features the artist's *Shadows and Flags*.

Go back onto Liberty Street and take in the **9/11 Memorial** and, if possible, the **Museum**. End the day by treating yourself to dinner at the lauded Japanese restaurant **Nobu Downtown** *(see p83)*.

See map on p78 ←

The Best of the Rest

1 Statue of Liberty
With a height of 305 ft (93m), the Statue of Liberty *(see pp20–21)* dominates the New York harbor and is an enduring symbol of freedom throughout the world.

2 Ellis Island
The historic Ellis Island *(see pp22–3)* is now a remarkable museum paying homage to the immigrant experience in America.

3 Governors Island
Nowhere in New York is quite like Governors Island. A blend of tranquil green spaces and historic buildings, this urban park *(see p56)* offers a welcome respite from busy city life.

4 The Oculus
MAP Q3 ■ 185 Greenwich St ■ Open 10am–8pm Mon–Fri, 10am–7pm Sat, 11am–6pm Sun
This striking structure by Santiago Calatrava houses a subway station and a Westfield shopping mall.

5 Pier A Harbor House
MAP R3 ■ 22 Battery Pl
This ornate 19th-century pier, located on the edge of Battery Park, may eventually serve as the terminal for Liberty Island.

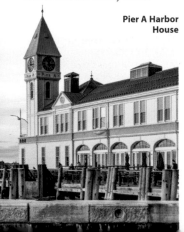

Pier A Harbor House

6 Stone Street
MAP Q4
Tucked between Hanover Square and Coenties Alley is Stone Street, a narrow, cobblestoned block of Greek Revival-style houses. The area is a great place to eat and drink, especially during the summer when it turns into a vast open-air beer garden with picnic tables covering the street.

Vietnam Veterans Memorial Plaza

7 Vietnam Veterans Memorial Plaza
MAP Q4 ■ 55 Water St ■ www.vietnamveteransplaza.com
A huge wall in this plaza is engraved with letters from servicemen and women who died in the Vietnam War.

8 Irish Hunger Memorial
MAP Q3 ■ 290 Vesey St, at North End Ave ■ Open 8am–6:30pm daily
This is a monument dedicated to the Irish people who starved to death during the Great Famine of 1845–52.

9 Skyscraper Museum
MAP R3 ■ 39 Battery Pl ■ Open noon–6pm Thu–Sat ■ www.skyscraper.org
This museum celebrates New York's architectural heritage.

10 Fraunces Tavern Museum
MAP R4 ■ 54 Pearl St ■ Open noon–5pm Wed–Sun
George Washington bade farewell to his officers in this tavern in 1783; it now displays exhibits interpreting early American history.

Restaurants

PRICE CATEGORIES
For a three-course meal for one with a glass of house wine, and all unavoidable charges including tax.

$ under $25 $$ $25–$75 $$$ over $75

1 The View at The Battery
MAP R4 ■ Battery Park, opposite 17 State St ■ 212 269 2323 ■ $$$

This restaurant offers decent New American fare with Asian accents plus stunning panoramic views of the harbor.

2 Le District
MAP Q3 ■ 225 Liberty St ■ 212 981 8588 ■ $$

This popular French food court at Brookfield Place has four restaurants and three themed areas: "market," "café," and "garden." Try to find a seat at the outdoor tables overlooking the river.

3 Adrienne's Pizzabar
MAP R4 ■ 54 Stone St, at William St ■ 212 248 3838 ■ $$

Enjoy delectable pizzas with red or white sauces and a variety of add-your-own toppings at this restaurant.

4 Eataly NYC Downtown
MAP Q4 ■ 101 Liberty St (4 World Trade Center, 3/F) ■ 212 897 2895 ■ $$

This branch of the lauded Italian food market hosts excellent restaurants like La Pizza & La Pasta .

Eataly NYC Downtown

5 Fraunces Tavern
MAP R4 ■ 54 Pearl St ■ 212 968 1776 ■ $$

This historic 18th-century tavern features a charming oak-paneled restaurant that serves traditional American fare along with specialty beers.

Fraunces Tavern

6 Harry's
MAP R4 ■ 1 Hanover Square, between Pearl & Stone Sts ■ 212 785 9200 ■ $$$

The historic India House is home to a downstairs café-steakhouse that draws Wall Street types in droves.

7 George's
MAP R3 ■ 89 Greenwich St, at Rector St ■ 212 269 8026 ■ $$

For hearty American diner fare downtown. Burgers, soups, omelets, sandwiches, and salads are on offer.

8 Nobu Downtown
MAP Q4 ■ 195 Broadway, between Dey & Futon Sts ■ 212 219 0500 ■ $$$

Nobu Matsuhisa's iconic restaurant moved to this luxurious space in 2017. Don't miss his famous black cod with miso.

9 Joseph's
MAP R4 ■ 3 Hanover Square ■ 212 747 1300 ■ $$

When Wall Streeters require Italian food, they often head for Joseph's. The menu includes *fettucine Alfredo* and fried calamari.

10 Ulysses
MAP R4 ■ 95 Pearl St/58 Stone St ■ 212 482 0400 ■ $$

This Stone Street mainstay knocks out a decent Guinness and pub food, including plenty of warming roasts on a Sunday.

See map on p78 ←

🔟 Civic Center and Seaport District NYC

Some of the finest architecture in New York City is to be found at its Civic Center, which serves as the headquarters for city government, including the police department and federal courts. The impressive buildings in this area span several centuries, from the 18th-century St. Paul's Chapel to the pioneering 20th-century Woolworth Building. The famous Brooklyn Bridge is located nearby, as well as the old maritime center of the city, Seaport District NYC. The piers and buildings of this area have been carefully restored and are home to a lively hub of cafés, restaurants, and museums.

Woolworth Building

CIVIC CENTER AND SEAPORT DISTRICT NYC

- ❶ Top 10 Sights
  see pp85–7
- ① Restaurants
  see p89
- ① Maritime Sights
  see p88

Brooklyn Bridge makes for an enjoyable stroll

1 Seaport District NYC
MAP Q4 ■ Museum open
Jan–Mar: 11am–5pm Fri–Sun;
Apr–Dec: 11am–5pm Wed–Sun
■ www.seaportdistrict.nyc

The cobbled streets, piers, and buildings that were the center of New York's 19th-century seafaring activity have been restored as a tourist center, although redevelopment is still in progress. There are shops, restaurants, bars, a museum with seafaring exhibits, a fleet of ships for boarding, and plenty of outdoor entertainment.

Seaport District NYC

2 Brooklyn Bridge
MAP Q4 ■ (Manhattan side)
Park Row near Municipal Building

Linking Manhattan and Brooklyn, this was the largest suspension bridge in the world when it was completed in 1883 and the first to be built of steel. It took 600 workmen and 16 years to build, claiming 20 lives during construction, including that of the designing engineer, John A. Roebling. Now an iconic symbol of New York, its 1-mile (1.8-km) span rewards those who walk it with fabulous views of city towers seen through the artistic cablework.

3 Woolworth Building
MAP Q4 ■ Broadway, between Park Pl & Barclay St ■ Open for tours only ■ www.woolworthbuilding.com

Built in 1913, this has one of New York's great interiors; marble walls, bronze filigree, a mosaic ceiling, and stained glass combine to magical effect (see p52). Architect Cass Gilbert also had a sense of humor – sculptures include Five and Dime mogul Woolworth counting nickels and Gilbert himself cradling a model of the building. It set the standard for the skyscrapers that followed in the 1920s and 1930s.

THE HIDDEN HISTORY OF THE AFRICAN BURIAL GROUND

It is estimated that enslaved Africans made up a quarter of the city's workforce in the 18th century and built much of colonial New York. This burial ground was originally the only place they were permitted to be buried (it was then outside the city). The site is just a tiny portion of a cemetery that covered five blocks between the 1690s and 1794.

Former AT&T Building
MAP Q4 ▪ 195 Broadway
▪ Open office hours

Completed in 1922, this is a monument to excess, but fun to see nevertheless. In its day, the facade was said to have more columns than any other building in the world; the vast lobby is a forest of marble pillars. Not far away at 120 Broadway, the former Equitable Building, built in 1915, is of note for another excess: its immense bulk was responsible for the nation's first sky-scraper zoning regulations.

5 St. Paul's Chapel
MAP Q4 ▪ 209 Broadway, between Fulton & Vesey Sts ▪ Open 8:30am–6pm daily ▪ Compline by Candlelight services 8pm Sun ▪ www.trinitywallstreet.org

Manhattan's oldest church was built in 1766 as an "uptown" chapel for Trinity Church and took on added importance while Trinity was being rebuilt after the great fire of 1776. St. Paul's Chapel was modeled after London's St. Martin-in-the-Fields. Situated one block away from Ground Zero, the church (see p54) has an 9/11 exhibit in the Chapel of Remembrance.

6 African Burial Ground
MAP P4 ▪ Duane St & Elk St ▪ Visitor Center: 290 Broadway ▪ Open 10am–4pm Tue–Sat ▪ www.nps.gov/afbg

In 1991, construction workers discovered the remains of 419 skeletons at this site, which was once part of a larger 18th-century African burial ground. After being examined, the remains were re-interred here in 2003, and were marked by an elegant black granite monument. The site is the oldest excavated burial ground for free and enslaved Africans in North America.

7 Municipal Building
MAP Q4 ▪ 1 Center St, at Chambers St

This building, which dominates the Civic Center area, straddling Chambers Street, was the first "skyscraper" by the prominent 20th-century architectural firm McKim, Mead, and White. The 25-story structure was completed in 1914. The top is a veritable wedding-cake fantasy of towers and spires topped by Adolph Weinman's famous statue, *Civic Fame*. The intricate terra cotta vaulting above the street is modeled on the entrance of the Palazzo Farnese in Rome, and the subway entrance at the south end, an arcaded plaza, is a dramatic vault of Guastavino tiles.

Municipal Building

8 New York County Courthouse
MAP P4 ▪ 60 Center St ▪ Open 9am–5pm Mon–Fri

Ascend the wide staircase of the 1926 New York County Courthouse (adjacent to the 31-story, pyramid-topped US Courthouse which dates from 1933), and enter to admire the marble-columned rotunda with its Tiffany lighting fixtures. Note, too, the ceiling murals depicting Law and Justice. The hexagonal building has a court room in each of its six wings.

Surrogate's Court/Hall of Records

⑨ Surrogate's Court/ Hall of Records

MAP Q4 ▪ 31 Chambers St ▪ Lobby open 9am–5pm Mon–Fri

With an interior inspired by the Paris Opéra, this 1907 Beaux Arts beauty boasts a magnificent central hall with marble stairways and ceiling mosaics. The facade features statues representing Justice, the seasons, and notable New Yorkers.

⑩ City Hall

MAP Q4 ▪ Broadway and Park Row ▪ Open noon Wed & 10am Thu for pre-arranged tours only, call 212 788 2656 ▪ www.nyc.gov

The seat of city government since 1812, City Hall is considered one of the most beautiful early 19th-century public buildings in the US (see p54). The rear of the building, facing north, was not clad in marble until 1954, since the architects, Mangin and McComb, Jr., never expected the city to develop further north.

New York City Hall's stunning facade

A WALK THROUGH CIVIC CENTER AND SEAPORT DISTRICT NYC

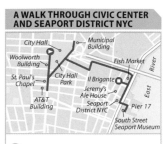

▶ MORNING

Most subway routes lead to **City Hall**. When you come up to street level, walk down Broadway to see the lobbies of the **Woolworth Building** (see p85) and the former **AT&T Building**, as well as the beautiful Georgian interior of **St. Paul's Chapel**.

Return via Park Row, once known as Newspaper Row because it was lined with the offices of various daily newspapers. Printing House Square has a statue of Benjamin Franklin holding a copy of his *Pennsylvania Gazette*. West of the Row lies small but beautiful **City Hall Park**, where the Declaration of Independence was read to George Washington's troops in July 1776. The park has a granite time wheel telling the city's history.

A walk along Center and Chambers Streets takes you past the ornate **Municipal Building**.

AFTERNOON

At midday, head east for a laid-back lunch of burgers and beer at **Jeremy's Ale House**. From here the East River is just across the street, offering excellent views of Brooklyn.

Spend the afternoon at **Seaport District NYC** (see p85), visiting the **South Street Seaport Museum** (see p88) and perhaps even taking a cruise on one of the ships. Head to **Fish Market** (see p89) for dinner, where you can enjoy Chinese and Malaysian food, or try some delicious Italian fare at **Il Brigante** restaurant (see p89).

See map on p84

Maritime Sights

Ambrose, South Street Seaport Museum

5 Ambrose
MAP Q4 ■ Pier 16, Seaport District NYC ■ Open Apr–Dec: 11am–5pm Wed–Sun ■ Adm

Part of the South Street Seaport Museum, this 1907 lightship remained in service until 1964.

6 Pilot House
MAP Q4
■ 89 South St (Pier 16)
■ Closed to public

Located in the center of Pier 16, this restored pilot house was once a part of *New York Central No. 31*, a steam tugboat built in 1923 by the New York Central Railroad.

7 Pier 17
MAP Q5 ■ Seaport District NYC

A pier with shops, restaurants, and a rooftop beer garden with views of the East River and Brooklyn Bridge.

8 Harbor Excursions
MAP Q4 ■ Pier 16, Seaport District NYC ■ Open May–Sep: Wed–Sun ■ Adm

The 1885 schooner *Pioneer* offers 90-minute family sails and 2-hour cruises in the afternoon and evening.

9 Titanic Memorial
MAP Q4 ■ Fulton St, at Water St

This lighthouse was built to commemorate the tragic sinking of the *Titanic*, the largest steamship ever made, in April 1912.

10 Fulton Market Building
MAP Q4 ■ 11 Fulton St

The former home of the Fulton Fish Market now contains several ritzy boutiques and a branch of the posh cinema chain iPic Theaters.

1 South Street Seaport Museum
MAP Q4 ■ 12 Fulton St ■ Open Jan–Mar: 11am–5pm Fri–Sun; Apr–Dec: 11am–5pm Wed–Sun ■ Adm ■ www.southstreetseaportmuseum.org

Housed in a unique ensemble of Federal-style houses, this museum exhibits a superb collection of maritime art. The historic ships on the nearby Pier 16 are also worth seeing.

2 Schermerhorn Row
MAP Q4 ■ Fulton St, between Front & South Sts

Federal-style houses built by Peter Schermerhorn in 1811–12 now houses the Seaport Museum, as well as shops and restaurants.

3 Wavertree
MAP Q4 ■ Pier 16, Seaport District NYC ■ Open Apr–Dec: 11am–5pm Wed–Sun ■ Adm

This graceful ship was built in Southampton (UK) in 1885, serving as a cargo ship until 1910.

4 Bowne & Co.
MAP Q4 ■ 211 Water St ■ Open 11am–5pm Wed–Sun

An atmospheric re-creation of a 19th-century print shop, complete with working printing presses.

Titanic Memorial

Restaurants

1 Nobu Downtown
MAP Q4 ■ 195 Broadway
■ 212 219 0500 ■ $$$

Lauded Japanese chef Nobu Matsuhisa's iconic restaurant features a stunning, calligraphy-inspired sculpture. Signature dishes include black cod with miso, umami sea bass, and wagyu dumplings.

Sushi chefs at Nobu Downtown

2 Crown Shy
MAP Q4 ■ 70 Pine St
■ 212 517 1932 ■ $$$

This restaurant serves innovative dishes that showcase a variety of styles and flavors. Try the gruyere fritters, razor clams with carrots, and roasted banana ice cream.

3 Jeremy's Ale House
MAP Q4 ■ 228 Front St, at Peck Slip ■ 212 964 3537 ■ $$

This local bar, with bras and ties hanging from the rafters, serves pints of draft beer, starting from $8, and excellent burgers.

4 Il Brigante
MAP Q4 ■ 214 Front St
■ 212 285 0222 ■ $$

Dig into hearty pastas, crisp pizzas from a wood-burning oven, and sausage ragù accompanied by silky red wines at this cozy trattoria.

5 Manhatta
MAP Q4 ■ 28 Liberty St, 60/F
■ 212 230 5788 ■ $$$

This modern American restaurant from Danny Meyer and chef Justin

PRICE CATEGORIES

For a three-course meal for one with a glass of house wine, and all unavoidable charges including tax.

$ under $25 $$ $25–$75 $$$ over $75

Bogle offers a seasonal menu that can include anything from poached cod to venison saddle.

6 Luchadores
MAP Q4 ■ 87 South St
■ 646 398 7499 ■ $$

No-frills, fresh Mexican cuisine is served up at this popular restaurant, named after the colorfully-masked Mexican wrestlers called *luchadores*.

7 Fish Market
MAP Q4 ■ 111 South St
■ 212 227 4468 ■ $$

Located on the site of a 19th-century fish market, this restaurant serves briny Malaysian-influenced staples in a wood-and-brick room.

8 Suteishi
MAP Q5 ■ 24 Peck Slip St
■ 212 766 2344 ■ $$

Nestled in the shadow of the Brooklyn Bridge, just to the north of Seaport District NYC, this spot is a favorite among area workers and nearby residents for its fresh, reasonably priced sushi.

9 Fresh Salt
MAP Q4 ■ 146 Beekman St
■ 212 962 0053 ■ $$

Come to this convivial bar and café for soups, gourmet sandwiches, and salads. Also on offer is a good weekend brunch.

10 The Fulton
MAP Q5 ■ 89 South St (Pier 17)
■ 212 838 1200 ■ $$$

Jean-Georges Vongerichten's sea-food restaurant offers sensational views of the Brooklyn Bridge and the East River. Brunch features sashimi, fresh scallops, king crab, and more.

See map on p84

TOP 10 Chinatown and Little Italy

Settled by immigrants in the 19th century, these two multicultural enclaves are among the most vibrant parts of the city. Little Italy has dwindled to a few blocks, but it is still an atmospheric center of authentic Italian food and shops. Chinatown, however, continues to grow – around 150,000 Chinese people now live here. The shops and sidewalk markets overflow with enticing foods, fine antiques, and novelty gifts.

Chinatown

CHINATOWN AND LITTLE ITALY

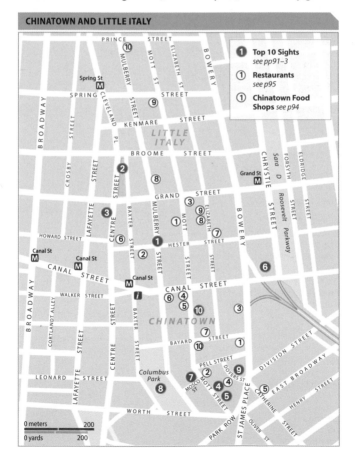

1 Top 10 Sights
see pp91–3

1 Restaurants
see p95

1 Chinatown Food
Shops see p94

Mulberry Street, Little Italy

1 Mulberry Street
MAP P4 ■ Mulberry St, between Broome & Canal Sts

There are many trendy shops on Mulberry Street from Houston down to Spring Street and though China- town is overrunning much of Little Italy, the section between Broome and Canal remains strictly Italian. It is filled with restaurants, coffee shops with tempting Italian pastries, and stores selling pasta-related gadgets, statues of saints, and T-shirts saying "Kiss Me, I'm Italian." The Feast of San Gennaro packs the street each September (see p74).

2 Old Police Headquarters Building
MAP P4 ■ 240 Centre St ■ Closed to public

After the boroughs merged into Greater New York in 1898, the city's police department expanded rapidly. This 1905 headquarters near Little Italy was the result – a monumental, columned Baroque structure fit for "New York's Finest," with an ornate dome tall enough to be seen from City Hall. The strange shape of the building fits a wedge- shaped lot. Empty for more than a decade

Old Police Headquarters

after the department relocated in 1973, the building has since been converted into luxury condos, the Police Building Apartments.

3 Museum of Chinese in America
MAP P4 ■ 211–215 Centre St ■ Opening hours vary, check website ■ Adm (free first Thu) ■ www.moca nyc.org

This fascinating museum, devoted to the Chinese experience in the West, features an exhibit called "Where is Home?," with personal stories, photographs, and poetry gathered from the community. Among the topics explored are women's roles, religion, and the "bachelor society." Changing exhibits range from art to the experience of the LGBTQ+ community. Books, area guides, and free flyers on cultural events are also available.

4 Wing On Wo & Co.
MAP P4 ■ 26 Mott St ■ www.wingonwoand.co

Founded in 1890, Wing On Wo & Co. is one of the oldest family-run shops in Chinatown. Originally a general store, W.O.W. is now a beautiful space selling a wide variety of Chinese and East Asian porcelain.

5 Mott Street Shopping
MAP P4 ▪ Mott St

Clustered on this street are a variety of shops with a wonderful selection of East Asian goods. New York Chinatown Souvenir Gift Center (No. 49) sells all manner of Chinese souvenirs, from paper umbrellas to prints. Vintage jewelry, bags, and candles are the specialty of Uniqulee (No. 36), while New Age Designer (No. 38), also known as Noble Madam, makes clothing to order in your choice of jewel-hued silks. For beautifully designed chopsticks, head to the Yunhong Chopsticks (No. 50).

6 Mahayana Buddhist Temple
MAP P4 ▪ 133 Canal St

This opulent Buddhist temple was built in 1997 in a classic Chinese design. The main altar contains a massive gold idol of the Buddha – 16 ft (5 m) – bathed in neon blue lighting and surrounded by candles. The 32 plaques that adorn the walls tell the story of Buddha's life.

7 Church of the Transfiguration
MAP P4 ▪ 29 Mott St ▪ Open 8:30am–3:30pm Fri & 1–6pm Sat, otherwise services only

Built by the English Lutheran Church in 1801 and sold to the Roman Catholic Church of the Transfiguration in 1853, this Georgian-style stone church with Gothic windows is typical of the influence of successive influxes of immigrants in New York. The church has changed with the nationalities of the community it serves, first Irish, then Italian, and now Chinese. As the focal point of today's Chinese Roman Catholic community, it offers classes and services to help newcomers and holds services in Cantonese and Mandarin.

Church of the Transfiguration

8 Columbus Park
MAP P4 ▪ Bayard & Mulberry Sts

Chinatown's only park was created in the late 1890s as a result of the campaigning of the newspaper reporter Jacob Riis and other social reformers. It filled a stretch of the city that at the time was New York's worst slum, where Riis reported a stabbing or shooting at least once a week. Though it features more concrete than greenery, the park is popular today, bustling with children playing,

Xiangqi **players in Columbus Park**

xiangqi (Chinese chess) players, and people practicing *tai chi*. On the weekends, Chinese fortune-tellers sometimes set up shop in the park.

9 Bloody Angle
MAP P4 ▪ Doyers St near Pell St

The name for this sharp curve on Doyers Street was coined by a newspaper because this was the site of so many gangland ambushes during the 1920s. It was a period when the Hip Sing and On Leong *tongs*, groups similar to criminal gangs, were fighting for control of the opium trade and gambling rackets in Chinatown. The *tong* wars continued off and on until at least the 1940s.

10 Eastern States Buddhist Temple
MAP P4 ▪ 64B Mott St ▪ Open 8am–6pm daily

Step into the incense-scented interior of this temple, where offerings of fresh fruit are piled high, and more than 100 gold Buddhas gleam in the candlelight. The temple takes advantage of Chinatown's tourist traffic by offering $1 fortunes for sale near the front.

Inside Eastern States Buddhist Temple

A STROLL AROUND CHINATOWN AND LITTLE ITALY

▶ MORNING

Take the No. 6 train to Spring Street, walk past Lafayette, and turn down **Mulberry Street** *(see p91)* for a stroll through Little Italy. Don't miss the old-fashioned food shops on Grand Street, such as cheese specialist **Alleva Dairy** *(188 Mulberry St at Grand)* and **Piemonte Ravioli Co.** *(190 Grand St)*, where two dozen shapes and varieties of pasta can be bought. Then stop by **Di Palo Fine Foods** *(206 Grand St)*, where you can watch fresh mozzarella being made. Take a break at a classic Italian café, such as **Caffè Roma**, *(385 Broome St)*, or **Ferrara's** *(195–201 Grand St)*.

Take Grand Street west to Centre Street, then turn left and you'll find an introduction to what's ahead, the **Museum of Chinese in America** *(see p91)*. Enjoy a dim sum lunch opposite the museum at **Jing Fong** *(202 Centre)*, then walk east back to Mott Street, the center of Chinatown.

AFTERNOON

Remaining on Mott Street, spend some time browsing the many shops, food stores, markets, and galleries lining the street. If in need of refreshment, step into **Ten Ren's Tea Time** *(73 Mott St)* for bubble tea: a tall glass of flavored tea served with "pearls" of tapioca in the bottom.

End the afternoon with a visit to the golden Buddhas of the **Eastern States Buddhist Temple** and have your fortune read.

See map on p90

Chinatown Food Shops

Market stall, Chinatown

1 Street Markets
MAP P4 ■ Chinatown, including Canal & Mott Sts

Canal Street and Mott Street are among the many blocks crowded with stands selling Chinese vegetables, fruits, and dried foods.

2 Taiyaki NYC
MAP P4 ■ 119 Baxter St

This tiny store has garnered a cult following for its Japanese ice cream served in fish-shaped waffle cones; the "Unicorn" option is especially popular.

3 Kamwo Meridian Herbs
MAP P4 ■ 211 Grand St

One of the better-known shops offering Chinese herbs said to cure anything from arthritis to impotence. Ginseng is available in teas or supplement form.

4 Fay Da Bakery
MAP P4 ■ 83 Mott St, at Canal St

Sample a delicious soft bun filled with roasted pork or beef for less than $2, then try almond cookies, red bean cakes, custard tarts, or cream buns for dessert.

5 Ten Ren's Tea & Ginseng Company
MAP P4 ■ 75 Mott St

An array of golden canisters holds many varieties of Chinese teas; knowledgeable clerks will explain the properties of each and how to brew them properly.

6 New Kam Man
MAP P4 ■ 200 Canal St

One of the largest food emporiums in Chinatown stocks tonics, teas, ginseng, vegetables of every shape, and row upon row of sauces.

7 Hong Kong Supermarket
MAP P4 ■ 157 Hester St, at Elizabeth St

This huge store offers all manner of dried seafood, noodles, imported goods, watermelon seeds, and food products from China. Try one of the inexpensive, wrapped hard candies.

8 Deluxe Food Market
MAP P4 ■ 79 Elizabeth St

Locals come here for prepared foods, marinated meats, and the fully stocked meat and fish counters.

9 Malaysia Beef Jerky
MAP P4 ■ 95A Elizabeth St

A tiny hole-in-the-wall specializing in Chinese Malaysian-style beef, pork, and chicken jerky (plus some extra spicy versions). Known as "Bak Kwa" in Malaysia, the pork jerky is a favorite over Chinese New Year.

10 Chinatown Ice Cream Factory
MAP P4 ■ 65 Bayard St, at Mott St

Ginger, lychee, pumpkin, mango, and red bean are among the flavors of ice cream that can be sampled at this popular dessert stop, a favorite with young visitors.

Chinatown Ice Cream Factory

Restaurants

PRICE CATEGORIES

For a three-course meal for one with a glass of house wine, and all unavoidable charges including tax.

$ under $25 $$ $25–$75 $$$ over $75

1 Great N.Y. Noodletown
MAP P4 ▪ 28½ Bowery St, at Bayard St ▪ 212 349 0923 ▪ No credit cards ▪ $$

The decor is simple and so is the menu, with wonderful soups, meat dishes, noodles, and creatively prepared seafood.

Peking Duck House in Chinatown

2 Peking Duck House
MAP P4 ▪ 28 Mott St ▪ 212 227 1810 ▪ $$

A pretty escape from Chinatown's surrounding bustle, the Peking Duck House serves diners its time-tested signature duck as well as elegant takes on Chinese classics.

3 Joe's Shanghai
MAP P4 ▪ 46 Bowery, between Canal & Bayard Sts ▪ 212 233 8888 ▪ No credit cards ▪ $$

The Chinatown branch of the Flushing (Queens) restaurant. Famous for its soup dumplings but the steamed buns are also delicious.

4 Chinese Tuxedo
MAP P4 ▪ 5 Doyers St, off Bowery ▪ 646 895 9301 ▪ $$

Elevated Chinese food – think stylish versions of spicy pork dumplings and chicken stir fries – served in a former opera house.

5 Golden Unicorn
MAP P4 ▪ 18 East Broadway, at Catherine St ▪ 212 941 0911 ▪ $$

Dim sum is the star but all the dishes are well prepared in this crowded, third-floor restaurant.

6 Jing Fong
MAP P4 ▪ 202 Centre St, between Hester & Grand Sts ▪ 212 964 5256 ▪ $$

This glittery room is packed daily for the vast selection of freshly made dim sum. Just point at your choices as the carts roll by.

7 Deluxe Green Bo
MAP P4 ▪ 66 Bayard St, between Mott & Elizabeth Sts ▪ 212 625 2359 ▪ No credit cards ▪ $$

This busy Shanghai spot is famous for its dumplings and scallion pancakes. Service is perfunctory, but the lines move quickly.

8 Da Nico
MAP P4 ▪ 164 Mulberry St, between Broome & Grand Sts ▪ 212 343 1212 ▪ $$

A rustic setting and a wonderful courtyard garden make this family run restaurant with a dozen varieties of pizza a favorite.

9 Lombardi's Pizza
MAP P4 ▪ 32 Spring St, between Mott & Mulberry Sts ▪ 212 941 7994 ▪ No credit cards ▪ $$

Pizza doesn't come much better than at "America's First Pizzeria." This unpretentious old-timer turns out delectable thin-crust pies.

Chef at Lombardi's Pizza

10 Parm
MAP P4 ▪ 248 Mulberry St ▪ 212 965 0955 ▪ $$

Known for its Italian-American cuisine, sensational sandwiches are served at this popular Nolita spot. Try their Turkey Hero or Saratoga Club.

See map on p90

TOP 10 Lower East Side and East Village

The Lower East Side still seems to echo the calls of immigrants living in the area's tenements. Early churches became synagogues for the Jews who came here in record numbers. Since the 1990s, Latin American and Chinese communities have added to the rich history of the area. Nearby is the East Village, an early Dutch enclave that changed from German to Jewish before becoming a hippie haven and the birthplace of punk rock. A Ukrainian community here has tenaciously survived these changes.

Steam iron, Tenement Museum

LOWER EAST SIDE AND EAST VILLAGE

1. **Top 10 Sights** see pp97–9
2. **Restaurants** see p101
3. **Bargain Stores and Boutiques** see p100

1 Lower East Side Tenement Museum

MAP N5 ■ 97 Orchard St ■ 212 431 0233 ■ Tours run regularly 10am–6pm daily from 103 Orchard St (call ahead) ■ Adm ■ www.tenement.org

Guided tours inside this tenement building give an insight into the lives of the several families who lived here; a German-Jewish clan in 1874, an Orthodox Jewish family from Lithuania in 1918, and a Sicilian Catholic family during the Depression in the 1930s. The "Under One Roof" exhibition at 103 Orchard Street explores the period post World War II.

2 Essex Crossing

MAP N5 ■ Essex St & Delancey St ■ www.essexcrossingnyc.com ■ International Center of Photography: opening times vary, check website; adm; www.icp.org

A vast megaproject, Essex Crossing covers nine blocks around Delancey and Essex Streets, and offers both residential and commercial spaces. It also features the historic Essex Market and the new International Center of Photography (ICP). Founded by Cornell Capa in 1974, the ICP has a collection of 12,500 original prints, which includes works by top photographers such as Ansel Adams, Henri Cartier-Bresson, and W. Eugène Smith.

3 New Museum

MAP N4 ■ 235 Bowery St ■ Open 11am–6pm Tue–Sun (to 9pm Thu) ■ Adm ■ www.newmuseum.org

This provocative museum mounts shows of experimental contemporary art work that other museums often overlook, particularly new multimedia forms, which sometimes include intriguing window displays. It moved into a cutting-edge building by Tokyo-based architects Sejima and Nishizawa in 2007, with a bookstore, theater, learning center, and café.

4 Museum at Eldridge Street

MAP P5 ■ 12 Eldridge St ■ Open 10am–5pm Sun–Fri ■ Tours every 30 mins ■ Adm (free Mon & Fri) ■ www.eldridgestreet.org

Constructed in 1887, the Eldridge Street synagogue was the country's first to be built by Jewish immigrants from Eastern Europe. As many as 1,000 people attended services here at the turn of the 20th century. As congregants left the neighborhood, attendance waned, and the temple closed in the 1950s. After a 20-year restoration initiative, the synagogue has been transformed into a museum and a vibrant cultural center, but remains a functioning house of worship.

Restored interior of the Museum at Eldridge Street

The counter at Russ & Daughters

5 Russ & Daughters
MAP N5 ■ 179 East Houston St ■ Open 8am–4pm daily (times may vary due to Jewish holidays) ■ www.russanddaughters.com

In 1907, Polish immigrant Joel Russ began selling schmaltz herring out of a barrel while he saved up to buy a handcart. In 1920, he opened this landmark store, which also sold salt-cured herring and salmon. Nowadays, a fourth generation of the family, Russ's great-grandchildren, are in charge. The smoked salmon (try it in a bagel) and other goods are always of top quality, and the caviar is a specialty.

6 Bialystoker Synagogue
MAP N5 ■ 7 Willett St, near the junction of Grand St & East Broadway ■ Tours by appointment only (call 212 374 4100 to confirm)

Built in 1826 as a Methodist church, this synagogue was purchased by the Beth Haknesseth Anshe Bialystok Congregation in 1905. With a grey stone facade, the synagogue's interior features beautifully restored stained glass, gold leaf, and murals of zodiac signs. A plaque commemorates the gangster Bugsy Siegel, who worshipped here as a child.

7 St. Mark's in-the-Bowery Church
MAP M4 ■ 131 East 10th St ■ Open 8:30am–4pm Mon–Fri, service 10:30am Sun

The second-oldest church in New York stands on land where Peter Stuyvesant, Dutch governor of the settlement in the 1600s, had his private chapel. He is also buried here. In the 1960s it served as one of the city's most politically committed congregations and continues to live on the avant-garde edge.

8 St. Mark's Place
MAP M4 ■ East 8th St, between 3rd Ave & Ave A

Once the heart of hippiedom, this block still has a counter-culture feel and is the headquarters of the East

The colorful St. Mark's Place

LITTLE TOKYO

Spurred by the boom in their country's economy, Japanese business folk moved to New York in the 1980s. Many of them set up shop in this tiny locality, located on and around East 9th and 10th streets in the East Village. Now, Little Tokyo is peppered with anime stores, Japanese clothes shops, steamy noodle joints, and quality sushi bars – such as Hasaki (210 East 9th).

Village youth scene. The sidewalks here are crowded until late into the night with people visiting noodle bars, tattoo parlours, and shops selling books, alternative and vintage clothing, and band posters.

⑨ Ukrainian Museum

MAP N4 ■ 222 East 6th St, between 2nd & 3rd Aves ■ Open 11:30am–5pm Wed–Sun ■ Adm ■ www.ukrainianmuseum.org

The museum showcases a beguiling collection of traditional Ukrainian wear (embroidered blouses, colorful sashes, sheepskin and fur vests) and wedding wreaths of yarn and ribbons. There are also jewelry, ceramics, and intricate Ukrainian Easter eggs known as *pysanky*.

Ukrainian costume

⑩ Merchant's House Museum

MAP N4 ■ 29 East 4th St ■ Open 1–5pm Thu–Sun (Jun–Aug open till 8pm Thu) ■ Adm ■ www.merchantshouse.com

This remarkable 19th-century Federal-style townhouse was bought in 1835 by Seabury Tredwell, a wealthy merchant, and stayed in the family until 1933. It was opened as a museum in 1936 and retains its original period furnishings. The first-floor parlors reveal how well New York's merchant class lived during the 1800s.

EAST SIDE EXPLORATION

▶ MORNING

From the Delancey Street Subway walk south to Grand Street and **Kossar's Bagels & Bialys** *(367 Grand)*, famous for chewy, onion-flavored rolls, or the **Doughnut Plant** *(379 Grand)*, where the treats achieve gourmet status. Walk east for an historic house of worship, the **Bialystoker Synagogue**, originally a Methodist church. Return along East Broadway, passing the Henry Street Settlement at No. 281. The community center at No. 197, the Manny Cantor Center, has good art exhibits. Walk to Orchard and pick up a bargain at the shops here or visit the **Lower East Side Tenement Museum** *(see p97)*. Try one of the 50 delicious flavors of ice cream at Il Laboratorio del Gelato *(188 Ludlow)*, then continue along East Houston Street and have lunch at **Katz's Delicatessen** *(see p101)*, or pick up some bagels at **Russ & Daughters**.

AFTERNOON

After lunch, walk uptown on 2nd Avenue. Turn left on East 6th to visit the **Ukrainian Museum**, a hidden gem of costumes and culture. Walk to St. Mark's Place, browsing the funky shops and bars on your way, then walk east on Stuyvesant Street, admiring the townhouses of the Renwick Triangle. Lastly, stop at **St. Mark's in-the-Bowery Church**, one of the oldest in the city, after which you can have dinner and drinks in one of the many restaurants and bars in the East Village.

See map on p96 ←

Bargain Stores and Boutiques

 Zarin Fabrics
MAP P5 ■ 72 Allen St

Since 1936, this mammoth show-room and workshop has provided upholstery and fabrics to the public at wholesale prices.

 Katinka
MAP M4 ■ 303 East 9th St

A miniature treasure trove, this colorful gift shop features Indian textiles, clothing, and jewelry for shockingly low prices.

3 L Train Vintage
MAP M5 ■ 204 1st Ave, between 12th & 13th Sts

Second-hand fashion store with a vast range of vintage T-shirts, jackets, coats, dresses, and suits. New merchandise comes in at least three times a week from all over the US.

4 Exit 9 Gift Emporium
MAP N5 ■ 51 Ave A

An independent store with a large collection of kitsch, gifts, and all sorts of novelties. This is a great places to pick up inexpensive, fun gifts, from inflatable moose heads to colorful tote bags.

 ExtraButter
MAP N5 ■ 125 Orchard St

This cult fashion store is best known for its designer sneakers but also sells shirts, tees, hoodies, shorts, and accessories.

6 A. W. Kaufman
MAP P5 ■ 73 Orchard St

Fine-quality European lingerie is sold here at an excellent price with personalized service. This third-generation store offers a range of underwear for men and women.

7 Jodamo
MAP N5 ■ 321 Grand St

An extensive range of European designer menswear can be found in this large store, including Versace, Valentino, and Missoni, as well as leather goods and shoes.

8 Altman Luggage
MAP N5 ■ 135 Orchard St

From computer cases to carry-ons, brand names like Lark, Travelpro, and American Tourister are sold for less at this well-stocked emporium.

9 Moo Shoes
MAP P5 ■ 78 Orchard St

You can shop for funky, colorful footwear at this vegan-owned store that sells cruelty-free shoes, bags, T-shirts, wallets, books, and various other accessories.

10 Economy Candy
MAP N5 ■ 108 Rivington St

Since 1937, this old-fashioned, family-run candy store has been doling out gumballs, hand-dipped chocolates, and fun New York-themed goodies.

Shelves filled with sweets at Economy Candy, a Lower East Side landmark

Restaurants

PRICE CATEGORIES

For a three-course meal for one with a glass of house wine, and all unavoidable charges including tax.

$ under $25 $$ $25–$75 $$$ over $75

Dirty French
MAP N5 ■ 180 Ludlow St, between Stanton and Houston Sts ■ 212 254 3000 ■ $$

This contemporary French bistro serves cleverly enhanced classics such as duck à l'orange and brook trout with sesame and apricots.

2 Katz's Delicatessen
MAP N5 ■ 205 East Houston St, at Ludlow St ■ 212 254 2246 ■ $$

Savor a pastrami sandwich on rye here and you'll understand how Katz's got its famous reputation.

3 Ivan Ramen
MAP N5 ■ 25 Clinton St ■ 646 678 3859 ■ $$

Enjoy sesame noodles, red chili ramen, and steamed pork buns from Chef Ivan Orkin, who returned to New York in 2012 after running successful ramen shops in Tokyo.

4 Dirt Candy
MAP N5 ■ 86 Allen St ■ 212 228 7732 ■ $$$

A stylish Lower East Side restaurant, Dirt Candy offers experimental vegetarian dishes. Dinner features a seasonal five course tasting menu.

5 Tim Ho Wan
MAP M4 ■ 85 4th Ave, at East 10th St ■ 212 228 2800 ■ $$

This Hong Kong-based dim sum chain, renowned for being one of the world's cheapest Michelin-starred restaurants, opened in NYC in 2017.

6 Veselka
MAP M4 ■ 144 2nd Ave, at 9th St ■ 212 228 9682 ■ $$

This funky and cozy Ukrainian diner is open late and for over 60 years has been serving well-priced borscht, blintzes, and pierogi. The tables at the back are quieter.

7 The Dumpling Man
MAP M4 ■ 100 St Mark's Place ■ 212 505 2121 ■ $

The pork, chicken, and vegetarian dumplings are a big draw, but save room for the shaved ice dessert.

8 Freemans
MAP N4 ■ Freemans Alley ■ 212 420 0012 ■ $$$

Hiding at the end of a graffitied alley, this hunting lodge-style restaurant serves a 1950s-inspired menu, from rum-soaked ribs to prunes wrapped in bacon, oozing Stilton cheese.

Freemans restaurant

9 Veniero's Pasticceria & Café
MAP M5 ■ 342 East 11th St, between 1st & 2nd Aves ■ 212 674 7264 ■ $

This old-school Italian gem, dating back to 1894, is known for its ricotta cheesecake and cannoli. You can order at the special take-out line or sit in the beautiful dining room.

10 Momofuku Noodle Bar
MAP M5 ■ 171 1st Ave, at East 11th St ■ 212 777 7773 ■ $$

David Chang's original restaurant is famed for its wide range of noodle bowls, Southern-style fried chicken, and Chinese-inspired buns.

See map on p96

TOP 10 SoHo and Tribeca

The area named for its shape (Triangle Below Canal) long consisted mostly of abandoned warehouses. When Robert De Niro set up his Tribeca Film Center in 1988, stylish restaurants opened, and the area started to draw celebrity residents. Now Tribeca is one of New York's hottest neighborhoods and home to the Tribeca Film Festival. SoHo's (South of Houston) once empty loft spaces first drew artists, then galleries, then crowds of browsers and restaurants to serve them. Only some galleries remain, and the streets are now lined with designer clothing and home furnishing boutiques. Both areas boast the famous New York cast-iron architecture.

Statue, Fire Museum

1 Greene Street
MAP N4

Cast-iron architecture flourished in New York in the late 1800s, as a way to produce decorative elements such as columns and arches and create impressive buildings inexpensively. Greene Street, between Canal and Grand streets, and between Broome and Spring streets, has 50 examples. The rows of columned facades creating a striking streetscape.

2 Color Factory
MAP N3 ■ 251 Spring St, at Varick St ■ 347 378 4071 ■ Open 9am–7pm Thu, Fri, Sun, 9am–8pm Sat, 10am–6pm Mon, Tue ■ Adm ■ www.colorfactory.co

This interactive exhibition arrived in SoHo on a semi-permanent basis in 2018. There are 16 immersive spaces celebrating the value of color in creativity. Highlights include the balloon-crammed room, the "Into the Blue" ball pit, and the luminous dance floor. Visitors are also entitled to free sweet cream gelato from Il Laboratorio Del Gelato and free rainbow macarons. Tickets must be purchased online.

3 Prada
MAP N4 ■ 575 Broadway, at Prince St ■ Open 11am–7pm Mon–Sat, 11am–6pm Sun

This extraordinary flagship store for trend-setting Italian designer Prada is a sign of SoHo's shift from art to fashion. Dutch architect Rem Koolhaas is responsible for the ultra-hip floating stairs, undulating walls, futuristic elevators, and hi-tech dressing rooms. A visit here is a must for fans of both high-end fashion and architecture.

Cast-iron buildings on Greene Street

SOHO AND TRIBECA

1 **Top 10 Sights**
see pp102–5

1 **Restaurants**
see p107

1 **Nightlife**
see p106

4 New York City Fire Museum

MAP N3 ■ 278 Spring St ■ Open 10am–5pm Wed–Sun ■ Adm ■ www.nycfiremuseum.org

A nostalgic treasure housed in a 1904 firehouse, this splendid collection includes the city's fire-fighting engines, equipment, garb, and memorabilia from the 18th century to the present. A moving photo display depicts the World Trade Center attack on September 11, 2001 and honors the many fire-fighters who lost their lives there.

New York City Fire Museum

Impressive cast-iron facade of the Haughwout Building

⑤ Haughwout Building
MAP P4 ■ 488–492 Broadway, at Broome St

A cast-iron masterpiece, this structure was built in 1857 to house a fashionable china and glassware emporium. The design of colonnaded arches flanked by taller Corinthian columns was adapted from the facade of the Sansovino Library in Venice. This motif is repeated 92 times across the front of the building. A 1995 renovation removed grime and restored the elegant original pale color. This building boasted the first Otis safety elevator, an innovation that made the skyscraper possible.

⑥ "Little" Singer Building
MAP N4 ■ 561–563 Broadway, between Prince & Spring Sts

By the early 1900s, cast iron was giving way to steel-framed brick and terra cotta. One notable example is Ernest Flagg's 1904 "Little" Singer Building (to distinguish it from a taller tower also built for Singer). Influenced by Parisian architecture of the period, it has a charming 12-story facade adorned with wrought-iron balconies and graceful arches painted in dark green.

⑦ Canal Street
MAP P3–4

The end of SoHo, the beginning of Tribeca, and a world of its own, no street better shows the contrasts of New York. Canal Street is crowded with peddlers selling fake Rolex watches and Gucci bags, electronics that may or may not be new, and bargain stores offering sneakers, jeans, and flea-market finds. Keep walking east into Chinatown, and the goods shift to vegetables and displays of live and dried fish.

"Little" Singer Building

8 Harrison Street
MAP P3

This group of Federal townhouses, built between 1796 and 1828, did not exist as a row until 1975, when the houses were moved to this site to be saved from the urban renewal that razed much of the area. At the end of the block (No. 6) is the former New York Mercantile Exchange, a Queen Anne building dating from 1884 and in use until 1977 when the Exchange moved to 4 World Trade Center.

9 The Drawing Center
MAP P4 ■ 35 Wooster St
■ **Open noon–6pm Wed–Sun**
■ **www.drawingcenter.org**

SoHo's legacy of fine art galleries is maintained at The Drawing Center (see p51), which focuses on changing exhibitions of historical and contemporary drawings. Each year an artist is invited to create a wall drawing in the gallery's main entryway and stairwell. The center has previously featured masters such as Marcel Duchamp, while recent exhibitors have included New York-based artist Catherine Chalmers and British-Sudanese artist Ibrahim El-Salahi.

10 Tribeca Film Center
MAP P3 ■ 375 Greenwich St

A turn-of-the-century coffee warehouse has been converted into office space for the film and entertainment industry. The guiding spirit was Robert De Niro, whose Tribeca Productions was founded in 1988. Miramax has set up offices here and the building is also home to the Tribeca Grill, owned by De Niro and restaurateur Drew Nieporent.

TRIBECA'S MOVIE BUSINESS

Robert De Niro organized the first Tribeca Film Festival in 2002 to help the neighborhood's recovery from the effects of the 9/11 attacks. The 10-day spring event is now one of the highest profile film festivals in the country. Outside the festival period, big name stars have been sighted heading for the Roxy Cinema at the Roxy Hotel (see p173).

A STROLL AROUND SOHO AND TRIBECA

Prince Street Subway
Franklin Bowles Galleries
Boqueria
Miu Miu
Staley-Wise Gallery
Greene Street
The Drawing Center
apexart
Roxy Bar
White Street
Harrison Street
The Odeon

▶ MORNING

Prince Street Subway is a good starting point to explore SoHo. Visit the interesting **Staley-Wise Gallery** *(100 Crosby St)*, which is known for its fashion photography. Then walk a block west and stop by the Italian designer boutique **Miu Miu** *(100 Prince St)*, before continuing on to one of SoHo's most respected art venues, the **Franklin Bowles Galleries** *(431 West Broadway)*.

Retrace your steps and head south on **Greene Street** *(see p102)* which has a number of interesting boutiques and designer stores, such as Louis Vuitton at No. 116, Stella McCartney at No. 112, and Tiffany & Co. at No. 97. At Spring Street, turn right and walk a couple of blocks to have lunch at **Boqueria** *(see p107)*.

AFTERNOON

After lunch, visit **The Drawing Center**, which exhibits work from emerging artists and has poetry readings. Then, proceed to Tribeca to take in the varied exhibits at **apexart** *(see p51)*.

Take a stroll along White Street to admire its historic architecture and then stop for a drink at the **Roxy Bar** *(see p106)*. From here walk over to **Harrison Street** to see stunning 19th-century rowhouses, before sampling the best of Tribeca cuisine with a meal at one of the area's leading restaurants, **The Odeon** *(see p107)*.

See map on p103 ←

Nightlife

1 Fanelli Café
MAP N4 ▪ 94 Prince St, at Mercer St ▪ 212 226 9412

Locals have been visiting bars on this site since 1847, but this former speakeasy opened its doors in 1922. A SoHo favorite.

2 Roxy Bar
MAP N3 ▪ Roxy Hotel Tribeca, 2 6th Ave ▪ 212 519 6600

Almost the entire ground floor of the hotel is devoted to this spacious bar with plush seats and a dramatic eight-story atrium.

3 Nancy Whiskey Pub
MAP P3 ▪ 1 Lispenard St ▪ 212 226 9943

This no-frills dive bar, popular with local workers, is one of Tribeca's most beloved neighborhood hang-outs. It promises burgers, whiskey, and shuffleboard games.

The popular Brandy Library

4 Brandy Library
MAP P3 ▪ 26 N Moore St, at Varick St ▪ 212 226 5545

The menu at this stylish lounge bar features single malt whiskeys, limited batch cognacs, and over 100 different cocktails.

5 Puffy's Tavern
MAP P3 ▪ 81 Hudson St, at Harrison St ▪ 212 227 3912

Cheap booze and Alidoro Italian sandwiches attract locals to this small, friendly neighborhood bar, which also has a dartboard and large flat-screen TVs playing sports events.

The bar at Ear Inn

6 Ear Inn
MAP P3 ▪ 326 Spring St, at Greenwich St ▪ 212 226 9060

This classy but cozy and casual spot is likely the oldest bar in the city (it dates to 1830). Fairly buzzy at night and at lunch, it's also good for a respectable cheap meal.

7 Grand Bar
MAP P3 ▪ SoHo Grand Hotel, 310 West Broadway, between Canal & Grand Sts ▪ 212 965 3588

The SoHo Grand is a neighborhood nightlife hub; comfortable and softly lit, with food if you want it.

8 Terroir Tribeca
MAP P3 ▪ 24 Harrison St ▪ 212 625 9463

Toast the New York night at this lively wine bar with wines from around the world and creative nibbles, from duck salad to mozzarella balls.

9 Paul's Casablanca
MAP N3 ▪ 305 Spring St ▪ 212 620 5220

This cocktail bar and nightclub has a loyal following among celebrities. The interior resembles a Moroccan palace, with mosaic tiles, lanterns, and leather beanbag chairs.

10 Kenn's Broome Street Bar
MAP P3 ▪ 363 West Broadway, at Broome St ▪ 212 925 2086

A SoHo institution with a decent range of beers and bar food.

Restaurants

PRICE CATEGORIES
For a three-course meal for one with a glass of house wine, and all unavoidable charges including tax.

$ under $25 $$ $25–$75 $$$ over $75

1 The Dutch

MAP N3 ▪ 131 Sullivan St ▪ 212 677 6200 ▪ $$$

Oysters and bold dishes, from strip steak to lamb neck, are the highlights at this wood-paneled tavern helmed by Andrew Carmellini.

Seafood platter at The Dutch

2 Tribeca Grill
MAP P3 ▪ 375 Greenwich St ▪ 212 941 3900 ▪ $$$

Partly owned by Hollywood star Robert De Niro, Tribeca Grill offers fine American dishes with Asian and Italian accents in an airy, brick-walled warehouse.

3 La Esquina
MAP P4 ▪ 114 Kenmare St ▪ 646 613 7100 ▪ $$

At this colorful Mexican spot, customers choose between the inexpensive *taquería* counter and the stylish cocktail lounge.

4 Locanda Verde
MAP P3 ▪ 377 Greenwich St ▪ 212 925 3797 ▪ $$$

Visit this casual Italian taverna for star chef Andrew Carmellini's exceptional creations. Try the porchetta sandwich, duck *arrosto* (roasted duck) or one of his superb pastas.

5 Bubby's
MAP P3 ▪ 120 Hudson St ▪ 212 219 0666 ▪ $$

In Tribeca, this sunny, family-friendly restaurant churns out comfort fare at all hours from a varied menu that includes full meals as well as light bites.

6 Grand Banks
MAP P2 ▪ Pier 25, North Moore St ▪ 212 660 6312 ▪ $$

Indulge in oysters and cocktails aboard the 1942 wooden schooner *Sherman Zwicker*, which is now a docked restaurant (summer only). Arrive early to get a seat.

7 Balthazar
MAP N3 ▪ 80 Spring St, at Broadway ▪ 212 965 1414 ▪ $$$

As close to a Parisian bistro as you're likely to find in SoHo, Balthazar's only problem is its continued popularity.

8 Raoul's
MAP N4 ▪ 180 Prince St, between Sullivan & Thompson Sts ▪ 212 966 3518 ▪ $$$

Another taste of the Left Bank in SoHo, with an updated French menu as well as a great garden.

9 The Odeon
MAP P3 ▪ 145 West Broadway, at Thomas St ▪ 212 233 0507 ▪ $$$

Art Deco decor, consistently good French-American food, and a star-studded crowd have been keeping the vibe right since 1980.

10 Boqueria
MAP N3 ▪ 171 Spring St ▪ 212 343 4255 ▪ $$

Head to lively Boqueria for superb tapas, such as blistered *padrón* peppers or juicy marinated lamb, all washed down with a jug of sangria.

See map on p103

TOP 10 Greenwich Village

It was different from the start, a unique pattern of streets that broke from the city's grid plan and reflected the boundaries of a rural hamlet. In the 20th century, Greenwich Village became a creative haven, its leafy lanes home to artists, beat poets, and musicians like the young Bob Dylan. Later it grew popular with the LGBTQ+ community, and today cafés and funky shops attract young people from all over the city. The Village really comes to life at night, when cafés, theaters, and clubs beckon at every turn.

New York University

1 Washington Square Park
MAP N3 ■ 5th Ave, between Waverly Pl & 4th St

In 1826, a marshy area was filled to form this popular park. The marble Washington Square Arch by Stanford White went up in 1892, replacing a wooden version that marked the centenary of George Washington's inauguration. Parents with strollers,

The iconic Washington Square Arch

GREENWICH VILLAGE

● **Top 10 Sights**
see pp108–11

① **Restaurants**
see p113

① **Literary Landmarks**
see p112

The mid-19th-century townhouses in Grove Court, Greenwich Village

chess players, and young lovers occupy the benches here. The fountain in the center is where Bob Dylan sang his first folk songs.

2 Whitney Museum of American Art

MAP M2 ■ 99 Gansevoort St ■ Open 10:30am–6pm Sun, Mon, Tue (Jul & Aug only), Wed, Thu, Sat; 10:30am–10pm Fri ■ Adm (7–10pm Fri is pay-what-you-wish) ■ www.whitney.org

Founded by Gertrude Vanderbilt Whitney, this museum (see p48) is the foremost showcase for American art of the 20th and 21st centuries. The sixth and seventh floors of this stunning building display pieces from the museum's collection – there isn't a permanent display, rather a constant rotation of works. The Whitney Biennial, held in even years, is the most significant exhibition of new trends of American art.

3 Grove Court

MAP N3 ■ Grove St near Bedford St

This group of six townhouses in a bend in the street was developed by grocer Samuel Cocks, who thought that having residents nearby would help his business at No. 18. But while such private courts are prized today, they were not considered respectable in the 1850s, and the disreputable types who moved in earned it the nickname "Mixed Ale Alley." American writer O. Henry later used the block as the setting for his 1902 novel The Last Leaf.

4 Washington Mews

MAP M3 ■ University Pl to 5th Ave

Another group of stables turned into houses around 1900, the mews attracted both writers and artists. No. 14A housed, at various times, author John Dos Passos and artists Edward Hopper, William Glackens, and Rockwell Kent. Writer Sherwood Anderson often stayed at No. 54 with his friend and patron, Mary Emmett. In contrast to the modern buildings in much of Manhattan, this type of quaint enclave is the reason many find the Village so appealing.

Washington Mews

5 Jefferson Market Courthouse

MAP M3 ■ 425 6th Ave, between 9th & 10th Sts ■ Open 10am–8pm Mon–Thu, 10am–5pm Fri & Sat, 1–5pm Sun

The site was a market in 1833, named after the former president, Thomas Jefferson. The fire lookout tower had a giant bell that alerted volunteer firefighters. When the courthouse was built in 1877, the bell was installed in its clock tower. The treasured Village landmark was saved from demolition after a spirited local campaign and converted into a branch of the New York Public Library *(see p128)* in the 1950s.

A restaurant on Bleecker Street

Jefferson Market Courthouse

6 Cherry Lane Theatre

MAP N3 ■ 38 Commerce St, between Bedford & Barrow Sts ■ 212 989 2020 ■ www.cherrylane theatre.org

In 1924, a warehouse was converted into one of the first Off-Broadway theaters and showcased plays by the likes of Edward Albee, Eugene Ionesco, David Mamet, Samuel Beckett, and Harold Pinter. Today, the "Cherry Lane Alternative" uses established playwrights to mentor talented newcomers.

7 Bleecker Street

MAP N3 ■ Between 6th Ave & LaGuardia Place

The present line-up of ordinary shops and restaurants belies the history of this street. James Fenimore Cooper lived at No. 145 in 1833, Theodore Dreiser stayed at No. 160 when he came to New York in 1895, and James Agee lived at No. 172 from 1941 to 1951. The café at No. 189, on the corner of Bleecker and MacDougal, was the San Remo bar, the favorite gathering place for William Burroughs, Allen Ginsberg, Gregory Corso, and Jack Kerouac, leading lights of the Beat Generation.

8 New York University

MAP N4 ■ Washington Square ■ www.nyu.edu

Founded in 1831, NYU enlarged the scope of early 19th-century study from its previous concentration on Greek and Latin to contemporary subjects: a "rational and practical education" for those aspiring to careers in business, industry, science, and the arts, as well as in law, medicine, and the ministry. It has grown into one of the largest private universities in America and now occupies buildings in many blocks around Washington Square.

9 Judson Memorial Church

MAP N3 ■ 55 Washington Square South ■ Open for services 11am Sun

An elegant work in Romanesque style by Stanford White, with stained glass by John La Farge, the church was built in 1888–93 as a memorial to Adoniram Judson, said to be the first American Baptist missionary in Asia. John D. Rockefeller, Jr. *(see p46)* contributed to the construction. White's novel use of mottled yellow brick and white terra cotta trim introduced light coloration into American church architecture.

10 75½ Bedford Street

MAP N3 ■ Between Morton & Barrow Sts

New York's narrowest home, just 9.5 ft (3 m) wide, was built in 1873 on a carriageway that led to former stables behind Nos. 75 and 77. Poet Edna St. Vincent Millay lived here, as did actors John Barrymore and, later, Cary Grant. No. 77 is the oldest house in the Village, dating from around 1799, and at No. 103 is "Twin Peaks," an 1830 structure that was remodeled in 1925 by Clifford Reed Daily to house artists and writers, who would presumably be inspired by the quirky architecture.

THE HALLOWEEN PARADE

Anything goes in this wildly gaudy annual parade of floats and amazing costumes **(below)**. Drawing more than 60,000 participants and reportedly two million spectators, it is the largest Halloween parade in the world. The parade route goes up 6th Avenue, from Spring Street in the Village to 23rd Street, starting at 7pm.

A VILLAGE STROLL

▶ MORNING

Begin at **Washington Square** *(see p112)* and the elegant townhouse row where Edith Wharton and Henry James once lived. Find the charming houses of **Washington Mews** *(see p109)* and MacDougal Alley *(East of MacDougal St, between 8th St & Waverly Pl)*, then stroll south along MacDougal Street, once a favorite haunt of the Beat Generation and Bob Dylan, to **Caffe Reggio** at No. 119. Open since 1927, the café is adorned with Italian antiques and paintings.

Walk down to **Bleecker Street** and follow it across 7th Avenue to see several iconic stores, including Rocco's, Murray's Cheese and Faicco's. Stroll down Sixth Avenue to find **Bedford Street**, one of the city's most attractive blocks, and visit **Grove Court** *(see p109)*. Have lunch at the lovely, pocket-size bistro, **The Little Owl** *(see p113)*. The apartment block above served as the exterior for Monica's apartment in *Friends*.

AFTERNOON

After lunch, while away a few hours browsing in the local shops on **West 4th Street**. There are also coffee houses, such as **Partners Coffee** *(44 Charles St)*, which are great for people-watching. Vintage-style designer clothing can be admired at shops such as **Odin** *(106 Greenwich Ave)*, while further west is the Meatpacking District, home to boutiques and restaurants. On the way, you can stop by the **NYC AIDS Memorial Park** *(76 Greenwich Ave)*, inaugurated in 2016 to commemorate all the New Yorkers who have died from AIDS since the 1970s.

See map on p108 ←

Literary Landmarks

 Washington Square
MAP N3

Prominent writers who lived here include Edith Wharton, at No. 7 in 1882. Henry James was born nearby at 2 Washington Place in 1843.

2 St. Luke's Place
MAP N3 ■ Between Hudson St & 7th Ave South

Poet Marianne Moore lived at No.14, and Theodore Dreiser wrote *An American Tragedy* at No. 16.

3 Patchin Place
MAP N3 ■ West 10th St

A charming pocket of 19th-century houses that later attracted e. e. cummings, John Masefield, and Eugene O'Neill, among various others.

4 Café Wha?
MAP N3 ■ 115 MacDougal St, between Bleecker & West 3rd Sts

Beat poet Allen Ginsberg was a regular at this venue that also hosted early appearances from Bob Dylan and Jimi Hendrix.

5 White Horse Tavern
MAP N3 ■ 567 Hudson St, at 11th St

Favorite hangout of Norman Mailer and Dylan Thomas, who announced one night in 1953, "I've had 18 straight whiskeys," and passed out. He died the next day.

6 Willa Cather Residence
MAP N3 ■ 5 Bank St, between Waverly Pl & Greenwich St ■ Closed to public

Willa Cather penned six novels in this house and her Friday "at homes" were attended by the likes of D. H. Lawrence.

 7 Mark Twain Residence
MAP M3 ■ 21 5th Ave, at 9th St ■ Closed to public

The former home (1904–8) of Mark Twain, designed by James Renwick, Jr., architect of St. Patrick's Cathedral, was demolished in 1954. Twain received guests while propped up in a carved bed.

Mark Twain

8 Emma Lazarus House
MAP M3 ■ 18 West 10th St ■ Closed to public

This Italianate brownstone was the home of Emma Lazarus, the author of the *New Colossus* poem, which adorns the Statue of Liberty.

9 James Baldwin Residence
MAP M2 ■ 81 Horatio St, between Washington & Greenwich Sts ■ Closed to public

Celebrated African American author James Baldwin lived in an apartment here from 1958 to 1961 while writing his third novel, *Another Country*.

10 West 10th Street
MAP M3

This street has had several literary residents. Mark Twain lived at No. 14 from 1900 to 1901, Hart Crane lived at No. 54 in 1917, and Edward Albee lived in the carriage house at No. 50 during the 1960s.

White Horse Tavern

Restaurants

1 Babbo
MAP N3 ▪ 110 Waverly Pl ▪ 212 777 0303 ▪ $$$

An attractive setting and the inventive Italian fare by restaurateur Joe Bastianich make this a very popular spot. Reserve in advance.

2 Il Mulino
MAP N3 ▪ 86 West 3rd St, between Sullivan & Thompson Sts ▪ 212 673 3783 ▪ $$$

Another top Italian. Quality is consistent, portions are large, and the brick-walled room is inviting.

3 Family Meal at Blue Hill
MAP N3 ▪ 75 Washington Pl, at MacDougal St ▪ 212 539 1776 ▪ $$$

Highly praised New American restaurant that serves shared plates of local, seasonal ingredients.

4 Gotham Restaurant
MAP M3 ▪ 12 East 12th St, between 5th Ave & University Pl ▪ 212 620 4020 ▪ $$$

Opened in 1984, this award-winning restaurant serves contemporary American cuisine. It's known for its steaks and international wine list.

5 John's of Bleecker Street
MAP N3 ▪ 278 Bleecker St ▪ 212 243 1680 ▪ $$

This old school, thin-crust pizza joint is also known for its graffiti-carved wooden booths.

6 Minetta Tavern
MAP N3 ▪ 113 MacDougal St ▪ 212 475 3850 ▪ $$$

While this classic tavern dates back to 1937 (Ernest Hemingway and Eugene O'Neill drank here), it's now best known for upscale bistro fare.

7 Red Farm
MAP N2 ▪ 529 Hudson St, between W 10th & Charles Sts ▪ 212 792 9700 ▪ $$

Local and seasonal produce drive this popular contemporary Chinese joint, with playful dim sum creations such as the "Pac-Man" shrimp dumplings.

8 Morandi
MAP M3 ▪ 211 Waverly Pl ▪ 212 627 7575 ▪ $$$

Enjoy a slice of rustic Italy at this wildly popular West Village restaurant, with excellent pastas, grilled meats and seafood.

9 The Little Owl
MAP N3 ▪ 90 Bedford St ▪ 212 741 4695 ▪ $$

This tiny but cozy restaurant run by Joey Campanaro has a great Italian-accented American bistro menu, serving everything from grilled scallops to Parmesan risotto with truffles.

10 Magnolia Bakery
MAP M2 ▪ 401 Bleecker St, at West 11th St ▪ 212 462 2572 ▪ $

There are many tasty baked goods on offer, but people come here for the heavenly and deservedly-famous multicolored cupcakes.

Magnolia Bakery

See map on p108 ←

🔟 Union Square, Gramercy Park, and Flatiron

This flourishing section of Manhattan is centered on Union Square, a major intersection but also a pleasant park, filled with statues and monuments. A Greenmarket fills it with fresh produce four times a week, and the surrounding neighborhood is attracting new apartments, shops, and restaurants. Shops and lively eating places extend up 5th Avenue into the once-neglected Flatiron District. Opposite the Flatiron Building that gives the area its name, Madison Square is home to some of the city's hottest restaurants as well as Madison Square Park. Gramercy Park continues to be the most European of the city's neighborhoods.

Union Square Greenmarket

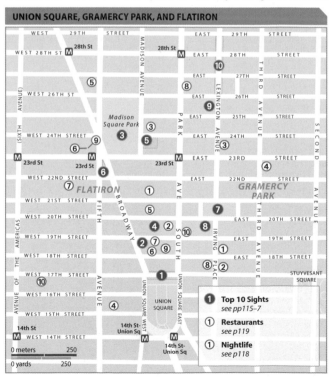

UNION SQUARE, GRAMERCY PARK, AND FLATIRON

① Top 10 Sights
see pp115–7

① Restaurants
see p119

① Nightlife
see p118

0 meters 250
0 yards 250

Madison Square Park

1 Union Square Greenmarket

MAP M4 ■ At Broadway & 17th St ■ Open 8am–6pm Mon, Wed, Fri, Sat

Herbs, berries, miniature vegetables, fresh flowers, homebaked pastries, newly woven yarns, hams, honey – all of these and more can be found at the bountiful Greenmarket that fills the inviting Union Square each Monday, Wednesday, Friday, and Saturday. Over 140 regional farmers take part in the market, each offering only goods that they have grown or made.

2 ABC Carpet & Home

MAP L4 ■ 888 Broadway, at East 19th St ■ Open 10am–6pm Mon–Sat, 11am–6pm Sun

The city's most eclectic emporium, with a landmark building that is part flea market, part antiques fair, and part Middle Eastern bazaar. Offerings include furniture, fabrics, accessories, bedding, flowers, and rugs. There are also the notable dining spaces ABC Cocina and ABC Kitchen.

3 Madison Square Park

MAP L3 ■ 23rd to 26th Sts, between Broadway & Madison Ave

The square opened in 1847 at the center of a residential area where politician Theodore Roosevelt and writer Edith Wharton were born. The original Madison Square Garden was here, at Madison Avenue and 26th Street. Development brought distinguished sites such as the Flatiron and Metropolitan Life Buildings. Today the park is home to the wildly popular burger spot Shake Shack (see p67).

4 Theodore Roosevelt Birthplace

MAP L4 ■ 28 East 20th St, between Broadway & Park Ave Sth ■ Open 10am–noon & 1–4pm Wed–Sun ■ Visits are by guided tour only, every 15 mins ■ www.nps.gov/thrb

The boyhood home where the 26th president of the United States was born in 1858 has been reconstructed. Exhibits trace his political career as well as his explorations, displaying everything from toys to campaign buttons, and emblems of the trademark "Rough Rider" hat Roosevelt wore in the Spanish-American War. The house offers a rare glimpse of a privileged 19th-century New York lifestyle.

Birthplace of Theodore Roosevelt

⑤ Metropolitan Life Tower
MAP L4 ▪ 1 Madison Ave, near 24th St ▪ Lobby open during office hours

This 54-story tower, built along the east side of Madison Square in 1909, was the world's tallest building at that time – an appropriate corporate symbol for the world's largest insurance company. Designed by Napoleon LeBrun & Sons, the tower follows the form of the campanile in Piazza San Marco in Venice. Although it was altered in the 1960s, when the entire structure was renovated, its ornate four-faced clock and crowning cupola remain a familiar landmark on the New York skyline. The clock tower now houses the New York Edition Hotel.

⑥ Flatiron Building
MAP L3 ▪ 175 5th Ave, at Broadway & 23rd St ▪ Lobby open during office hours

Though dwarfed by taller structures today, this unusual building – its shape conforming to a triangular plot of land – remains striking, a symbol of the beginning of the skyscraper

Flatiron Building

THE CITY'S SQUARES

Manhattan has only four London-style squares: Union, Madison, Stuyvesant, and Gramercy Park, all formed in the 1800s by real estate speculators hoping to profit by selling surrounding lots to the wealthy. The squares provide welcome breaks among the city's dense, tall buildings, but only Gramercy Park (below) has remained private.

era. Its slim, rounded facade is as proud as a ship's prow sailing up the avenue. Completed in 1902, it anchored the north end of the prestigious Ladies' Mile shopping district, located between Union and Madison Squares. The designer, famous Chicago architect Daniel Burnham, included detailed Italian Renaissance decoration on the building from top to bottom, much of it in terra cotta.

⑦ Gramercy Park
MAP L4 ▪ Lexington Ave, between 20th & 21st Sts ▪ Closed to public

Samuel Ruggles laid out this neighborhood around a private park in the 1830s. It remains the city's only private park and a desirable place to live. Architect Stanford White remodeled No. 16 in 1888 for Edwin Booth, who founded the Players Club here. Booth's statue (see p118) can be seen standing in the park.

⑧ National Arts Club
MAP L4 ▪ 15 Gramercy Park South ▪ Open 10am–5pm daily ▪ www.nationalartsclub.org

Originally the home of Samuel Tilden, a governor of New York and opponent of the notorious William "Boss" Tweed, this Gothic Revival brownstone was designed by Calvert Vaux, of Central Park fame. The National Arts Club, whose members have included leading American artists since 1898, bought the building in 1906. Each member is asked to donate a work to the club. Though it is a private club, its galleries are open to the public.

The National Arts Club brownstone

⑨ 69th Regiment Armory
MAP L4 ▪ 68 Lexington Ave, between 25th & 26th Sts ▪ Closed to public

This 1906 Beaux Arts building was used as the drill hall and offices of a military unit privately formed in 1848. In 1913, the controversial exhibition of modern art known as the Armory Show was held here, including works by Van Gogh, Duchamp, and Brancusi. The show was widely panned in the press, but it brought modern art to New York on a large scale and had a profound and lasting effect on American art.

⑩ "Curry Hill"
MAP L4 ▪ Lexington Ave, between 26th & 29th Sts

Despite changes around it, this three-block corridor just south of Murray Hill remains filled with Indian shops selling saris and gifts, and is lined with restaurants that are a boon for diners (particularly vegetarians) in search of Indian food at reasonable prices. Kalustyan's, 123 Lexington Avenue, is a treasure trove of spices and grains, with some 31 different kinds of rice.

EXPLORING GRAMERCY PARK AND FLATIRON

▶ MORNING

Book-lovers should start on 12th Street, where the city's biggest used bookstore, the **Strand**, is located at No. 828. From here, head north up Broadway to Union Square, visiting the **Union Square Greenmarket** (see p115). Continue walking up Broadway to get to the **Paragon Sports** superstore (867 Broadway, at 18th St), and **Fishs Eddy** (889 Broadway, at 19th St), which sells both vintage and new china and glassware. The fascinating **ABC Carpet & Home** awaits at No. 888 (see p115).

At the **Flatiron Building**, turn east to **Madison Square Park** (see p115), then stop to have lunch at the iconic Shake Shack or, if it's a Saturday, the gourmet **Eleven Madison Park** (see p119). Several restaurants on **"Curry Hill"** also offer affordable lunches – these include Pongal (110 Lexington Ave), and the popular Saravanaa Bhavan (81 Lexington Ave).

AFTERNOON

While in the neighborhood, check out the range of intriguing spices at **Kalustyan's** (123 Lexington Ave).

More shops can be found on **Fifth Avenue** between 14th and 23rd Streets, including Free People at No.79, Zara at No. 101, Lululemon at No.114, and H&M at No. 111.

End your day in the **Gramercy Park** neighborhood. Stroll up **East 19th Street**, known as the "Block Beautiful," for its elegant 1920s houses.

See map on p114 ←

Nightlife

1 Pete's Tavern
MAP L4 ▪ 129 East 18th St
▪ 212 473 7676

Opened in 1864, Pete's Tavern is known for being writer O. Henry's local hangout – he supposedly wrote *The Gift of the Magi* here.

2 Bar Jamón
MAP M4 ▪ 125 E 17th St, at Irving Place ▪ 212 253 2773

A Spanish-style bar, Bar Jamón offers a variety of wine and sherry, plus Spanish tapas. Its sister restaurant, Casa Mono, is next door.

3 Broken Shaker
MAP L4 ▪ 23 Lexington Ave
▪ 212 475 1920

This outpost of the celebrated Miami cocktail bar is located on the roof of the Freehand Hotel and serves fabulous cocktails and posh bar bites.

4 Molly's
MAP L4 ▪ 287 3rd Ave, between East 22nd & East 23rd Sts
▪ 212 889 3361

Operating since the 1960s, Molly's is an old-school Irish pub with friendly bartenders.

5 230 Fifth Rooftop Bar
MAP L3 ▪ 230 Fifth Ave
▪ 212 725 4300

This chic bar and roof garden affords great views of the Empire State Building. Heated "igloos" are available from November to May.

6 SERRA by Birreria
MAP L3 ▪ 200 5th Ave (Eataly NYC Flatiron) ▪ 212 937 8910

Eataly's bright rooftop is part beer garden, part Italian trattoria. The menu here changes seasonally, but it's always a great place to sample Italian IPAs.

7 Undercote
MAP L3 ▪ 16 West 22nd St
▪ www.cotenyc.com

With walls covered in plants, this subterranean cocktail bar is a jungle oasis in the heart of Manhattan. Booking is essential; the drinks are exceptional.

8 Dear Irving
MAP M4 ▪ 55 Irving Place
▪ www.dearirving.com

Inspired by Woody Allen's film *Midnight in Paris*, this cocktail bar features spaces depicting different historical eras, such as a Baroque French palace area and a JFK-inspired room.

9 Old Town Bar
MAP L4 ▪ 45 E 18th St, between Broadway & Park Ave ▪ 212 529 6732

An atmospheric bar dating back to 1892, Old Town features much of its original decor – including the weathered dumbwaiter and a fine mahogany bar.

10 Raines Law Room
MAP M3 ▪ 48 W 17th St, between 5th & 6th Aves ▪ 212 213 1350

A modern-day speakeasy, Raines Law Room is tucked away in what appears to be a normal townhouse; you have to ring the doorbell to get in.

230 Fifth Rooftop Bar

Restaurants

1 Cosme

MAP L4 ▪ 35 East 21st St
▪ 212 913 9659 ▪ $$

This contemporary Mexican restaurant from Enrique Olvera stays true to its roots while sourcing local and seasonal ingredients from the Hudson Valley. It also serves a superb margarita.

2 Gramercy Tavern
MAP L4 ▪ 42 East 20th St
▪ 212 477 0777 ▪ $$$

Unpretentious fine dining (see p67) where the inventive American cuisine is universally praised. The desserts are great too.

3 Eleven Madison Park
MAP L4 ▪ 11 Madison Ave, at East 24th St ▪ 212 889 0905 ▪ $$$

Chef Daniel Humm has made Eleven Madison Park a chic spot with his imaginative New American cuisine (see p66), which is served up in elegant Art Deco surroundings.

4 15EAST at Tocqueville
MAP M4 ▪ 1 East 15th St, between Union Square West & 5th Ave ▪ 212 647 1515 ▪ $$$

French cuisine is prepared with Japanese touches in this hidden gem, which also has an award-winning wine list.

5 Sugarfish
MAP L4 ▪ 33 East 20th St, between Park Ave & Broadway
▪ 347 705 8100 ▪ $$

This lauded LA-based sushi chain, helmed by Japanese sushi chef Kazunori Nozawa, serves ultra fresh salmon, tuna, sea bream, and yellowtail.

6 ABC Kitchen
MAP M4 ▪ 35 East 18th St, between Park Ave South & Broadway
▪ 212 475 5829 ▪ $$$

This upscale New American joint is spearheaded by French celebrity chef Jean-Georges Vongerichten.

PRICE CATEGORIES
For a three-course meal for one with a glass of house wine, and all unavoidable charges including tax.

$ under $25 $$ $25–$75 $$$ over $75

7 ABC Cocina
MAP L4 ▪ 38 East 19th St
▪ 212 677 2233 ▪ $$

Farm-to-table fine dining with a Latin-American fusion feel is on offer here. Great seasonal menu and creative tapas.

8 Bread and Tulips
MAP L4 ▪ 365 Park Ave South
▪ 212 532 9100 ▪ $$

A cozy homestyle Italian restaurant, sleek but welcoming, with a fantastic wine list. Great value in the area.

Italian food emporium Eataly

9 Eataly

MAP L3 ▪ 200 5th Ave
▪ 212 229 2560 ▪ $$

At this sprawling emporium of all things edible and Italian there are multiple dining options, from quick takeaway counters to sit-down gourmet eateries.

10 Union Square Café
MAP L4 ▪ 101 East 19th St, at Park Ave South ▪ 212 243 4020 ▪ $$$

Danny Meyer's first and most famous restaurant offers exquisite New American fare just a few blocks from where it spent its first thirty years.

See map on p114 ←

🔟 Chelsea and Herald Square

Chelsea Flea market

A neighborhood that has seen a great deal of change, Chelsea was a quiet enclave of 19th-century brownstones that never made it as a fashionable address. Now it is a hub for New York's LGBTQ+ community and a center for avant-garde art galleries. Superstores and discount outlets occupy 6th Avenue, and Chelsea Piers has transformed the waterfront. Uptown, the Garment District begins around 27th Street, with Herald Square and Macy's at the heart of the city's busiest shopping area.

CHELSEA AND HERALD SQUARE

❶ **Top 10 Sights**
see pp121–3

① **Restaurants**
see p125

① **Chelsea Galleries**
see p124

Shops along 6th Avenue

1 6th Avenue Shopping
MAP L3 ■ 6th Ave, West 18th to 23rd Sts

This was once a popular district known as "Fashion Row." The 1876 cast-iron facade of the Hugh O'Neill Dry Goods Store at Nos. 655–71 exemplifies the era, when the arrival of the elevated line provided easy access to the district. As Manhattan's commercial center moved north, these cast-iron palaces were left deserted until the 1990s, when they found new life as bargain fashion outlets and superstores.

2 Chelsea Flea
MAP L3 ■ 29 West 25th St, between 5th & 6th Aves ■ Open 8am–4pm Sat & Sun ■ Adm

On weekends, year-round, in the shadow of the Cathedral of St. Sava, sprouts one of the city's most popular markets, a tradition since 1976. Around 50 to 60 vendors set up booths selling clothing, silver, jewelry, furniture, art, and "junktiques." Many prize antiques can be discovered at The Showplace (open 10am–6pm daily), 40 West 25th Street, with more than 200 galleries spread over four floors.

3 The High Line
MAP L2–M2 ■ Gansevoort to 34th Sts ■ Open 7am–10pm daily ■ www.thehighline.org

What was once a disused elevated railroad track, overgrown with weeds, is now a city park, planted with native grasses, trees and shrubs. The High Line, which runs through Chelsea and the Meatpacking District, attracts more than five million visitors annually, who come to enjoy the great views, beautiful gardens, and pop-up art installations and events.

The High Line

Chelsea Market

4 Chelsea Market

MAP M2 ■ 75 9th Ave, between 15th and 16th Sts ■ Open 7–2am Mon–Sat, 8am–10pm Sun ■ www.chelseamarket.com

An unmissable destination for foodies, this market features an enclosed food court and shopping mall as well as the Food Network's TV production facility. A range of gourmet ingredients, international dishes, and charming gifts are on offer here. Make sure to explore the small stores and kiosks selling artisanal products and visit the colorful shops nearby.

5 Chelsea Historic District

MAP L2 ■ Between 9th & 10th Aves, 20th & 21st Sts

Clement Moore, author of *A Visit from St. Nicholas*, developed this land during the 1830s. The finest of the townhouses built here are the seven known as "Cushman Row," Nos. 406–18 West 20th Street, which are among the city's best examples of Greek Revival architecture. Houses at Nos. 446–50 West 20th are in the Italianate style, for which Chelsea is also known.

6 Hudson Yards and the Edge

MAP L2 ■ West 30th to 33rd Sts, between 10th and 11th Aves ■ Edge open 10am–10pm daily ■ www.hudsonyardsnewyork.com.

Opened in 2019, this neighborhood of soaring skyscrapers has a shopping mall and Thomas Heatherwick's "Vessel", a 150-ft- (45-m-) tall spiral copper staircase, which affords stunning views of the city and the river. Other highlights include the Shed, an arts center that features works by emerging artists, and the Edge, an open-air observation deck with sensational views of the city.

7 Rubin Museum of Art

MAP F3 ■ 150 West 17th St ■ Open 11am–5pm Thu–Sun ■ Adm (free 6–10pm on Fri) ■ www.rubinmuseum.org

This museum has a collection of 2,000 paintings, sculptures, and textiles, predominately from the Himalayan region. The Tibetan Buddhist Shrine Room recreates an authentic shrine with ritual items, flickering lamps, and an installation on the four main Tibetan religious traditions that rotates every two years. The museum hosts exhibitions and programs, with concerts and films. The Café Serai, housed within the musuem, serves wine, coffee, tea, and light snacks.

Chelsea Historic District

8 Fashion Institute of Technology (F.I.T.)

MAP L3 ■ 227 West 27th St, at 7th Ave ■ Museum open noon–8pm Wed–Fri, 10am–5pm Sat & Sun ■ www.fitnyc.edu/museum

Founded in 1944, the Fashion Institute of Technology is a prestigious school teaching art, fashion design, and marketing. The institute boasts many famous alumni, including Calvin Klein, Norma Kamali, and David Chu. Students benefit from internships with New York's leading stores and designers. The museum at F.I.T. has changing exhibits, often drawn from the school's own textile and clothing collections.

9 Herald Square

MAP K3 ■ Broadway at 6th Ave

This was the center of a rowdy theater district known as the Tenderloin in the 1870s and 80s. The Manhattan Opera House was then razed in 1901 to make way for Macy's, and other stores soon followed. The clock where Broadway meets 6th Avenue is all that is left of the building that housed the *New York Herald* until 1921.

Herald Square clock

10 Macy's

MAP K3 ■ 151 West 34th St, between Broadway & 7th Ave ■ Open 10am–9pm daily (to 10pm Tue, Fri & Sun) ■ www.macys.com

Former whaler Rowland Hussey Macy founded the store *(see p70)* in 1858 on 6th Avenue and 14th Street; the red star logo was inspired by Macy's tattoo, a souvenir of his sailing days. Innovations to the retail industry included pricing goods a few cents below a full dollar and offering a money-back guarantee. The original store was sold in 1888 and moved to the present building.

A DAY AROUND CHELSEA

▶ MORNING

Wind your way through Chelsea, starting with the megastores now occupying former "Fashion Row," on **6th Avenue** *(see p121)* between 18th and 23rd streets. Walk west on 16th Street to 9th Avenue and **Chelsea Market**, a one-time Nabisco factory where the first Oreo cookies were made, now a block-long line of stalls offering all manner of food. The Food Network tapes its TV shows in a street-level studio here.

Continue up 9th Avenue to 20th Street, for the **Chelsea Historic District** and **The High Line** *(see p121)*. Browse the art on "Gallery Row," from 21st to 27th streets, 10th to 11th avenues. A good lunch bet is the **Empire Diner**, an Art Deco railcar serving upscale diner food *(see p125)*.

AFTERNOON

Walk east on 23rd Street to view the wrought-iron balconies of the Chelsea Hotel, and when you get to 6th Avenue, turn uptown for the antiques market and colorful Flower District around 27th Street. A stroll for one block further west on 27th brings you to the **Fashion Institute of Technology**, where the museum usually has interesting displays.

There is a great hidden treasure in this area, **St. John the Baptist Church** *(210 West 31st St)*, whose dingy facade belies a glowing Gothic interior. Continue to 34th Street for **Herald Square** and **Macy's**.

See map on pp120–21 ←

Chelsea Galleries

The exterior of the Gagosian gallery

1 Gagosian
MAP L2 ■ 555 & 541 West 24th St & 522 West 21st St ■ Open 10am–6pm Tue–Sat

Gagosian (see p50) is one of the premier names in New York's modern gallery scene.

2 Matthew Marks
MAP L2 ■ 523 West 24th St, between 10th & 11th Aves; 522 & 526 West 22nd St, between 10th & 11th Aves ■ Open 10am–6pm Tue–Sat

The Matthew Marks Gallery maintains a huge exhibition space in Chelsea, showing large-scale works and contemporary art (see p51).

3 Paula Cooper
MAP L2 ■ 521, 529 & 534 West 21st St ■ Open 10am–6pm Tue–Sat

The lofty setting of this gallery (see p51) is worth a visit. Many of Cooper's shows are controversial.

4 Kasmin
MAP M2 ■ 509 West 27th St ■ Open 10am–6pm Tue–Sat

Son of a British art dealer, Kasmin nurtured many newcomers. Exhibitions at this gallery (see p51) have featured Kenny Scharf, Robert Indiana, Deborah Kass, and Barry Flanagan.

5 Gladstone Gallery
MAP L2 ■ 515 West 24th St, between 10th & 11th Aves ■ Open 10am–6pm Tue–Sat

A dramatic backdrop for large-scale video and photography pioneers.

6 David Zwirner
MAP L2 ■ 537 West 20th St, between 10th & 11th Aves; 525 West 19th St ■ Open 10am–6pm Tue–Sat

A prominent name in the New York art scene, Zwirner relocated to Chelsea from SoHo in 2002. He's especially known for showing Felix Gonzalez-Torres, Luc Tuymans, and Yayoi Kusama.

7 Marlborough
MAP L3 ■ 545 West 25th St, between 10th & 11th Aves ■ Open 10am–6pm Tue–Sat

Opened in New York in 1963, Marlborough exhibits modern sculptures and paintings.

8 Hauser & Wirth
MAP L2 ■ 542 West 22nd St, between 10th & 11th Aves ■ Open 10am–6pm Tue–Sat

This major Swiss-based gallery was purpose-built by Selldorf Architects with 36,000 sq ft (3,345 sq m) of exhibition space.

9 Lehmann Maupin
MAP L2 ■ 501 West 24th St, at 10th Ave ■ Open 10am–6pm Tue–Sat

Representing early pop artists, and still on the lookout for new trends, this gallery is a powerful presence in the art world.

Visitors at Lehmann Maupin

10 Pace Gallery
MAP L2 ■ 540 West 25th St ■ Open 10am–6pm Tue–Sat

World-class gallery of established and emerging artists' work.

Restaurants

 Da Umberto
MAP M3 ■ 107 West 17th St, between 6th & 7th Aves ■ 212 989 0303 ■ $$$

Popular over the years thanks to the sophisticated Tuscan fare and the long list of daily specials on offer.

 **Cookshop**
MAP L2 ■ 156 10th Ave ■ 212 924 4440 ■ $$

Countrified restaurant with a menu rooted in local farmers' markets, from grilled squid with capers to organic buckwheat pasta with brussels sprouts and sage.

A wine bar in Mercado Little Spain

 **Mercado Little Spain**
MAP L2 ■ 10 Hudson Yards (10th Ave & 30th St) ■ 646 495 1242 ■ $$

A spanish-themed food hall at Hudson Yards, Mercado was created by celebrity chefs José Andrés and the brothers Ferran and Albert Adrià.

 Empire Diner
MAP L2 ■ 210 10th Ave, at West 22nd St ■ 212 335 2277 ■ $$

This latest incarnation of the iconic Art Deco dining car is helmed by chef John DeLucie. The menu features updated diner fare.

PRICE CATEGORIES

For a three-course meal for one with a glass of house wine, and all unavoidable charges including tax.
....
$ under $25 $$ $25–$75 $$$ over $75

 Buddakan
MAP M2 ■ 75 9th Ave, at 16th St ■ 212 989 6699 ■ $$$

The star of this trendy spot is not the good Asian fusion food, but the decor.

 La Nacional
MAP M3 ■ 239 West 14th St, between 7th & 8th Aves ■ 212 929 7873 ■ $$

This historic Spanish restaurant serves authentic tapas-based dishes at reasonable prices.

 Hill Country
MAP L3 ■ 30 West 26th St ■ 212 255 4544 ■ $$

Known on the barbecue scene for its brisket and sausages. Live music Thursday to Saturday evenings.

8 Koloman
MAP L3 ■ 16 West 29th St ■ 212 790 8970 ■ $$

This contemporary Austrian restaurant is located in the Ace Hotel. It's helmed by Chef Markus Glocker and serves inventive dishes like roasted beets "Linzer".

9 El Quijote
MAP L3 ■ 226 West 23rd St ■ 212 518 1843 ■ $$

Founded in 1930 inside the legendary Chelsea Hotel, this Spanish restaurant serves tapas and classics like Andalusian spiced rotisserie chicken. Ornate murals decorate the interior.

10 Cho Dang Gol
MAP K3 ■ 55 West 35th St, between 5th & 6th Aves ■ 212 695 8222 ■ $$

In the heart of Koreatown, this place is best known for tofu and *jjigae* (spicy Korean stews and soups).

See map on p120

🔟 Midtown

The lights of Times Square, the Rockefeller Center, the spires of the Empire State and Chrysler buildings, stores on Fifth Avenue, museums, theaters, and grand buildings galore – all are found in New York's midtown. Fifth Avenue, the dividing line between the East and West sides, is in many ways the Main Street of Manhattan, and in itself offers a generous sampling of the city's riches, from architecture to commerce. Midtown also reflects the city's characteristic diversity, with attractions that range from the bustling retail outlets of the Diamond District, to the stately halls of the New York Public Library.

Detail, 30 Rockefeller Plaza entrance

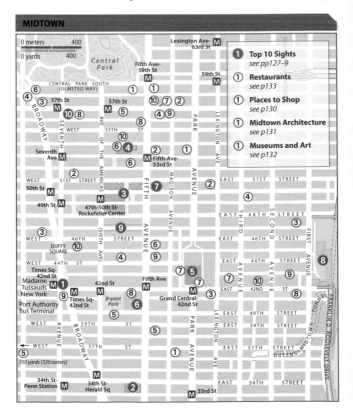

MIDTOWN

1 **Top 10 Sights** see pp127–9

1 **Restaurants** see p133

1 **Places to Shop** see p130

1 **Midtown Architecture** see p131

1 **Museums and Art** see p132

Bright lights and advertising hoardings of Times Square

1 Times Square

The city's most famous intersection, dazzling Times Square is a symbol of New York's beloved theater district (see pp28–31). It's also known for hosting a lively New Year's Eve party every year.

2 Empire State Building

New York's best-known sky-scraper (see pp12–13) is an iconic feature of the city's skyline. Since the structure was completed in 1931 more than 120 million visitors have admired the views across the city from its observatories.

3 Rockefeller Center

Rockefeller Center (see pp16–17) is the hub of midtown New York, alive with activity day and night, integrating shops, gardens, dining and office space, and its own aerial vantage point.

4 Museum of Modern Art (MoMA)

The Museum of Modern Art (see p36–9) is New York City's premier destination for art lovers. The collection features masterpieces such as Vincent Van Gogh's *Starry Night* and Frida Kahlo's *Self Portrait*. The museum also houses a popular sculpture garden, which offers an oasis of calm in the center of the city.

5 Grand Central Terminal

MAP J–K4 ■ 42nd St, between Park & Lexington Aves ■ Open 5:30am–2am daily ■ www.grandcentralterminal.com

One of the world's great rail terminals, the outstanding Beaux Arts building (see p55) is New York's most visited, with 500,000 people passing through it daily. Since restoration work was completed, its admirers are no longer limited to travelers. Grand Central has become an attraction in its own right, with many shops, restaurants and food vendors, and a branch of the New York City Transit Museum.

Grand Central Terminal clock

New York Public Library

6 New York Public Library

MAP K3 ■ 5th Ave, at 42nd St ■ 917 275 6975 ■ Open 10am–6pm Mon, Thu–Sat, 10am–8pm Tue & Wed, 1–5pm Sun ■ www.nypl.org

Carrère and Hastings won a competition for the design of this great Beaux Arts building *(see p55)*. Their genius reached its height in the Main Reading Room, a paneled space as majestic as a cathedral, extending almost two city blocks, with enormous arched windows, 18 grand chandeliers, and an elaborately decorated, vaulted ceiling.

7 St. Patrick's Cathedral

MAP J3 ■ 5th Ave, between 50th & 51st Sts ■ Open 6:30am–8:45pm daily ■ www.saintpatricks cathedral.org

America's largest Roman Catholic cathedral is a place where up to 3,000 people worship every Sunday. When Archbishop John Hughes decided to build a cathedral here in 1850, many criticized the choice of a site so far from the city's center at the time. Today the archbishop's foresight has given James Renwick's church *(see p54)* one of the best locations in Manhattan.

8 United Nations Headquarters

MAP J5 ■ 1st Ave, at 46th St ■ Open 9am–4:30pm Mon–Fri for tours ■ Adm ■ www.un.org

John D. Rockefeller, Jr. donated $8.5 million to purchase the 18-acre East River site, and American Wallace Harrison worked with international consultants to create this striking headquarters. The United Nations was formed in 1945 to work for global peace and economic and social well-being. Currently, 193 members meet in the General Assembly, the closest thing to a world parliament. Guided tours allow visitors to see the various council chambers, the General Assembly Hall, and many of the works by prominent artists, including Marc Chagall and Henry Moore.

United Nations Headquarters

9 Diamond District

MAP J3 ■ 47th St, between 5th & 6th Aves

Jewels glisten in every window of this block, the center of the city's retail and wholesale trade,

A diamond ring on display

handling 80 per cent of the diamonds coming into the US. Developed largely by Orthodox Jews, the district grew in importance during World War II when thousands fled the diamond centers of Europe to escape Nazism and settled here. Above the shops are the workshops where the stones are cut and set.

Carnegie Hall

10 Carnegie Hall

MAP H3 ■ West 57th St, at 7th Ave ■ Museum open 11am–4:30pm Mon–Sat ■ www.carnegie hall.org

New York almost lost its most famous concert hall when the New York Philharmonic moved to the newly built Lincoln Center in the 1960s. However, a coalition, led by violinist Isaac Stern, saved the building from demolition. It was bought by the city in 1960 and became a National Historic Landmark in 1964. A major 1986 renovation restored much of the original appearance while updating technical facilities in the hall (see p54). Musical memorabilia fills the halls and the Rose Museum. Tours are available for a fee.

A DAY EXPLORING MIDTOWN

[map showing Midtown locations: Salon de Ning, Bergdorf Goodman, Museum of Modern Art, Tiffany & Co., Paley Center for Media, Grand Central Terminal, Chrysler Building, Ford Foundation, Diamond District, New York Public Library, United Nations HQ, Morgan Library & Museum, Daily News Building, Tudor City]

▶ MORNING

Start at the **Morgan Library & Museum** (see p49) and see Morgan's opulent study, then proceed to 42nd Street and turn east for a tour through **Grand Central Terminal** (see p127). Continue east on 42nd Street, stopping to see the outstanding lobbies of the **Chrysler Building** (see p127), the **Daily News Building** (see p131), and the **Ford Foundation** (see p131), and climbing the stairs to see the Tudor City complex (see p131).

End the morning with a tour of the **United Nations HQ**. If you reserve ahead, you can lunch in the special U.N. delegate's dining room (212 963 7626).

AFTERNOON

Take the 42nd Street crosstown bus back to 5th Avenue and visit the **New York Public Library**. Walk uptown to 47th Street and turn west for the **Diamond District**, then pay a quick visit to the **Paley Center For Media** (see p132) on 52nd Street, between 5th and 6th Avenues. Head to the **Museum of Modern Art** (see p48) for a coffee in the museum's second-floor café, and take in some of the splendid exhibits.

Return to 5th Avenue and pass by the uptown shops – take a look at the windows of jewels at **Tiffany and Co.** (see p14) or the stylish displays at **Bergdorf Goodman** (see p14). Round the day off at **Salon de Ning** (see p69) in the Peninsula Hotel, with stunning views over Fifth Avenue.

See map on p126 ←

Places to Shop

 Apple Fifth Avenue
MAP H3 ▪ 767 5th Ave, at 59th St
This 32-ft- (9.75-m-) tall glass cube is worth a visit. The below-ground sales floor is open 24 hours.

2 Microsoft Experience Center
MAP H3 ▪ 677 5th Ave, at 53rd St
Flagship store of the iconic software company, now showcasing its own laptops and tablets.

3 Nordstrom
MAP H3 ▪ 225 West 57th St & Broadway
One of the most attractive stores in the city, Nordstrom *(see p70)* features designer fashions and a notable selection of cosmetics.

4 Tiffany & Co.
MAP H4 ▪ 727 5th Ave
Immortalized in Truman Capote's 1958 novel *Breakfast at Tiffany's*, this jewelry store is a must-see for fans of the book and film alike. The huge building on Fifth Avenue is the flagship.

5 Department Stores
MAP K3–H3 ▪ 5th Ave, between 38th & 58th Sts
Bountiful stocks of beautiful clothing, accessories, and jewelry can be found at famous department stores such as Bergdorf Goodman, Saks Fifth Avenue, and Bloomingdale's.

6 Museum of Modern Art Design Shop
MAP J3 ▪ 44 West 53rd St, between 5th Ave & 6th Aves
Lamps, furniture, toys, jewelry, posters, books – whatever the item, you can be sure it will be the epitome of good design.

7 Designer Boutiques
MAP H4 ▪ 57th St, between 5th & Madison Aves
57th Street is lined with impressive designer boutiques, including Burberry, Saint Laurent, Chanel, and Dior. Prada is at No. 724 5th Avenue.

8 Harry Winston
MAP H4 ▪ 701 5th Ave
You will likely only be window shopping here; the diamonds and gems, many of which Harry Winston supplies to the rich and famous, are very expensive.

9 NBA Store
MAP J3 ▪ 545 5th Ave, at 45th St
A high-tech shopping destination, this store sells sportswear and merchandise for the National Basketball Association (NBA).

10 Louis Vuitton
MAP H4 ▪ 1 East 57th St
Perhaps the flashiest of the high-end stores from the outside, Louis Vuitton's windows are imprinted with the same iconic pattern as is on the handbags.

Saks Fifth Avenue

Midtown Architecture

 Lever House
MAP J4 ■ 390
Park Ave ■ Lobby
and plaza open
during office hours
This 24-story
glass-and-steel
building *(see p53)*
built by Gordon
Bunshaft was
New York's first
"glass box".

Lever House

 General Electric Building
MAP H4 ■ 570 Lexington Ave
■ Closed to public
This 1931 Art Deco building has
a clock crowned by disembodied
arms grasping at lightning bolts.

③ **Chanin Building**
MAP K4 ■ 122 East 42nd St
■ Lobby open during office hours
One of the great early Art Deco
skyscrapers (c.1929) notable for its
terra cotta frieze and bronze band
illustrating the theory of evolution.

④ **NY Yacht Club**
MAP J3 ■ 37 West 44th St
■ Closed to public
The window bays of this 1899 private
club are the carved sterns of ships,
sailing on a sea of sculpted waves.

⑤ **American Standard Building**
MAP K3 ■ 40 West 40th St ■ Lobby
open during office hours
Raymond Hood's first New York
skyscraper is an ornate black tower
built in 1924. It is now a hotel.

⑥ **Fred F. French Building**
MAP J3 ■ 551 5th Ave ■ Lobby
open during office hours
Built in 1927 for the best-known real
estate firm of its day, this opulent
building has a stunning lobby.

⑦ **Chrysler Building**
MAP J3 ■ 405 Lexington Ave,
at 42nd St ■ Lobby open 8am–6pm
Mon–Fri
The shimmering spire of this skyscraper is one of New York's great
landmarks *(see p52)*. The grand Art
Deco lobby was once used as a
showroom for Chrysler cars.

⑧ **Tudor City**
MAP J4–K4 ■ 1st to 2nd Aves,
40th to 43rd Sts ■ Lobby open during
office hours
Fred F. French created this mock-
Tudor enclave in the 1920s, designed
to prove that middle-class housing
could succeed in Midtown.

⑨ **Ford Foundation**
MAP J4 ■ 320 East 43rd St,
at 1st Ave ■ Lobby open 8am–6pm
Mon–Fri
Headquarters of Ford's philanthropic
arm, this is considered one of the
city's best modern designs (1967).
Every office opens onto a sky-lit, 12-
story atrium with lush landscaping.

⑩ **Daily News Building**
MAP K4 ■ 220 East 42nd St,
at 2nd Ave ■ Lobby open during
office hours
The *Daily News* has moved on, but
this fine 1930 building is still an Art
Deco classic. Step inside and marvel
at the revolving globe.

The globe in the Daily News Building

See map on p126 ←

Museums and Art

Morgan Library

1 Morgan Library and Museum

MAP K4 ■ 225 Madison Ave, at 36th St ■ Open 10:30am–5pm Tue–Sun (to 7pm Fri) ■ Adm (free entry Fri 5–7pm, reservations required) ■ www.themorgan.org

The library holds a private collection of rare books, prints, and manuscripts (see p49). The steel-and-glass pavilion houses an impressive performance hall.

2 Adelson Galleries

MAP H4 ■ The Fuller Building, 595 Madison Avenue ■ Open 11am–6pm Mon–Fri ■ www.adelson galleries.com

Renowned art gallery focused on American Impressionism, Realism, and Modernism.

3 Japan Society

MAP J5 ■ 333 East 47th St ■ Open noon–7pm Wed–Sun (to 9pm Fri) ■ Adm (free entry 6–9pm Fri) ■ www.japansociety.org

Explore Japanese culture, from contemporary art to Kabuki dance, at this esteemed cultural institution.

4 Museum of Arts and Design

MAP H3 ■ 2 Columbus Circle ■ Open 10am–6pm Tue–Sun (to 9pm Thu) ■ Adm ■ www.madmuseum.org

The permanent collection includes 2,000 craft exhibits.

5 Marian Goodman Gallery

MAP H3 ■ 24 West 57th St ■ Open 10am–6pm Mon–Sat ■ www.marian goodman.com

Works by Giovanni Anselmo, Thomas Struth, Steve McQueen and others are exhibited in this art space.

6 Paley Center for Media

MAP J3 ■ 25 West 52nd St, between 5th & 6th Aves ■ Open noon–6pm Wed–Sun ■ Adm ■ www.paley center.org

Watch your favorites from over 60,000 radio and TV programs.

7 Transit Museum Gallery Annex

MAP K3 ■ Shuttle Passage, Grand Central Terminal ■ Open 11:30am–6pm Tue–Sat ■ www. nytransitmuseum.org

Displays images and objects from the Brooklyn museum (see p59).

8 New York Public Library Galleries

MAP K3 ■ 5th Ave, at 42nd St ■ Open 10am–5pm Mon, Thu–Sat, 10am–6pm Tue & Wed, 1–5pm Sun

Rare prints, vintage posters, paintings, and changing exhibitions.

9 Sculpture Garden at 590 Madison

MAP J3 ■ 590 Madison Ave, at 57th St

The zen-like atrium of the IBM building houses a rotating cast of sculptures within its glass walls.

10 Museum of Broadway

MAP J3 ■ 145 West 45th St ■ Open 10am–10pm daily ■ Adm ■ www.themuseumofbroadway.com

This museum tells the story of Broadway's theater district through art, videos, and immersive technology.

Restaurants

PRICE CATEGORIES
For a three-course meal for one with a glass of house wine, and all unavoidable charges including tax.
....
$ under $25 $$ $25–$75 $$$ over $75

(1) The Palm Court
MAP H3 ▪ The Plaza, 768 5th Ave, at Central Park South ▪ 212 546 5300 ▪ $$$

Set under an elegant stained-glass dome with tall palm trees and custom furnishings, this iconic spot is renowned for its afternoon tea.

(2) Le Bernardin
MAP J3 ▪ 155 West 51st St, at 6th Ave ▪ 212 554 1515 ▪ $$$

The acclaimed French chef Eric Ripert does wonders here with every kind of fish and seafood. The dining experience at this restaurant *(see p66)* is nothing short of perfection.

(3) Blue Fin
MAP J3 ▪ 1567 Broadway, at 47th St ▪ 212 918 1400 ▪ $$

One of the trendiest places in the area, this restaurant is dedicated to serving the highest quality seafood dishes, including sushi and raw bar selections.

(4) Smith & Wollensky
MAP J4 ▪ 797 3rd Ave, at East 49th St ▪ 212 753 0444 ▪ $$$

Fill up on a *Flintstones*-esque sirloin steak and irresistible fries amid classic surroundings of wooden floors and black-and-white photographs of New York.

(5) Chef's Table at Brooklyn Fare
MAP K2 ▪ 431 West 37th St, between Ninth & Tenth Aves ▪ 212 216 9700 ▪ $$$

This lauded restaurant from chef César Ramirez offers incredible tasting menus that feature a blend of Japanese flavors and French techniques.

(6) Marea
MAP H3 ▪ 240 Central Park South ▪ 212 582 5100 ▪ $$$

Dine on razor clams and sea bass or enjoy a variety of oysters and antipasti. The weekend brunch is great.

(7) Grand Central Oyster Bar and Restaurant
MAP K4 ▪ Grand Central Terminal, lower level, 42nd St, at Lexington Ave ▪ 212 490 6650 ▪ $$$

A New York classic, this bustling and ever-popular restaurant serves only the freshest seafood.

Lavish interiors of Russian Tea Room

(8) Russian Tea Room
MAP H3 ▪ 150 West 57th St, at 7th Ave ▪ 212 581 7100 ▪ $$$

Although not as famous as its original counterpart, this opulent Russian restaurant knocks out a delicious stroganoff and a stunning chicken kiev.

(9) The Counter
MAP K3 ▪ 7 Times Square at 41st St & Broadway ▪ 212 997 6801 ▪ $

An innovative chain, The Counter serves custom-made burgers that are a notch above other fast food outlets.

(10) La Bonne Soupe
MAP H3 ▪ 48 West 55th St, between 5th & 6th Aves ▪ 212 586 7650 ▪ $$

This theater district favorite has a distinct French bistro charm and is a great spot for a meal after a show. Try the famous French onion soup.

See map on p126

TOP 10 Upper East Side

New York's upper crust moved to the Upper East Side over a century ago. Most of their Beaux Arts mansions around Fifth Avenue are now occupied by embassies or museums; today's elite live in apartment buildings on 5th and Park Avenues, convenient for Madison's exclusive boutiques. Only churches and a few restaurants remain of German Yorkville or the Hungarian and Czech neighborhoods that used to fill the blocks east of Lexington. Young families now occupy the newer buildings in this area. For visitors, the Upper East Side is home to many of the city's best museums.

Buddha statue at the Met

1 Central Park

Designed in the 19th century, the 843-acre (341-ha) swathe of green *(see pp32–3)* in the city center provides recreation and beauty for more than 40 million annual visitors, from rowboat and bicycle rental to flowers and sculptures.

2 Metropolitan Museum of Art

More a collection of museums than a single one, the Met *(see pp34–7)* displays over two million pieces spanning more than 5,000 years of global culture, from Ancient Egypt to 20th-century Afghanistan.

The Reservoir at Central Park during autumn

Previous pages Aerial view of the Manhattan skyscrapers at night

Guggenheim Museum's spiral design

③ Solomon R. Guggenheim Museum

MAP E4 ■ 1071 5th Ave, at 89th St
■ Opening hours vary, check website
■ www.guggenheim.org

A notable collection of modern art is located in Frank Lloyd Wright's iconic building, which is the only edifice in New York he designed. The main gallery is used for temporary exhibits.

④ Museum Mile

MAP D4–F4 ■ 5th Ave from 82nd to 104th Sts ■ Opening times vary

Eight museums are situated within one mile. They unite for a free open-house day one Tuesday in June. Participants include the Metropolitan Museum of Art (see pp34–7), Africa Center, Cooper-Hewitt, Smithsonian Design Museum, Solomon R. Guggenheim Museum (see pp38–9), Jewish Museum, Neue Galerie, Museum of the City of New York (see p49), and El Museo del Barrio. There is street entertainment and music, and 5th Avenue closes to traffic.

UPPER EAST SIDE

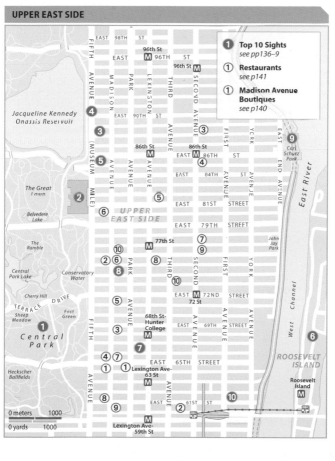

Top 10 Sights
see pp136–9

① Restaurants
see p141

① Madison Avenue Boutiques
see p140

⑤ Neue Galerie

MAP E4 ▪ 1048 5th Ave, at East 86th St ▪ Open 11am–6pm Thu–Mon ▪ Adm ▪ www.neuegalerie.org

Dedicated to early 20th-century art from Austria and Germany, this enchanting museum is housed in an ornate 1914 mansion. Once the residence of New York socialite Grace Vanderbilt and her millionaire husband Cornelius Vanderbilt III, the building was converted into a museum, largely due to the efforts of art collectors Serge Sabarsky and Ronald S. Lauder. The star attraction of the gallery is Gustav Klimt's *Portrait of Adele Bloch-Bauer I* (1907).

⑥ Roosevelt Island

MAP H5 ▪ Trams every 15 mins from Tram Plaza, 2nd Ave, at 59th St

Take the short, scenic aerial tram ride to this East River area. Once known as "Welfare Island," when it was home to a prison, poorhouse, and hospital, the 147-acre (60-ha) island was renamed and redeveloped in the 1970s according to a master plan drawn up by Philip Johnson and John Burgee, intended to create a quiet, almost traffic-free residential community. The plan was not fully developed, although more than 3,000 apartments were built, and while there is a subway stop from Manhattan, the only access by car is via a bridge in Queens.

Aerial tram to Roosevelt Island

ST. NICHOLAS RUSSIAN ORTHODOX CATHEDRAL

An unexpected slice of Russia at 15 East 97th Street, this building (below) was constructed in 1902 in Muscovite Baroque style with a facade of red brick, white stone, and blue and yellow tiles. The incense-filled interior has marble columns and an altar enclosed by wooden screens trimmed with gold. Mass is still said in Russian.

⑦ Park Avenue Armory

MAP G4 ▪ 643 Park Ave, at 66th St ▪ 212 616 3930 ▪ Open during public programming only ▪ Tour days vary, check website ▪ armoryonpark.org

The socially prominent members of the Seventh Regiment, formed in 1806, constructed an armory in 1877–89, with a drill room 200 by 300 feet (60 by 90 m) and 100 feet (30 m) high, and an administration building in the form of a medieval fortress. The rooms within the fortress are filled with lavish Victorian furnishings. The drill room is used for the prestigious Winter Antiques Show every January. Following a $150-million renovation project, the space now allows for the development of unconventional performing and visual art.

⑧ Frick Madison

MAP G4 ▪ 945 Madison Ave, at East 75th St ▪ Open 10am–6pm Thu–Sun ▪ Adm ▪ www.frick.org

The remarkable art collection *(see p49)* of steel magnate Henry Clay Frick will be exhibited in the Breuer Building until at least the end of 2023 (when it should move back to 1 East 70th St). Most of the collection has been displayed over three floors. The second floor contains Dutch and Flemish paintings – these include

Vermeer's *Officer and Laughing Girl* in Room 6, and Rembrandt's *Self-Portrait* in Room 4. In Room 2 are two famous works by Hans Holbein the Younger. The third floor contains El Greco's *St. Jerome* and Giovanni Bellini's masterpiece *St. Francis in the Desert*, while the fourth floor features Impressionist masterpieces and British portraiture.

9 Gracie Mansion and Carl Schurz Park

MAP E5 ■ East End Ave, at 88th St ■ 212 639 9675 ■ Free tours 10:30am & noon Mon ■ www.graciemansion.org

The wooden country home built by merchant Archibald Gracie in 1799 was the original home of the Museum of the City of New York and became the official mayoral residence under Fiorello LaGuardia in 1942. It is located at the northern end of a park laid out in 1891, with a wide promenade that stretches along the East River. The park was named for Carl Schurz, a statesman and newspaper editor who lived nearby.

Gracie Mansion

10 Mount Vernon Hotel Museum and Gardens

MAP H5 ■ 421 East 61st St, between 1st & York Aves ■ Opening hours vary, check website ■ Adm ■ www.mvhm.org

This was the stone carriage house of a 1799 estate. When it burned in 1826, the carriage house was converted into an inn and became a fashionable resort for New Yorkers in what was then still countryside. The building and garden were restored by the Colonial Dames of America in 1939.

A DAY EXPLORING UPPER EAST SIDE

▶ MORNING

Start at the **Solomon R. Guggenheim Museum** (see p137) and admire Frank Lloyd Wright's great architectural achievement before seeing the modern art collection. "Must sees" include Chagall's *Paris Through the Window*, Modigliani's *Nude*, and Picasso's *Woman Ironing*. Stop for coffee at the café.

Head east along 92nd Street to see two rare remaining wooden houses, **No. 120**, built in 1859, and **No. 122**, in 1871. Continue east for **Gracie Mansion** and **Henderson Place** (East End Ave, between 86th & 87th Sts) and rest on a bench with a river view in **Carl Schurz Park**. Take a taxi or subway and recharge at **Serendipity 3** (see p141), famous for its small plates and desserts.

AFTERNOON

Walk over to Madison Avenue and head uptown, browsing the designer boutiques. Detour down the side streets in the upper 60s and 70s to see the townhouses of affluent New Yorkers. Pay a visit to the **Frick Madison**, then stop for coffee at one of the cafés on Madison Avenue. Alternatively, get another dose of fine art at **Neue Galerie**, further along 5th Avenue.

Spend the rest of the afternoon at the **Metropolitan Museum of Art** (see p136) and admire Rembrandt's *Self-Portrait*, *Cypresses* by Van Gogh, and Michelangelo's Sistine Chapel studies. End the day with a meal at **Sistina** (see p141).

See map on p137 ←

Madison Avenue Boutiques

1 Bottega Veneta

MAP G4 ■ 740 Madison Ave, between 64th & 65th Sts

The first in the Madison Avenue boutique line-up, known for luxury leather goods, shoes, and fashion.

2 Carolina Herrera
MAP G4 ■ 954 Madison Ave, at East 75th St

Beautifully crafted ready-to-wear clothing, fragrances, and accessories from the famous Venezuelan-American fashion designer.

3 Valentino
MAP G4 ■ 821 Madison Ave, at 69th St

If you can afford it, join the rich and famous; many of Valentino's gowns are worn at the Oscars.

4 Giorgio Armani
MAP G4 ■ 761 Madison Ave, at 65th St

The New York flagship of the Italian master, known for his superb tailoring, offers a good range from his collection.

5 Ralph Lauren

MAP G4 ■ 867 Madison Ave, at 72nd St

The 1898 Rhinelander Mansion is the backdrop for the king of preppy fashion. Ralph Lauren sportswear is in a separate shop across the street.

Facade of the Ralph Lauren store

Christian Louboutin boutique

6 Christian Louboutin
MAP F4 ■ 965–967 Madison Ave, between East 75th and 76th Sts

You can spot celebrities at this chic outpost selling the world-famous red-lacquered shoes.

7 Michael Kors
MAP F4 ■ 790 Madison Ave, at East 67th St

Drop in for handbags, stylish watches, and ready-to-wear fashion apparel from the ever-popular American menswear designer Michael Kors.

8 Jimmy Choo
MAP H4 ■ 699 Madison Ave, between East 62nd & East 63rd Sts

Head here for stylish mens and womens shoes from this British-based designer (whose brand is now owned by Michael Kors). Top-of-the-range purses, bags, and sunglasses are also available.

9 Schutz
MAP H4 ■ 655 Madison Ave, at 60th St

US flagship store for the high-end Brazilian brand, known for its colorful women's footwear and accessories, from high heels to wedge sneakers.

10 Vera Wang
MAP F4 ■ 991 Madison Ave, at 77th St

The flagship store of the esteemed designer of wedding gowns also features ready-to-wear fashion and accessories.

Restaurants

1 Daniel
MAP G4 ■ **60 East 65th St, at Park Ave** ■ **212 288 0033** ■ **$$$**

A flower-filled dining room at this restaurant *(see p66)* provides the setting for Daniel Boulud's award-winning seasonal French menus.

2 Serendipity 3
MAP H4 ■ **225 East 60th St** ■ **212 838 3531** ■ **$$**

Famous for its sinful concoctions, including massive sundaes, this dessert emporium is an old favorite with celebratory couples and families.

3 Café d'Alsace
MAP F4 ■ 1703 2nd Ave, at 88th St ■ 212 722 5133 ■ $$

Dessert at Serendipity 3

A charming bistro that blends French regional and contemporary New York cuisines. The highlights include a great lunchtime prix-fixe menu and a huge beer selection.

4 Heidelberg Restaurant
MAP F4 ■ **1648 2nd Ave, between East 85th & East 86th Sts** ■ **212 628 2332** ■ **$$**

This 1930s remnant of German Yorkville is great fun, with a kitsch interior, German beer, and authentic food – from liver-dumpling soup to *schweinshaxe* (pork shank).

5 Toloache
MAP F4 ■ **166 East 82nd St** ■ **212 861 4505** ■ **$$**

This lively restaurant serves terrific Mexican cuisine, from creamy guacamole and tangy ceviches to tacos that are spilling over with fresh shrimp or grilled chicken, and topped with salsa.

6 Sistina
MAP F3 ■ **24 East 81st St, between Madison and 5th Aves** ■ **212 861 7660** ■ **$$**

They don't come more romantic than this elegant Italian restaurant, with a cozy winter garden room and a menu of well-prepared classics (try the especially good crab or lobster pasta).

7 Uva
MAP F4 ■ **1486 2nd Ave, between 77th & 78th Sts** ■ **212 472 4552** ■ **$$**

An intimate, cozy wine bar serving genuine Italian cuisine at reasonable prices, Uva is the go-to spot for the city's wine connoisseurs.

8 Orsay
MAP G4 ■ **1057 Lexington Ave, at 75th St** ■ **212 517 6400** ■ **$$**

This chic French brasserie is busy and cozy, serving modern and authentic brasserie fare. There is a definite Gallic vibe to the place, with mahogany-paneled walls and Art Nouveau chandeliers.

9 The Meatball Shop
MAP F4 ■ **1462 2nd Ave, at 76th St** ■ **212 257 6121** ■ **$$**

Calling all meatball lovers: this friendly spot serves juicy meatballs every which way, including smothered in tomato sauce, Parmesan cream, mushroom gravy, or pesto.

10 E. J.'s Luncheonette
MAP G4 ■ **1271 3rd Ave, at 73rd St** ■ **212 472 0600** ■ **No credit cards** ■ **$$**

A family-friendly diner that serves large portions of well-prepared American breakfasts. Great pancakes are served all day, along with granola and fresh fruit.

See map on p137

Top 10 Upper West Side

Soldiers' and Sailors' Monument

This area did not begin to develop until the 1870s, when the 9th Avenue El went up, making it possible to commute to Midtown. When the Dakota, New York's first luxury apartment building, was completed in 1884, it was followed by others on Central Park West and Broadway, while side streets were filled with handsome brownstones. The West Side remains a desirable neighborhood with much of the city's best residential architecture. The creation of the Lincoln Center in the 1960s was a great boost to the area, and the fantastic American Museum of Natural History is also a draw.

1 American Museum of Natural History

The mammoth museum's holdings include more than 32 million artifacts and specimens *(see pp40–43)*.

2 Lincoln Center for the Performing Arts

MAP G2 ▪ Columbus to Amsterdam Aves, between 62nd & 66th Sts ▪ **Tours twice daily** ▪ **Adm**

Built on 15 acres (6 ha) during the 1960s, transforming slums into a giant cultural complex, the Lincoln Center houses an array of venues *(see pp62–3)* and organizations: the Metropolitan Opera, the New York City Ballet, the New York Philharmonic, the Vivian Beaumont and Walter Reade theaters, David Geffen and Alice Tully halls, and the Julliard

School. In the summer, Mostly Mozart concerts take place, and free concerts are held in the adja-cent park. The Jazz at Lincoln Center headquarters is located in the Deutsche Bank Center at Columbus Circle.

3 New York Historical Society

MAP G2 ▪ 170 Central Park West at West 77th St ▪ **Open 11am–5pm Tue–Sun (to 8pm Fri)** ▪ **Adm** ▪ **www.nyhistory.org**

New York's oldest museum, founded in 1804, reopened in 2011 after an extensive renovation that saw $70 million invested over three years. The museum features more than 40,000 objects divided into such areas as paintings, sculpture, furniture, silver, tools, and, notably, Tiffany lamps. Other galleries within the museum are used to display changing exhibits. The New York Historical Society also maintains a children's gallery, as well as a research library.

4 Columbus Circle

MAP H2 ▪ Columbus Circle

One of the largest building projects in New York's history, Columbus Circle transformed this once neglected urban plaza into an important public site. The redevelopment has attracted

Lincoln Center for the Performing Arts

national and international business, such as German financial giant Deutsche Bank, which has its New York headquarters in an 80-story skyscraper. The Deutsche Bank Center contains shops, entertainment, restaurants, and the Mandarin Oriental hotel. It is also home to Jazz at Lincoln Center, the world's first performing arts facility dedicated to jazz. Other structures around Columbus Circle include the Museum of Arts and Design and the USS Maine Monument.

Skyscrapers behind Columbus Circle

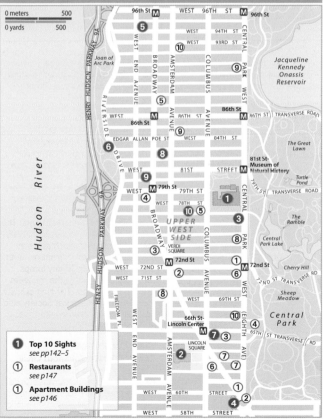

UPPER WEST SIDE

- **1** Top 10 Sights
  see pp142–5
- **1** Restaurants
  see p147
- **1** Apartment Buildings
  see p146

Pomander Walk

5 Pomander Walk

MAP E2 ■ 261–7 West 94th St, between Broadway & West End Ave

This double row of small brick and stucco, timbered, Tudoresque townhouses, hidden on a private street, is one of the many delightful surprises to be discovered in Manhattan. The developer, a restaurateur named Thomas Healy, took his inspiration in 1921 from the sets used for a popular play by Louis Parker called *Pomander Walk*, hoping to recreate the village atmosphere depicted in the romantic comedy. Gloria Swanson, Rosalind Russell, and Humphrey Bogart are among the actors who have lived here.

6 Riverside Drive and Park

MAP C1–E1 ■ Park open 6am–1am daily

Riverside Drive is one of New York City's most attractive streets, with lovely shaded views of the Hudson River. It is lined with opulent late 19th-century townhouses, in addition to some modern apartment buildings. Riverside Park, a woodsy band of green desgined by Frederick Law Olmsted, follows Riverside Drive for 70 blocks and boasts playgrounds, sports fields, a promenade, and a few monuments. It is one of only eight official "scenic landmarks" in the city.

7 American Folk Art Museum

MAP G2 ■ 2 Lincoln Square (Columbus Ave, at West 66th St) ■ Open 11:30am–6pm Tue–Sun ■ www.folkartmuseum.org

The home for the appreciation and study of American folk art is conveniently located opposite the Lincoln Center complex. Founded in 1961, the museum *(see p49)* holds over 8,000 artworks dating from the 18th cen-tury to the present day. With colorful quilts, impressive portraits, and major works by self-taught, contemporary artists, the selection is remarkable. Especially worth seeking out are Henry Darger's watercolors, and the incredible urban commen-taries of Ralph Fasinella.

8 Children's Museum of Manhattan

MAP F2 ■ 212 West 83rd St, at Broadway ■ Open 10am–5pm Tue–Sun ■ Adm ■ www.cmom.org

Founded in 1973, in a former school building, this museum is dedicated to the principle that children learn best through self-discovery *(see p58)*. It uses a variety of participatory activities and fantasy world environ-ments to engage its young visitors in learning that is fun. The museum's range of activities include exhibits to intrigue older children, while the popular Adventures with Dora and Diego provides a distraction for two- to six-year-olds at the same time as educating them about animals and their natural habitats.

Riverside Park

UPPER WEST SIDE ARCHITECTURE

The Upper West Side's side streets are lined with fine rows of the typical brownstones favored by New York's 19th-century middle classes. Built of inexpensive, local, brown sandstone, the narrow buildings are usually three or four stories high, and have a flight of steps called a "stoop" that leads from street level to the living floors.

9 Zabar's

MAP F2 ■ 2245 Broadway, at 80th St ■ Open 8am–7:30pm Mon–Sat, 9am–6pm Sun ■ www. zabars.com

A monument to New York's obsession with finding the best foods and a landmark since 1934, this always-crowded store sells smoked salmon, sturgeon, and other Jewish delicacies, along with a big selections of oils, vinegars, olives, and gourmet gift baskets. The second floor is filled with cooking equipment, and the adjacent coffee counter at the 80th Street corner offers delicious baked goods, sandwiches, and coffees.

Deli counter at Zabar's Café

10 Grand Bazaar NYC

MAP F2 ■ 100 West 77th St, at Columbus Ave ■ Open 10am–5pm Sun ■ www.grandbazaarnyc.org

Flea market junkies throng this school yard every Sunday, hoping for finds among the piles of vintage clothing, books, jewelry, prints, and memorabilia. On a good day as many as 300 booths occupy the premises. A weekly green market shares the same space and is worth checking out.

WALK ON THE WEST SIDE

▶ MORNING

Begin at **Lincoln Center** *(see p142)* and admire the plaza, the Chagall windows at the Metropolitan Opera, and the Henry Moore statue in front of Vivian Beaumont Theater. The New York Public Library for the Performing Arts on Amsterdam Avenue, behind the theater, is notable for its enormous collection of books about the performing arts.

Make your way up Broadway, window shopping and noting some of the landmark buildings such as the **Ansonia Hotel** *(see p146)* and the **Apthorp Apartments** *(see p146)*. Almost any side street will reveal examples of the area's great line-up of brownstone townhouses. West Side is famous for its gastronomic palaces, such as Fairway at 74th Street and **Zabar's**. For lunch, head to Zabar's Café to grab a delicious smoothie and a grilled panini.

AFTERNOON

A visit to the **American Museum of Natural History** *(see pp40–43)* can easily fill an entire afternoon, and the **New York Historical Society** *(see p142)* has an amazing collection on show.

Stroll down Central Park West and admire the landmark apartment buildings *(see p146)* that can be seen here, then head to **Central Park** *(see pp32–3)*, the city's vast "backyard". Take a boat out on the lake, or enjoy a gondola ride around it, followed by drinks at the **Tavern on the Green** *(see p147)*, ⬤ the perfect end to an afternoon.

See map on p143 ←

Apartment Buildings

The Dakota, John Lennon's last home

1 The Dakota
MAP G2 ■ 1 West 72nd St, at Central Park West ■ Closed to public

Infamous as the site of John Lennon's murder, the building is thought to be named The Dakota because it was located so far west in 1884.

2 Dorilton
MAP G2 ■ 171 West 71st St, at Broadway ■ Closed to public

A flamboyant example of the Beaux Arts era, this 1902 apartment house has an iron gate fit for a palace.

3 Ansonia
MAP G2 ■ 2109 Broadway, between 73rd & 74th Sts ■ Closed to public

This 20th-century apartment-hotel has soundproof partitions, a feature that has attracted many distinguished musicians.

4 Apthorp
MAP F2 ■ 2211 Broadway, between 78th & 79th Sts ■ Closed to public

Modeled after an Italian Renaissance palazzo, this 1908 full-block building includes a huge interior courtyard.

5 Belnord
MAP F2 ■ 225 West 86th St, at Amsterdam Ave ■ Closed to public

Even larger than the Apthorp, and also with its own large interior courtyard, this 1908 Renaissance Revival structure is where Nobel Prize-winning author Isaac Bashevis Singer lived and wrote.

6 Majestic
MAP G2 ■ 115 Central Park West, between 71st & 72nd Sts ■ Closed to public

The first of architect Irwin Chanin's two 1931 landmarks, and one of the original four twin towers that dominate the West Side skyline.

7 Century
MAP H2 ■ 25 Central Park West, between 62nd & 63rd Sts ■ Closed to public

Irwin Chanin's second twin tower, consisting of 30 stories, is the tallest on the block, and an Art Deco icon.

8 San Remo
MAP G2 ■ 145–6 Central Park West, between 74th & 75th Sts ■ Closed to public

Architect Emery Roth's 1930 Art Deco masterpiece is an extremely sophisticated adaptation of Renaissance forms. The twin towers hide water tanks.

San Remo's twin towers

9 Eldorado
MAP E2 ■ 300 Central Park West, between 90th & 91st Sts ■ Closed to public

Another Art Deco design by Emery Roth. Past celebrity tenants have included Groucho Marx and Marilyn Monroe.

10 Hotel des Artistes
MAP G2 ■ 1 West 67th St, between Central Park West & Columbus Ave ■ Closed to public

Built in 1918 as artists' studios and apartments, with double-height windows, the spaces are much coveted. Residents have included Noël Coward and Isadora Duncan.

Restaurants

PRICE CATEGORIES

For a three-course meal for one with a glass of house wine, and all unavoidable charges including tax.

$ under $25 $$ $25–$75 $$$ over $75

① Jean-Georges

MAP H2 ■ 1 Central Park West, Trump International Hotel ■ 212 299 3900 ■ $$$

Jean-Georges Vongerichten's namesake restaurant *(see p66)* is among the finest in New York.

② Per Se

MAP H2 ■ Deutsche Bank Center, 10 Columbus Circle ■ 212 823 9335 ■ $$$

Book well in advance for this critically acclaimed restaurant *(see p67)* owned by well-known restaurateur Thomas Keller.

Octopus à la Plancha at Boulud Sud

③ Shun Lee West

MAP G2 ■ 43 West 65th St ■ 212 769 3888 ■ $$

This clean-lined, black-and-white dim sum cafe is arguably the best one to be found north of Chinatown.

④ Tavern on the Green

MAP G2 ■ 67th Street & Central Park West ■ 212 877 8684 ■ $$$

Open since 1934 (the building dates from the 1880s and used to house sheep), this iconic Central Park restaurant serves seasonal dishes in wood panelled dining rooms. The lovely outdoor area is especially charming on a summer night.

Tavern on the Green's outdoor area

⑤ Covacha

MAP F2 ■ 368 Columbus Ave, between West 77th & West 78th Sts ■ 212 712 2929 ■ $$

Savor Mexican favorites at this lively spot, and wash them down with tangy margaritas.

⑥ Rosa Mexicano

MAP H2 ■ 61 Columbus Ave, at 62nd St ■ 212 977 7700 ■ $$

This is a branch of one of the city's most popular Mexican restaurants, famous for its excellent guacamole that is made to order and its power-packed margaritas.

⑦ Boulud Sud

MAP F4 ■ 20 West 64th St ■ 212 595 1313 ■ $$$

Daniel Boulud celebrates flavors of the Mediterranean at this elegant restaurant, with dishes like grilled octopus with Marcona almonds.

⑧ Café Luxembourg

MAP G2 ■ 200 West 70th St, at Amsterdam Ave ■ 212 873 7411 ■ $$$

A classic Parisian bistro with a zinc-topped bar and a hip clientele. The steak-frites can't be beaten.

⑨ Jacob's Pickles

MAP F2 ■ 509 Amsterdam Ave, between West 84th & 85th Sts ■ 212 470 5566 ■ $$

Enjoy classic Southern fare such as pancakes and fried chicken, plus tangy pickles, at this great Upper West Side restaurant.

⑩ Gennaro

MAP E2 ■ 665 Amsterdam Ave, between 92nd & 93rd Sts ■ 212 665 5348 ■ No credit cards ■ $$

This popular restaurant serves authentic Italian food. Try the pastas or the braised lamb shank. Arrive early to avoid waiting in line.

See map on p143

TOP 10 Morningside Heights and Harlem

The area between Morningside Park and the Hudson River is dominated by Columbia University and two important churches. Extending north is Harlem, America's best-known African American community. Irish, Italian, and Jewish families occupied large townhouses here in the 1880s, but by the 1920s Black families predominated. The Harlem Renaissance, when Black artistic and intellectual culture flourished, ended with the Depression. Nevertheless, development is reviving the area, causing some to declare a second Renaissance.

Statue of St. John the Divine

1 Columbia University

MAP C3 ■ West 116th St, at Broadway ■ www.columbia.edu

One of America's oldest universities, noted for its law, medicine, and journalism schools, Columbia was founded in 1754 as King's College. It moved in 1897 to its present campus, designed by American Beaux Arts architect Charles McKim. Notable buildings include McKim's 1898 Low Memorial Library and St. Paul's Chapel, which has three stained-glass windows by La Farge.

2 Cathedral Church of St. John the Divine

MAP C3 ■ 1047 Amsterdam Ave, at 112th St ■ Open 9:30am–5pm Mon–Sat, noon–5pm Sun ■ Adm ■ www.stjohndivine.org

The mother church of the Episcopal Diocese of New York, begun in 1892 and still incomplete, is one of the world's largest cathedrals. Over 600 ft (180 m) long and 320 ft (96 m) wide, the church is a mix of Romanesque and Gothic styles (see p54). Features include the west entrance, the rose window, and the Peace Fountain on the south lawn. The medieval stone carving techniques used on the building are now taught in workshops.

St. Paul's Chapel, Columbia University

3 **Riverside Church**
MAP C1 ■ 490 Riverside Drive, between 120th and 122nd Sts
■ Open 9am–5pm Thu–Sun (tower tours 11am & 2pm, plus 2:30pm Sun)
■ www.trcnyc.org

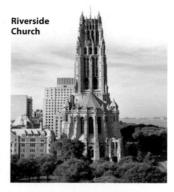

Riverside Church

This Gothic church, financed by John D. Rockefeller Jr. in 1930, has a 21-story tower with wonderful views. The tower houses the world's largest carillon, dedicated to Rockefeller's mother. The stained-glass windows are copies of those at Chartres cathedral with four exceptions: the Flemish windows on the east wall.

MORNINGSIDE HEIGHTS AND HARLEM

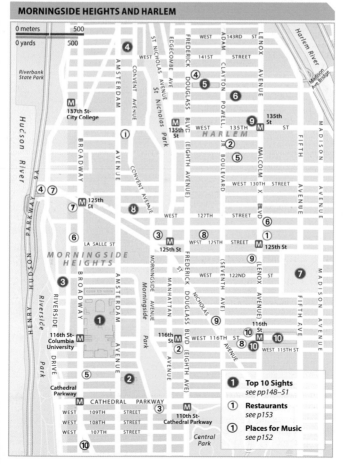

1 Top 10 Sights
see pp148–51

1 Restaurants
see p153

1 Places for Music
see p152

Hamilton Heights Historic District

④ Hamilton Heights Historic District

MAP A2 ■ West 141 St to West 145th St

Once part of the country estates of the wealthy, like Alexander Hamilton whose 1802 home, Hamilton Grange, is here, this location on a hill above Harlem became desirable in the 1880s when an elevated rail line was built. Fine residences went up between 1886 and 1906, and in the 1920s and 1930s they attracted Harlem's elite, when the area was dubbed Sugar Hill. Chief Justice Thurgood Marshall and musicians Count Basie, Duke Ellington, and Cab Calloway were among those who lived here.

⑤ St. Nicholas Historic District (Strivers' Row)

MAP A3 ■ 202–250 West 138th St, between Powell & Frederick Douglass Blvds

These fine houses, originally known as the King Model Houses, were built in 1891 when Harlem was a neighborhood for the gentry. Three architects, including McKim, Mead, and White, managed to blend Renaissance, Georgian, and Victorian styles to create a harmonious whole. Successful African Americans, such as congressman Adam Clayton Powell Jr. *(see p47)*, moved here in the 1920s and 1930s, giving rise to the nickname Strivers' Row.

⑥ Abyssinian Baptist Church

MAP A3 ■ 132 West 138th St, at Powell Blvd ■ Sunday services at 11am ■ www.abyssinian.org

One of the oldest and most influential African American churches in the US was organized in 1808 by a group protesting segregation within the Baptist church. The congregation became politically active (starting in 1908) under such leaders as congressman Adam Clayton Powell, Jr. Today the church is popular for its gospel choir.

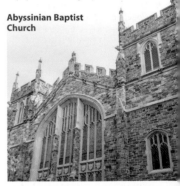

Abyssinian Baptist Church

⑦ Marcus Garvey Park

MAP B3 ■ West 120th to West 124th Sts, between Malcolm X Blvd & 5th Ave

A Black nationalist who encouraged emigration to Africa, Marcus Garvey became a hero of the Black Pride movement, and the park's name was changed from Mount Morris in 1973 to honor him. It adjoins the Mount Morris Historical District of handsome houses and churches from an earlier, German-Jewish era. In the 1920s, as Harlem's African American population grew, the synagogues became churches, and the houses were divided up.

Studio Museum 127

8 Studio Museum 127
MAP B2 ■ 429 West 127th St
■ Open noon–6pm Thu–Sun
■ Donations ■ www.studio
museum.org

Opened in 1967 as an artists' studio, this organization has become an important center for work by Black artists. The main building at 144 West 125th Street, which opened in 1982, is undergoing renovation and is expected to be closed until 2024. Visitors can check out new exhibitions in the temporary space at 429 West 127th Street instead.

9 Schomburg Center for Research in Black Culture
MAP A3 ■ 515 Malcolm X Blvd at 135th St ■ Open 10am–6pm Mon–Sat

This complex, opened in 1991, houses the largest research center for African and African American culture in the US. The immense collection was assembled by Arthur Schomburg. The original building was the unofficial meeting place for the Black literary renaissance of the 1920s; the present building includes a theater and two art galleries.

10 Masjid Malcolm Shabazz/Harlem Market
Mosque: MAP C3; 102 West 116th St; open by appointment ■ Harlem Market: MAP C3; 52–60 West 116th St, between 5th Ave & Malcolm X Blvd; open 10am–9pm daily

The Malcolm Shabazz Mosque was the ministry of the late Malcolm X, and the area around it has become the center of an active Muslim community. Harlem Market nearby sells African art.

A DAY IN HARLEM AND MORNINGSIDE HEIGHTS

▶ MORNING

Begin late Sunday morning and take the No. 2 or No. 3 subway uptown to 135th Street and Lenox Avenue, also known as Malcolm X Boulevard. Walk to Odell Clark Place and turn west to hear the fabulous choir at the **Abyssinian Baptist Church**.

Continue west along the street to see the fine 1890s homes of the **St. Nicholas Historic District** and stop on 8th Avenue to enjoy a gospel brunch at **Londel's** (see p152).

AFTERNOON

Retrace your steps to Lenox Avenue and head downtown to 125th Street to browse the shops. Turn west for the famous **Apollo Theater** (see p152) and excellent displays of African American art at the **Studio Museum 127**. Stop for coffee at **I Like It Black** (409 West 125th St).

Walk or take the M60 bus from 125th Street and Amsterdam Avenue to West 120th Street and Broadway. Walk down to **Riverside Church** (see p149) for views over the Hudson River. Across the street is the tomb of the 18th US president, Ulysses S. Grant. At 116th Street, head east two blocks to Broadway and the entrance to **Columbia University** (see p148). One block east on Amsterdam Avenue is the **Cathedral Church of St. John the Divine** (see p148) with its immense interior. End the day with a meal at **Miss Mamie's** (see p153) and return to Broadway for the No. 1 subway back downtown.

See map on p149 ←

Places for Music

Harlem Stage auditorium

1 Harlem Stage
MAP A2 ■ City College campus, 150 Convent Ave, at West 135th St

Home to jazz series, as well as ballet, modern dance, opera, and the Harlem Stage on Screen film festival.

2 Shrine
MAP B3 ■ 2271 Adam Clayton Powell, Jr. Blvd

Open since 1968, this dive bar is a neighborhood favorite and offers live jazz performances every night with no cover charge.

3 Showman's Jazz Club
MAP B2 ■ 375 West 125th St, between St. Nicholas & Morningside Dr

Live jazz and blues performances have pulled in the crowds at this cool club since it opened in 1942.

4 Londel's
MAP A3 ■ 2620 Frederick Douglass Blvd (8th Ave), between West 139th & 140th Sts

Part of the new Harlem, with an upscale ambience, Londel's features waiters in tuxedos, delicious Southern fare, and live jazz on weekends.

5 Bill's Place
MAP B3 ■ 148 West 133rd St

A Harlem hideaway modeled after the speakeasies that once dotted this neighborhood. There are great jazz sets by saxophonist Bill Saxton on Fridays and Saturdays at 7pm and 9pm, and you can bring your own alcohol (none is sold inside).

6 Sylvia's
MAP B3 ■ 328 Malcolm X Blvd, between West 126th & 127th Sts

Sylvia Woods founded this soul food restaurant in 1962. The place is jammed for Saturday and Sunday gospel brunches, and always fun despite the crowds.

7 Cotton Club
MAP B2 ■ 656 West 125th St, at Riverside Dr

Duke Ellington and Cab Calloway are long gone, and the location has changed, but the famous club of the 1920s is making a comeback.

The famous Apollo Theater

8 Apollo Theater
MAP B3 ■ 253 West 125th St, between 7th & 8th Aves

This is Harlem's famous showcase, where Ella Fitzgerald and James Brown launched their careers.

9 Minton's Playhouse
MAP C4 ■ 206 West 118th St

Bebop was born at this legendary club that has a nightly lineup of jazz, along with cocktails and food from The Cecil Steakhouse, which is next door.

10 Smoke
MAP D2 ■ 2751 Broadway, at West 106th St

Music lovers congregate here to hear top-notch jazz groups every weekend.

Restaurants

PRICE CATEGORIES

For a three-course meal for one with a glass of house wine, and all unavoidable charges including tax.

$ under $25   **$$** $25–$75   **$$$** over $75

1 Red Rooster
MAP B3 ■ 310 Malcolm X Blvd ■ 212 792 9001 ■ $$

Celebrity chef Marcus Samuelsson brings Downtown style to Harlem, drawing in an eclectic crowd to enjoy a cutting-edge menu that honors the area's colorful culinary history.

2 BLVD Bistro
MAP C2 ■ 2149 Frederick Douglass Blvd ■ 212 678 6200 ■ $$

Relax into the night at this engaging wine bar and restaurant. Enjoy classic American dishes with a soul food twist, like pan-fried chicken and cornmeal-crusted grouper.

3 Miss Mamie's Spoonbread Too
MAP D2 ■ 366 Cathedral Pkwy (West 110th St), between Manhattan Ave & Columbus Ave ■ 212 865 6744 ■ $$

This cheerful café is run by Norma Jean Darden, who knows her Southern cooking. The excellent food has attracted the likes of former US president Bill Clinton to eat here.

4 Dinosaur Bar-B-Que
MAP B1 ■ 700 West 125th St, at Riverside Dr ■ 212 694 1777 ■ $$

The generous portions live up to the name of this roadhouse-style BBQ joint. A wide selection of microbrews along with pit-smoked meats.

5 Tom's Restaurant
MAP C2 ■ 2880 Broadway ■ 212 864 6137 ■ $$

Immortalized as a location in Suzanne Vega's *Tom's Diner* and the popular *Seinfeld* TV series, this restaurant is known for its filling portions of affordable diner classics.

6 Pisticci
MAP B1 ■ 125 La Salle St, between Broadway & Claremont Ave ■ 212 932 3500 ■ $$

A cozy Italian restaurant serving up pasta dishes to a mostly local crowd.

7 Jin Ramen
MAP B1 ■ 3183 Broadway, between Tiemann Pl & 125th St ■ 646 559 2862 ■ $$

This Japanese restaurant attracts patrons with its bowls of ramen, tasty pork buns, and other specialties.

8 Le Baobab
MAP C3 ■ 120 West 116th St, at Lenox Ave ■ 212 864 4700 ■ No credit cards ■ $$

The Senegalese cooking and the tab are both agreeable here.

9 Harlem Shake
MAP D2 ■ 100 West 124th St ■ 212 222 8300 ■ $

Fill up on juicy burgers, all-beef hot dogs and creamy milkshakes at this playful restaurant.

10 Amy Ruth's
MAP C3 ■ 113 West 116th St, between A. C. Powell & Malcolm X Blvds ■ 212 280 8779 ■ $$

A cheerful café with an updated slant on Southern classics. Waffles are a house specialty.

Interior of Amy Ruth's

See map on p149

🔟 The Outer Boroughs

Manhattan is just one of New York's five boroughs, each of which has its own unique character and attractions. Brooklyn alone, with its fine brownstone neighborhoods and numerous top-class sights, would be one of the largest cities in the US. The Bronx, to the north, features the New York Botanical Garden, the Bronx Zoo, and Yankee Stadium,

while bustling Queens is famous for its engaging, family-friendly museums, international restaurants, and numerous sports events. The ferry to Staten Island leads to New York's only restored historic village.

World Fair Unisphere, Flushing Meadows-Corona Park

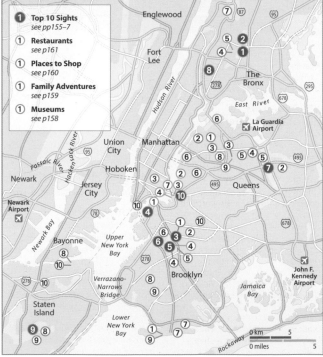

THE OUTER BOROUGHS

1 **Top 10 Sights**
see pp155–7

1 **Restaurants**
see p161

1 **Places to Shop**
see p160

1 **Family Adventures**
see p159

1 **Museums**
see p158

The tropical JungleWorld at Bronx Zoo

① Bronx Zoo

Bronx River Parkway & Boston Rd, Bronx ■ Subway (2, 5) West Farms Square/East Tremont Ave ■ Open Apr–Oct: 10am–5pm Mon–Fri, 10am–5:30pm Sat, Sun, & hols; Nov–Mar: 10am–4:30pm daily ■ Adm ■ www.bronxzoo.com

Established in 1895, this sprawling zoo is one of the best managed in the country. Exhibits include Madagascar!, JungleWorld, Tiger Mountain and the 6.5-acre (2.6-ha) Congo Gorilla Forest, an African rainforest habitat, which brings visitors nose to nose with the inhabitants. The Bug Carousel and the Children's Zoo are particularly appealing to young children.

② New York Botanical Garden

Bronx River Parkway & Kazimiroff Blvd, Bronx ■ Subway (B, D, 4) Bedford Park Blvd ■ Open 10am–6pm Tue–Sun (to 5pm Jan–Feb) ■ Adm ■ www.nybg.org

One of the oldest and largest botanical gardens in the world, this National Historic Landmark covers 250 acres (101 ha), which includes 50 gardens and plant collections, and 50 acres (20 ha) of forest, the only remains of woods that once covered New York. The Enid A. Haupt Conservatory, a restored Victorian glass house, is home to tropical rain forest and arid desert plants. A tram makes it easy to see the highlights; guided tours are offered. The Leon Levy Visitor Center has a shop, a visitor orientation area, and a café.

③ Brooklyn Botanic Garden

900 Washington Ave, Brooklyn ■ Subway (2, 3) Eastern Pkwy ■ Open Mar–Oct: 8am–6pm Tue–Fri, 10am–6pm Sat, Sun, & hols; Nov–Feb: 10am–3:30pm Tue–Sun ■ Adm (free Sat & Sun Nov–Feb) ■ www.bbg.org

This 52-acre (21-ha) garden designed by the Olmsted brothers in 1910 is home to more than 12,000 plantings. It is best known for the Cranford Rose Gardens, where thousands of roses cascade down arches and climb lattices, and the authentic Japanese Hill-and-Pond Garden, planted in 1915. It is also famous for its Cherry Esplanade and Cherry Walk, one of the foremost cherry-blossom sites outside Japan. The Steinhardt Conservatory houses tropical and desert plants, and a large bonsai collection.

New York Botanical Garden, Bronx

④ Brooklyn Heights Historic District

Court St to Furman St, between Fulton & State Sts ■ Subway (2, 3) Clark St

Overlooking the East River and lower Manhattan skyline, this district is an enclave of old-world charm. Along its quaint streets are preserved Federal, wooden and brick townhouses of the 1820s and even grander Greek Revival homes of the following decades.

Soldiers' and Sailors' Arch at the main entrance to Prospect Park, Brooklyn

5 Prospect Park
Between Eastern Pkwy & Parkside Ave, Brooklyn ■ Subway (2, 3) Grand Army Plaza

Frederic Olmsted and Calvert Vaux considered this park, opened in 1867, their masterpiece. The 90-acre (36-ha) Long Meadow is the longest unbroken green space in the city. The pools and weeping willows of the Vale of Cashmere are particularly fine, along with Vaux's Oriental Pavilion and Concert Grove.

BIRTHPLACE OF HIP HOP TOUR
New York is the home of hip hop. The Bronx scene emerged in the mid-1970s with pioneers such as DJ Kool Herc. The famous hip hop group Run-DMC **(below)** was formed in Queens, while Fab Five Freddy hailed from Brooklyn. Hush Hip Hop Tours *(www.hushtours. com)* runs the "Birthplace of Hip Hop Tour" through Harlem and the Bronx.

6 Park Slope Historic District
Prospect Park West to 8th Ave, between 14th St & St. John's Pl, Brooklyn ■ Subway (F) 7th Ave

These blocks on the western edge of Prospect Park became desirable places to live after the opening of the Brooklyn Bridge in 1883. The Victorian brownstones from the late 19th and early 20th centuries are outstanding US Romanesque Revival and Queen Anne residences.

7 Flushing Meadows-Corona Park
Queens ■ Subway (7) 111th St, Willets Pt–Shea Stadium

The site of two World Fairs, this is now a park with picnic areas, fields for cricket and soccer, paths for bikers and skaters, boating lakes, and many other attractions. The New York Mets' Citi Field, the US Tennis Center, the New York Hall of Science, and the Queens Museum of Art are also here. The Unisphere, the symbol of the 1964 World Fair, still stands.

8 Yankee Stadium
East 161st St & River Ave, Bronx ■ Subway (B, D, 4) 161st St Yankee Stadium ■ Opening times vary ■ Adm

This sports shrine, completed in 1923 and known as "The House that Ruth Built" for the legions of fans who came to see superhero Babe Ruth, was retired in 2008. Other legendary heroes of America's most successful baseball team include Joe DiMaggio and Mickey Mantle. The new Yankee stadium across the street incorporates Monument Park and exhibits statues of the greatest players.

⑨ Historic Richmond Town
441 Clarke Ave, Staten Island
■ Bus S74 from ferry ■ Open late May–early Oct: 11am–5pm Wed–Sun; early Oct–late May: 11am–5pm Fri–Sun ■ Tours at noon, 1pm, 2pm, & 3pm ■ Adm ■ www.historicrichmond town.org

This restored village has 29 buildings from the town of Richmond, Staten Island's seat of government from 1729. Other historic buildings were moved here from other sites. The Dutch-style Voorlezer's House (1695) is the island's oldest home on its original site.

Wythe Hotel bar, Williamsburg

⑩ Williamsburg
Bedford Ave, Brooklyn
■ Subway J, M, Z to Marcy Ave & G to Metropolitan Ave; Bus B39 or B61

This was mostly a community of Hasidic Jews, Puerto Ricans, and Italians until the 1990s when artists from Manhattan began to move here. The heart of Williamsburg is Bedford Avenue, where you'll find stores promoting local designers, as well as bars and restaurants. Attractions here include the Russian Orthodox Cathedral of the Transfiguration, the Brooklyn Brewery, Smorgasburg, and McCarren Park. The area is also a noted indie rock venue.

A DAY OUT IN BROOKLYN

River Café
Brooklyn Heights Historic District
Borough Hall Subway
Atlantic Avenue
Bergen Street Subway
Brooklyn Heights Promenade
Long Island Bar
5th Avenue
Eastern Parkway Subway
Gorilla Coffee
Brooklyn Museum
Prospect Park
Brooklyn Botanic Garden

▶ MORNING

Take the No. 2 or 3 subway train to Eastern Parkway – Brooklyn Museum, for the world-class **Brooklyn Museum** *(see p49)*. The museum is part of a civic complex that includes the stately Grand Army Plaza, the **Brooklyn Botanic Garden** *(see p155)*, with its well-known Japanese garden, and neighboring **Prospect Park**.

Along the western edge of Prospect Park is the beautiful Park Slope Historic District. Stop for coffee at **Gorilla Coffee** *(472 Bergen St)*, before taking in the area's historic residences. Browse the hip lineup of small shops along **5th Avenue**, and stop for lunch at one of the area's many cafés.

AFTERNOON

Return by train to Borough Hall and head for the **Brooklyn Heights Historic District** *(see p155)*. Walk along Pierrepont, Willow, and Cranberry streets to see some 19th-century houses; Truman Capote wrote *Breakfast at Tiffany's* in the basement of No. 70 Willow, and Arthur Miller once owned the property at No. 155.

A short walk east brings you to **Atlantic Avenue** *(see p160)*. Look in on the spice shops here, and stop for refreshments at the **Long Island Bar** *(110 Atlantic Ave)*. Head back to Brooklyn Bridge, stopping at the **Brooklyn Heights Promenade** for dramatic vistas of Lower Manhattan's towers. End the day with dinner at the romantic **River Café** *(see p161)*.

See map on p154 ←

Museums

(1) Brooklyn Museum
200 Eastern Parkway, Brooklyn ▪ Subway (2, 3) Eastern Pkwy ▪ Open 11am–6pm Wed–Sun, 11am–10pm first Sat of month (except Sep) ▪ Adm (free from 5pm first Sat of month)
The permanent collection *(see p49)* has it all, from ancient Egyptian objects to contemporary art.

(2) Noguchi Museum
9-01 33rd Rd at Vernon Blvd, Queens ▪ Bus 103 to Vernon Blvd ▪ Open 11am–6pm Wed–Sun ▪ Adm (free first Fri of month)
Thirteen galleries and a serene Japanese sculpture garden.

(3) Museum of the Moving Image
6-01 35th Ave, at 37th St, Queens ▪ Subway (M, R) Steinway St ▪ Open 12–6pm Thu, 2–8pm Fri, noon–6pm Sat & Sun ▪ Adm (free 2–6pm Thu)
Artifacts and screenings show the history and techniques of film and TV.

(4) New York Hall of Science (NYSCI)
47-01 111th St, Queens ▪ Subway (7) 111th St ▪ Open 10am–5pm Wed–Sun ▪ Adm
A science and technology museum with hands-on exhibits on color, light, and physics, and outdoor play area. The museum also features a 3D theater.

Hall of Science

(5) Queens Museum
New York City Building, Queens ▪ Subway 111th St ▪ Open 11am–5pm Wed–Sun ▪ Adm
Art exhibitions plus artefacts from the World's Fairs. The New York Panorama scale model has over 800,000 buildings.

(6) MoMA PS1
22–25 Jackson Ave, at 46th Ave, Queens ▪ Subway (E, V) 23rd St-Ely Ave ▪ Open noon–6pm Thu–Mon (to 8pm Sat) ▪ Adm
MoMA's Queens center displays contemporary art and provides studio space for artists.

(7) Van Cortlandt House Museum
Van Cortlandt Park, Broadway and West 246th St, Bronx ▪ Subway (1) 242nd St ▪ Open 11am–4pm Tue–Sun; last tickets 30 mins before closing ▪ Adm
This restored 1748 Georgian house is the Bronx's oldest building.

(8) Jacques Marchais Museum of Tibetan Art
338 Lighthouse Ave, Staten Island ▪ Bus S74 from ferry ▪ Open 1–5pm Wed–Sun ▪ Suggested donation of $6
A collection of Tibetan art in a Himalayan-style building.

(9) Historic Richmond Town
441 Clarke St, Staten Island ▪ Bus S74 from ferry ▪ Opening times vary ▪ Adm
The museum housed in the County Clerk's office, built in 1848, is just one of 27 buildings in the museum village.

(10) Snug Harbor Cultural Center
1000 Richmond Terrace, Staten Island ▪ Bus S40 from ferry ▪ Opening times vary ▪ Adm
Chinese garden, performance spaces, art center, children's museum, and a maritime collection.

Family Adventures

1 New York Aquarium
Surf Ave & West 8th St, Brooklyn ■ Subway (F, Q) W 8th St ■ Open Jun–Aug: 10am–6pm daily (last entry at 5pm); Sep–May: 10am–4:30pm daily ■ Adm

Walk through a swamp, stay dry beneath a waterfall, and admire the more than 350 species at New York's beloved aquarium. The shark tunnel is a highlight.

Brooklyn Children's Museum

2 Brooklyn Children's Museum
145 Brooklyn Ave, at St. Marks Pl, Brooklyn ■ Subway (3) Kingston ■ Open 10am–5pm Wed–Sun; free 2–5pm every Thu ■ Adm

Founded in 1899, this is said to be the first children's museum in the US. The hands-on exhibits have informed and entertained countless children.

3 New York Transit Museum
99 Schermerhorn St, Brooklyn ■ Subway (4, 5) Borough Hall ■ Open 10am–4pm Thu–Sun ■ Adm ■ www.nytransitmuseum.org

Charting the evolution of the city's public transit system, this museum (see p59) features a range of interactive displays.

4 Prospect Park Carousel
Prospect Park, Brooklyn ■ Subway (B, Q) Prospect Park ■ Open noon–5pm Thu–Sun & holidays ■ Rides $3

This 1912 carousel came here from Coney Island in 1950.

5 Lefferts Historic House
Prospect Park, Brooklyn ■ Subway (B, Q) Prospect Park ■ Opening hours vary, check website ■ www.prospectpark.org

This rare 18th-century Dutch farmhouse shows early farm life.

6 Puppetworks
338 6th Ave, at 4th St, Brooklyn ■ Subway (F) 7th Ave (Brooklyn) ■ Performance times vary ■ Adm (reservations required)

Hand-carved marionettes are used to present children's classics.

7 Sheepshead Bay Fishing Boats
Emmons Ave, Brooklyn ■ Subway (B, Q) to Sheepshead Bay ■ Boats leave 6:30–9am, 1, & 7pm, or can be chartered ■ Adm

A fishing fleet takes passengers for day and evening trips.

8 Staten Island Children's Museum
1000 Richmond Terrace, Staten Island ■ Bus S40 from ferry ■ Open 10am–1pm Wed–Sun (also 2–5pm Sat & Sun) ■ Adm ■ www. sichildrens museum.org

A kinetic porpoise welcomes you to this interactive museum for children.

9 Luna Park
1000 Surf Ave, Coney Island ■ Subway (D, F, N, Q) Coney Island-Stillwell Ave ■ Open Apr–Oct ■ Adm ■ www.lunaparknyc.com

This legendary amusement park features spine-tingling rides, including the Cyclone rollercoaster.

10 Staten Island Ferry
Bus to St. George Terminal, Staten Island ■ Boats every 15 mins–1 hr, 24 hours daily from Whitehall and South Sts

A free ride (see p72) with fabulous views of the Statue of Liberty. St. George Terminal buses go to Staten Island's sights.

See map on p154 ←

Places to Shop

1 Broadway, Astoria
Broadway, Astoria, Queens
■ Subway (N, Q) Broadway

Astoria has the largest Greek community outside Greece, with restaurants, coffee shops, and bakeries on Broadway.

2 Main Street, Flushing
Main St, Flushing, Queens
■ Subway (7) Main St

Flushing's Chinatown offers gifts, herbal remedies, and acupuncture, as well as bakeries and restaurants. Queensborough Library has material in 40 languages.

3 74th Street, Jackson Heights
74th St, Jackson Heights, Queens
■ Subway (E, F, R) Roosevelt Ave

The shop windows of New York's Indian community are filled with ornate gold jewelry and rich saris. The food stores are redolent with delicious spices.

4 Arthur Avenue, Bronx
Arthur Ave, Bronx ■ Subway (4) Fordham Rd

In this Italian neighborhood, dozens of small, family-run stores sell everything from Italian wines, handmade pastas, and sausages to rosaries and votive candles.

Italian food stall, Arthur Avenue

5 Roosevelt Avenue, Jackson Heights
Jackson Heights, Queens ■ Subway (E, F, R) Roosevelt Ave

Around the corner from Indian 74th Street, loudspeakers play Latin American rhythms, street vendors sell hot churros (fried dough), and shops offer music, hats, and piñatas.

6 Nassau Avenue, Greenpoint
Nassau Ave, Greenpoint, Brooklyn
■ Subway (G) Nassau

Shops in America's largest Polish community are full of homemade *kielbasas* (sausages), *babkas* (cakes), statues of saints, books, and music.

7 Brighton Beach Avenue, Brooklyn
Brighton Beach Ave, Brooklyn
■ Subway (B, Q) Brighton Beach

Everything from fish to *matryoshka* dolls are sold in "Little Odessa", where Russian is the first language.

8 13th Avenue, Borough Park
13th Ave, Borough Park, Brooklyn
■ Subway (D) 55th St

The main street of America's largest Orthodox Jewish community bustles with shops filled with religious articles, baked goods, and linens.

9 18th Avenue, Bensonhurst
18th Ave, Bensonhurst, Brooklyn
■ Subway (D) 18th Ave

Though the old-world Italian community is slowly giving way to other nationalities, the street still offers generous samplings of traditional Italian foods.

10 Atlantic Avenue, Brooklyn
Atlantic Ave, Brooklyn ■ Subway (R) Court St

This Middle-Eastern shopping hub offers baklava and many varieties of olives, dried fruits, and spices.

Restaurants

River Café under the Brooklyn Bridge

PRICE CATEGORIES
For a three-course meal for one with a
glass of house wine, and all unavoidable
charges including tax.

$ under $25 $$ $25–$75 $$$ over $75

River Café
1 Water St, Brooklyn ■ Subway
(A, C) High St ■ 718 522 5200 ■ Men
require jackets after 5pm ■ $$$

Lobster, duck, and seafood are
among the many specialties served
here. Dessert choices include a mini
chocolate Brooklyn Bridge.

Paulie Gee's
60 Greenpoint Ave, Brooklyn
■ Subway (G) Greenpoint Ave ■ 347
987 3747 ■ $$

Paulie Giannone serves some of
the best pizzas in New York. Try
the "Hellboy", which is made with
fresh mozzarella, tomatoes, spicy
soppressata, Parmigiano-Reggiano,
and chili-infused honey.

Peter Luger Steak House
178 Broadway, Brooklyn
■ Subway (J, M, Z) Marcy Ave ■ 718
387 7400 ■ No credit cards ■ $$$

Beef lovers flock to Peter Luger's
beer hall-style location for what have
long been considered New York's best
steaks. It is necessary to book ahead.

Smorgasburg
Marsha P. Johnson State Park,
90 Kent Ave; Prospect Park, Breeze
Hill ■ www.smorgasburg.com ■ $

Open-air food market Smorgasburg
has over 100 tempting stands in
Williamsburg on Saturdays and in
Prospect Park on Sundays (Apr–Oct).

Dominick's Restaurant
2335 Arthur Ave, Bronx
■ Subway (D) Fordham Rd ■ 718
733 2807 ■ No credit cards ■ $$

There's no menu at this traditional
joint; order your favorite Italian dish
or trust the waiter's choice.

Agnanti
19-06 Ditmars Blvd, Queens
■ Subway (N, Q) Ditmars Blvd-Astoria
■ 718 545 4554 ■ $$

Greek favorites, perfectly cooked,
in a charming location with a shady
terrace in the summer.

Marlow & Sons
81 Broadway, Brooklyn ■ Sub-
way (7) Main St ■ 718 384 1441 ■ $$

This whimsical restaurant serves
a Mediterranean-accented menu.

SriPraPhai
64-13 39th Ave, Woodside,
Queens ■ Subway (7) 61 St-Woodside
■ 718 899 9599 ■ $$

New Yorkers love the classic menu
at this authentic Thai spot, which
also features specials like soft shell
crab with mango sauce.

Jackson Diner
37–47 74th St, Queens
■ Subway (E, F, G, R, V) Roosevelt Ave
■ 718 672 1232 ■ No credit cards ■ $$

The best-known Indian restaurant in
the area. The curries are a must-try.

Denino's Pizzeria
524 Port Richmond Ave, Staten
Island ■ Bus SIM3 ■ 718 442 9401
■ No credit cards ■ $$

Staten Island's favorite pizzeria since
1937. Try the signature clam pie or the
"garbage pie" (sausage, meatballs,
pepperoni, mushrooms, and onions).

See map on p154

Streetsmart

Yellow New York cabs on 8th Avenue

Getting Around

Arriving by Air

New York can be reached by air direct from most major cities. Allow extra time at the airport, both at arrival and departure, for the careful passport and security checks in the US. The two main international airports in the New York City area are **John F. Kennedy International (JFK)** and **Newark Liberty International (EWR)**. Both also handle domestic flights. The third major airport is **LaGuardia (LGA)**, which handles mostly domestic flights. All three airports offer connecting flights to most US cities.

Cab fares to Manhattan from JFK are fixed at $74 ($79 4–8pm Monday to Friday), inclusive of various charges, plus any tolls, on each trip. From Newark, the fare ranges between $85 and $100 on the meter (inclusive of tolls and tips), and from LaGuardia, it ranges between $40 and $45 on the meter.

Airlink NYC vans operate door-to-door and cost less than taxis. They pick up several passengers, so allow plenty of time for the journey. Prices start at $27 from JFK to Manhattan and $40 from Newark. Coaches, like **Newark Airport Express** (from $18.70), offer transport from the airports to central Midtown points. Alternatively, from JFK, take the **AirTrain** to the A, E, J, and Z subway trains into Manhattan. From Newark, take the AirTrain to **New Jersey Transit** or Amtrak into Manhattan. Take the M60 SBS bus from LaGuardia, to 125th St, where you can catch the subway, including the 4, 5, and 6 lines or the A, B, C, and D lines. The LaGuardia Link Q70 runs directly from LaGuardia to the Jackson Heights/Roosevelt Ave subway hub, serving the 7, E, F, M, and R trains.

Train Travel

Amtrak, the US passenger rail service, Long Island Rail Road (**LIRR**) and New Jersey Transit (NJT) commuter trains all pull in to the Moynihan Train Hall at Penn Station, situated on Seventh and Eighth avenues and 31st and 34th streets. Amtrak has its own designated area in Penn Station for ticket sales, and waiting rooms for coach and high-speed passengers.

Metro-North regional trains use Grand Central Terminal, located at 42nd Street and Park Avenue in Midtown Manhattan.

Tickets can be bought on the day of travel, or ahead of your trip online or over the phone. Prepaid tickets can be collected at ticket windows or automated kiosks at the station. If you collect tickets at the window, photo ID will be requested.

To ensure you get the cheapest fares, book your tickets in advance. You can buy tickets for multiple journeys with Amtrak's USA Rail Pass, which allows eight journeys over a 30-day period for $499.

The most popular train service from New York is Amtrak's Northeast Corridor route between Boston, New York, Philadelphia, and Washington, DC. Most of the trains on this route have unreserved seating, but Amtrak's high-speed **Acela Express** trains offer an hourly service with reserved first and business-class seating plus electrical outlets.

Amtrak also offers long-distance sleeper services (to Atlanta, Chicago, New Orleans, and Florida). Included in the service is a private cabin and restroom, a complimentary meal onboard, and private lounge access.

Long-Distance Bus Travel

Intercity buses are a great and economical way to get to New York City, or to travel farther afield around the state with the city as your starting point.

Coach and intercity buses from all over the US, as well as New York City commuter lines, arrive at the Port Authority Bus Terminal (**PABT**), which is the central hub for interstate buses in New York City.

Taxis can be found on the Eighth Avenue side of the terminal; the A, C and E subway stops are located on the lower floors in the terminal; and a one-block-long tunnel leads to Times Square station along with other subway connections. Buses from the Port Authority connect with all three airports, and the terminal also serves many busy commuter bus lines to New Jersey. With over 6,000 buses arriving and departing daily, the atmosphere can be hectic at rush hour.

Greyhound offers low-cost bus routes between New York and Philadelphia (2 hours), Washington, DC (4 hours), Boston (4.5 hours), Toronto (11.5 hours), and Montreal (8.5 hours), among other cities.

Discount long-distance bus services, such as **Megabus** and **FlixBus**, depart and arrive at various street and avenue stops around Manhattan's midtown districts.

Public Transportation

New York City's extensive bus and subway transportation system is operated by the Metropolitan Transportation Authority (**MTA**). Useful information can be found on the MTA website.

Buses and subways are busiest during the rush hours: 7–9:30am and 4:30–6pm Monday to Friday. However, more services do run during these times. At other times of day and during certain holiday periods, the traffic is often much lighter. Note that public transportation runs a reduced service during major holidays.

Tickets

OMNY, MTA's new fare payment system, works on all buses and subway

trains. It accepts all contactless credit, debit, and prepaid cards, as well as digital wallets from Google, Apple, and Samsung. Wearables such as Apple Watch and Fitbit are also accepted. Travelers simply have to wave their card or device over the reader to pay. Once you've spent $33 in fares (equivalent to 12 trips) you receive free, unlimited rides for the rest of that week (Mon–Sun).

The current MetroCard system will be retired in 2024; however, Metro-Cards and SingleRide tickets are still valid on buses and the subway until then. Cards may be purchased for any number of individual rides. One free transfer ride is allowed between the subway and bus (and vice versa), or between two different bus lines. This must be used within 2 hours of first use. This transfer policy also applies to OMNY.

A single trip costs $3 with a SingleRide paper ticket and a SingleRide MetroCard, or $2.75 with a Pay-Per-Ride MetroCard, no matter how far you travel. If you are making several trips, buy a weekly unlimited ticket for $33. MetroCards and tickets are sold at drugstores, and all subway stations. They can be purchased for amounts from $5.50 to $80. Seven-day ($33) or 30-day ($127) unlimited-ride options are also available. The MTA charges a $1 "new card fee" for the purchase of a new MetroCard. By reusing your current MetroCard, you can avoid this fee.

DIRECTORY

ARRIVING BY AIR

AirTrain
w jfkairport.com/to-from-airport/air-train

Airlink NYC
w goairlinkshuttle.com

John F. Kennedy International (JFK)
w jfkairport.com

LaGuardia (LGA)
w laguardiaairport.com

Newark Liberty International (EWR)
w newarkairport.com

Newark Airport Express
w coachusa.com/airport-transportation/newark-airport

New Jersey Transit
w njtransit.com

TRAIN TRAVEL

Acela Express
w amtrak.com/acela-train

Amtrak
w amtrak.com

LIRR
w new.mta.info/agency/long-island-rail-road

Metro-North
w mta.info/mnr

LONG-DISTANCE BUS TRAVEL

FlixBus
w flixbus.com

Greyhound
w greyhound.com

Megabus
w megabus.com

Port Authority Bus Terminal (PABT) MAP K2
w panynj.gov/bus-terminals/en/port-authority.html

PUBLIC TRANSPORTATION

MTA
w mta.info

Subway

The subway is the fastest way to get around, with over 472 stations across the boroughs, and routes that fan out to the farthest reaches of New York City. The subway runs 24 hours a day, though late-night service patterns change.

Generally, the 1, 2, 3, 4, 5, 6, A, B, C, D, Q trains cover the main parts of the city, running north–south, originating in Upper Manhattan or the Bronx and, with the exception of the 1 and 6, all continue east to Brooklyn. The L train runs east–west across Manhattan along 14th Street to Brooklyn. The 7 train runs along 42nd Street to Queens. The E, F, M, N, R, and W originate in Queens and make a few stops in the city before continuing into Brooklyn (except for the E which terminates in Lower Manhattan).

Buses

Most buses run every 3–5 minutes during the morning and evening rush hours, and every 7–15 minutes from noon to 4:30pm and from 7 to 10pm. A reduced service operates on weekends and holidays. Certain buses on the busiest crosstown routes ("Select Bus") require you to enter the MetroCard into the kiosks at the bus stop to get a receipt for your journey. Inspectors do check occasionally, and riders without a receipt are fined.

Many lines run 24 hours, but check the schedule posted at your stop. After 10pm, many buses run every 20 minutes or so.

From midnight to 6am, expect to wait 30–60 minutes for a bus.

Bus Tours

One of the most popular ways to see the sights is on a hop-on-hop-off bus tour. Get off wherever you like, stay as long as you want, and catch another bus when you're ready.

Big Bus Tours is the best-known company. Routes include a Downtown loop, Uptown loop, and night and holiday lights tours (not hop-on-hop-off). Buy a 48- or 72-hour pass, and you can see a great deal of New York this way.

Taxis

Manhattan's iconic yellow taxis can be hailed any-where and can be found waiting outside most hotels and stations. The light atop the cab goes on when it is available. All cabs accept cash and should also accept credit cards. For any taxi com-plaints, you can call 311.

The green Boro taxis operate in areas of New York not commonly served by yellow cabs – north of West 110th Street and East 96th Street in Manhattan, the Bronx, Queens (excluding the airports), Brooklyn, and Staten Island. They can drop you off anywhere in the city, but cannot pick up passengers in Manhattan below 96th and 110th Streets.

All taxis are metered and can issue printed receipts. The meter starts ticking at $4.50. The fare increases 70 cents after each addi-tional fifth of a mile or

every 60 seconds of waiting time. There is an additional $1 charge from 8pm to 6am, and an extra $2.50 charge 4–8pm on weekdays. There is also a New York State Congestion Surcharge of $2.50 for all trips south of 96th Street. Tolls are extra and are added to the fare. The minimum fare for an **Uber** is $7.19, with an additional $1.55 per mile. Lyft and Gett offer similar rates.

Driving

Busy traffic, lack of park-ing, and expensive rental cars make driving in New York a frustrating experi-ence. To get around stress-free, opt for public trans-port outside of rush hour.

Car Rental

Rental car companies are located at airports, major stations, and other loca-tions in the city.

Most companies will only rent cars to drivers 25 years and older in the US. A valid driving license and clean record are essential. All agencies require a major credit card. Damage and liability insurance is recommended just in case something unexpected should happen. It is advis-able to return the car with a full tank of gas; other-wise you will be required to pay an inflated fuel price.

Be sure to check for any pre-existing damage to the car and note this on your contract before you leave the rental lot.

Parking

If you do decide to drive in the city, check with your hotel to see if they offer parking; this will usually add at least $25 per night to your bill. Otherwise, there are parking meters across the city, where you can park for up to 12 hours, starting at $3.50 per hour (meters do not have to be paid on Sundays), and you will have to return every 1 or 2 hours to top up. If not, a parking fine will cost at least $65.

New York also has numerous parking lots, but these can be expensive, starting from an average of $50 per day.

Rules of the Road

All drivers are legally required to carry a valid driver's licence and must be able to produce registration and insurance documents. Most foreign licenses are valid, but if your license is not in English, or does not have a photo ID, apply for an International Driving Permit (IDP).

Traffic drives on the right-hand side of the road, and the speed limit is usually 25 mph (40 km/h) in New York City. Seat belts are compulsory in front seats and the back. Children under three years old must ride in a child seat in the back. It is also compulsory to wear seat belts in cabs.

Most streets are one-way, and there are traffic lights at almost every corner. Unlike the rest of New York State, you can never turn right on a red light unless there is a sign indicating otherwise. If a school bus stops to let passengers off, all traffic from both sides must stop and wait for the bus to drive off.

A limit of 0.08 per cent blood alcohol is strictly enforced. For drivers under the age of 21 there is a zero tolerance policy for drink-driving. Driving while intoxicated (DWI) is a punishable offense that incurs heavy fines or even a jail sentence. It is advisable to avoid drinking altogether if you do plan to drive.

In the event of an accident or breakdown, drivers of rental cars should contact their car rental company first. Members of the American Automobile Association (**AAA**) can have their vehicle towed to the nearest service station to be fixed. For simple problems like a flat tire or a dead battery, the AAA will fix it or install a new battery on site for a fee.

Cycle Hire

It takes courage to cycle alongside busy traffic in Midtown. Bike trails along the East River and Central Park are more pleasant. **Bike Rent NYC** offers daily bike rentals and guided tours in the city. Hourly, half-day, full day, or 24hr rentals are available. **Citibike** has 25,000 bicycles at over 1,500 stations all over the city; reserve at a particular address through the app or use a credit card at the pickup location.

There is no law requiring adult cyclists to wear a helmet, but it is highly advisable. Children under 14 must wear one.

Walking

New York City is always busy, so streets have pedestrian walk lights at most intersections; some also have audio cues. Exploring by foot is a great way to experience the city, but central attractions are quite spread out, so pack a pair of comfortable shoes.

Boats and Ferries

New York Waterway ferries connect New Jersey and Manhattan. You can buy tickets online or at the ferry terminals. **NYC Ferry** connects Manhattan, Brooklyn, Queens and the Bronx. The 24-hour Staten Island Ferry is free and offers spectacular views of Lower Manhattan and the Statue of Liberty.

The NYC Ferry app provides route maps, schedules, and transport links for New York's ferry services. The app also allows users to buy paperless tickets and present their phone as proof of purchase.

DIRECTORY

BUS TOURS
Big Bus Tours
w bigbustours.com

TAXIS
Uber
w uber.com

RULES OF THE ROAD
AAA
w aaa.com

CYCLE HIRE
Bike Rent NYC
w bikerent.nyc

Citibike
w citibikenyc.com

BOATS AND FERRIES
New York Waterway
w nywaterway.com

NYC Ferry
w ferry.nyc

Practical Information

Passports and Visas

For entry requirements, including visas, consult your nearest US embassy or check the **US Department of State**.

Canadian visitors just require a valid passport to enter the US. Citizens of Australia, New Zealand, the UK, and the EU do not need a visa, but must apply to enter in advance via the Electronic System for Travel Authorization (**ESTA**) and have a valid passport. Visitors from all other regions will require a tourist visa and passport to enter. A return airline ticket is required to enter the country.

Government Advice

Now more than ever, it is important to consult both your and the US government's advice before travelling. The **UK Foreign, Commonwealth and Development Office**, the **Australian Department of Foreign Affairs**, and the US State Department offer the latest information on security, health and local regulations.

Customs Information

You can find information on the laws relating to goods and currency taken in or out of the US on the **US Customs and Border Protection Agency** website. Passengers may carry $100 in gifts; 1 liter of alcohol as beer, wine, or liquor (if aged 21 years or older); 200 cigarettes, 100 cigars (not Cuban) or two kilograms (4.4 lbs) of smoking tobacco into the US without incurring tax.

Insurance

We recommend that you take out a comprehensive insurance policy covering theft, loss of belongings, medical care, cancellations and delays, and read the small print carefully. Medical insurance is highly recommended for international travelers to the US, as costs for medical and dental care can be high. Car rental agencies offer vehicle and liability insurance, but check your policy before traveling.

Health

The US has a world-class healthcare system. It is possible to visit a doctor or dentist in New York without being registered, but you will be asked to pay in advance. Keep receipts to make a claim on your insurance later. Payment of hospital and other medical expenses is the patient's responsibility. As such it is always important to arrange comprehensive medical insurance before you travel.

There are plenty of walk-in medical clinics and emergency rooms, as well as 24-hour pharmacies, throughout New York. **Mount Sinai** offers walk-in or by-appointment services for adults and children at locations around the city, from the West Village to Midtown. Another option is **NYC**

Health + Hospitals. Hospital emergency treatment is available 24 hours a day. If you are able, call the number on your insurance policy first, and check which hospitals your insurance company deals with. For immediate treatment in an emergency, call an ambulance.

There are also numerous 24-hour pharmacies across the city, including **Duane Reade/Walgreens**. For dental issues, visit Beth Israel or contact **NYU Dentistry**.

For information regarding COVID-19 vaccination requirements, consult government advice.

Unless otherwise stated, tap water is always safe to drink.

Smoking, Alcohol, and Drugs

The legal minimum age for drinking alcohol in the US is 21, and you will need photo ID as proof of age in order to purchase alcohol and be allowed into bars. It is illegal to drink alcohol in public parks or to carry an open container of alcohol in your car, and penalties for driving under the influence of alcohol are severe.

Smoking is prohibited in all public buildings, bars, restaurants, and stores. Cigarettes can be purchased by those over 21 years old; proof of age will be required.

Though marijuana is now legal in New York (for over 21s), smoking rules still apply, and all other narcotics are prohibited.

ID

It is not compulsory to carry ID at all times in New York City. If you are asked by police to show your ID, a photocopy of your passport photo page should suffice. You may be asked to present the original document within 12 or 24 hours.

Personal Security

New York is one of the safest urban centers in the US. Petty crime does exist, so be alert to your surroundings and leave your valuables and passport in a hotel safe, get a receipt for stored luggage, and be discreet with expensive jewelry. Most city parks are safe during the day, but it's best to avoid them after dark.

If you leave property on a bus, subway or taxi, call 311 to report the loss. The best way to keep track of the taxis you have traveled in is to ask for receipts, which contain identifying numbers.

If you have anything stolen, report the crime within 24 hours to the nearest police station and take ID with you. Get a copy of the crime report in order to claim on your insurance. Contact your embassy if you have your passport stolen, or in the event of a serious crime or accident. For **emergency** police, ambulance or fire brigade services dial 111.

As a rule, New Yorkers are very accepting of all people, regardless of their race, gender or sexuality. Same-sex marriage has been legal since 2011 and 1969's Stonewall Riots are considered to be one of the most important events leading to the gay liberation movement in the US. If you do feel unsafe, the **Safe Space Alliance** pinpoints your nearest place of refuge.

Travelers with Specific Requirements

New York City law requires that facilities built after 1987 provide entrances and accessible restroom facilities for those with specific requirements. All city buses now have steps that can be lowered to allow wheelchair access, and most street corners also have curb cuts for wheelchairs.

The **YAI** is a valuable resource for those with intellectual and developmental disabilities. The website provides information on access to New York's cultural institutions and art centers.

The **Mayor's Office for People with Disabilities** provides services to residents with disabilities and also has information on city facilities. The website highlights a wide range of events such as verbal description tours in museums and galleries including MoMA and the Whitney.

The city's **Theater Development Fund** runs the Theater Access Project, which aims to increase access to theater for those who are hearing- and sight-impaired, as well as for those with other disabilities.

The **Lighthouse Guild** offers tips on exploring New York for those who are visually impaired.

Time Zone

New York is on Eastern Standard Time (EST), five hours behind GMT (UK time) and three hours ahead of PST (California time). Australia is 15 hours ahead of EST and New Zealand is 17 hours ahead.

Money

The US currency is the dollar ($), which is made up of 100 cents. Most establishments accept major credit, debit, and prepaid currency cards. Contactless payments are becoming increasingly common, and the MTA has introduced a contactless payment system on all of its subway and bus routes.

Cash is still required on some New York buses and by some smaller businesses and street vendors. ATMs are available at nearly every bank and street corner in Manhattan.

Larger banks are able to exchange foreign currency. Be prepared to show a passport or other photo identification when changing currency. ATMs (Automated Teller Machines) are available at nearly every bank.

Electrical Appliances

The US uses a 115–120V electrical current, rather than the 220V current used in Europe and other countries. Most computers and electronic devices are equipped with an automatic conversion switch, but some 220V appliances will need adapters, which are available in airport shops and some department stores. The US also uses two-prong plugs, so an adapter will be required for use of all European electrical appliances.

Mobile Phones and Wi-Fi

Most cell phones are compatible with US services, though it is key that you confirm roaming charges with your service provider at home, as these can be very expensive. Many mobile phone networks have special offers to help mitigate international charges, so make sure to inquire before traveling. Another economical option is to use a US SIM card, which works with some phones.

Most hotels offer free Wi-Fi access, but some do charge and fees can be as high as $10–$15 a day – always check before you book. Free Wi-Fi is available at all public libraries, Starbucks, McDonald's, Bryant Park, Battery Park, and a number of bookstores and subway stations in the city.

Postal Services

Post offices are open from 9am to 5pm Monday to Friday. Some are open on Saturday. The **General Post Office** is open 7am to 10pm Monday to Friday, 9am to 9pm on Saturday, and 11am to 7pm on Sunday.

Stamps can be bought from post offices, drugstores, and newsstands. Most hotels also sell stamps and mail letters for their guests. On-street mailboxes are usually blue, or red, white, and blue.

Postage for letters sent within the US costs $0.60 for the first ounce (28 g), and $0.14 for additional ounces; stamps for postcards cost $0.44. To send mail internationally, postcards cost $1.40, and letters start at $1.40 for the first ounce.

Weather

New York has distinct seasons, with average temperatures ranging from 26° to 38° F (–3° to 3° C) in the winter and from 67° to 84° F (19° to 29° C) in the summer. Despite the averages, the weather can be unpredictable and change very quickly – so it's best to pack layers for your trip. The winter months can be very cold, with snow sometimes coating the city streets and icy winds blowing in.

The months of March and August have the heaviest rainfall, but an umbrella and raincoat are useful all year round.

Opening Hours

Business hours are usually weekdays 9am to 5pm. Shops in the city open at 9 or 10am Monday to Saturday; smaller shops may close at 6 or 7pm, but department stores stay open until 8 to 10pm, often with extended hours during the holidays. Sunday shop hours are generally from 10am to 6 or 7pm.

Some museums in the city close on Mondays or

Tuesdays, or both, though the majority are open every day.

Museums, attractions, post offices, banks, and many businesses close for state and federal holidays. It is best to check with individual venues for specific closures ahead of your visit.

The COVID-19 pandemic proved that situations can change suddenly. Always check before visiting attractions and hospitality venues for up-to-date hours and booking requirements.

Visitor Information

NYC & Company, the official tourist office for the city, operates a central visitor center, located inside Macy's at Herald Square. NYC & Company also has travel apps, including apps for cabs and the subway.

New York City offers visitor passes and discount cards for events, exhibitions, museum entry, and even transport. These include **City Pass, Go City Pass**, and **The New York Pass**. They are available online and from participating tourist offices. The cards are not free, so consider carefully how many of the offers you are likely to take advantage of before purchasing.

Big Apple Greeter is a lovely way to explore the city if you're on a budget. A volunteer guide takes small groups on a free 2- to 4-hour tour of New York's varied neighborhoods.

Local Customs

There is a knack to navigating New York City's busy streets. Always walk on the right side of the sidewalk and stairwells. If you want to take a picture or consult a map while walking, move to the side first. Avoid walking three or four abreast. The locals will be quick to tell you if you are doing something wrong.

When visiting churches, cathedrals, and synagogues, try to dress respectfully. Cover your torso and upper arms, and ensure shorts and skirts cover your knees.

Language

New York City is a cosmopolitan city in which you will hear many languages spoken. Tour companies, such as **Free Tours by Foot**, offer audio tours as well as guided tours in different languages.

Taxes and Refunds

A sales tax of around 9 per cent is added to most items, including meals. Waiters generally receive 20 per cent of the bill, including tax. A quick way to calculate restaurant tips is simply to double the tax, which adds up to about 18 per cent.

Accommodation

With over 130,000 hotel rooms available, New York offers hotels to suit all budgets. The city's top hotels are among the most expensive in the US, but there are also many budget and mid-priced hotels, family-run B&Bs,

and hostels. Prices vary accordingly. The sky is the limit for upscale hotels, mid-range accommodation hovers around $250 to $400 per night, and budget hotels start around $100 – though prices can fluctuate frequently. The good news is that every neighborhood, from Midtown to Downtown, has a good mix of hotels, so you can generally find one to suit your budget.

Regardless of where you stay, book early – hotels fill up quickly, no matter what the season. Accommodation is usually busiest during the week, when business travelers are in the city, so most hotels offer budget weekend packages.

Note that hotel rooms are subject to a total 14.75 per cent tax, plus a $3.50 room fee per night.

Places to Stay

Luxury Hotels

Michelangelo

MAP J3 ■ 152 West 51st St, New York, NY 10019 ■ 212 765 0505 ■ www.michel angelohotel.com ■ $$

A handsome New York outpost of a luxury Italian chain, Michelangelo has unusually spacious rooms that blend contemporary and Neo-Classical design with Italian flair.

Algonquin Hotel

MAP J3 ■ 59 West 44th St, New York, NY 10019 ■ 212 840 6800 ■ www.algon quinhotel.com ■ $$$

This literary landmark is famous for the clique of writers known as the "Round Table," which met for regular luncheons here in the early 20th century. The Algonquin remains an oasis of civility, with antique lighting fixtures and *New Yorker* cartoon wallpaper in the halls.

Carlyle

MAP G4 ■ 35 East 76th St, New York, NY 10021 ■ 212 744 1600 ■ www. rosewoodhotels.com/en/ the-carlyle-new-york ■ $$$

Antiques set the stage for this luxury hotel that has long attracted the rich and famous with its hushed European ambience and spacious quarters decorated in understated taste. Café Carlyle is the poshest cabaret in New York City.

Baccarat Hotel

MAP H3 ■ 28 West 53rd St, New York, NY 10019 ■ 212 790 8800 ■ www. baccarathotels.com ■ $$$

This lavish hotel features Baccarat crystals in every room, elegant Parisian decor, and an amazing swimming pool. A personal host is provided with each reservation.

The Ritz-Carlton New York, Central Park

MAP H3 ■ 50 Central Park South, New York, NY 10019 ■ www.ritzcarlton. com ■ $$$

Recent renovations have transformed this iconic hotel into a stylish luxury retreat, with townhouse-inspired rooms adorned with work by local artists. The spa and club lounge have also been revamped and there is a new Movement Studio..

St. Regis

MAP H4 ■ 2 East 55th St, New York, NY 10022 ■ 212 753 4500 ■ www. marriott.com ■ $$$

The elegant guest rooms and suites at this Beaux Arts beauty come complete with Louis XVI furnishings, silk wall coverings, chandeliers, and a butler tending to your every need. The famed King Cole Bar, which serves food as well as its renowned cocktails, is attached to the hotel.

Mandarin Oriental

MAP H2 ■ 80 Columbus Circle, New York, NY 10023 ■ 212 805 8800 ■ www.mandarinoriental. com ■ $$$

There is no better way to spoil yourself than to stay at this luxurious hotel with views over Central Park and the city skyline. Guests can enjoy the hotel's world-class spa.

Loews Regency Hotel

MAP H4 ■ 540 Park Ave, New York, NY 10021 ■ 212 759 4100 ■ www.loews hotels.com/regency-hotel ■ $$$

A tranquil sanctuary favored by show-business moguls, this hotel has sleek, stylish rooms, some with views of Park Avenue, and oversize suites. The restaurant serves excellent food and is a power breakfast favorite.

Lotte New York Palace

MAP J4 ■ 455 Madison Ave, at 50th St, New York, NY 10022 ■ 212 888 7000 ■ www.lottenypalace.com ■ $$$

This legendary hotel incorporates the opulent 1882 Villard Houses and a 55-story tower, with a choice of classic and elegantly appointed Palace rooms as well as luxurious Tower rooms and suites. It is also home to a French bakery and a cocktail bar.

Four Seasons

MAP H4 ■ 57 East 57th St, New York, NY 10022 ■ 212 758 5700 ■ www. fourseasons.com ■ $$$

For luxury in a modern mode, this dramatic, pale-hued tower by I. M. Pei is the ultimate offering. The rooms here are among the largest in New York City, and every amenity is available. The hotel bar and restaurant draw the city's elite.

1 Hotel Central Park

MAP H3 ▪ 1414 6th Ave, New York, NY 10019 ▪ 212 703 2001 ▪ www.1hotels.com ▪ $$$
Designed using reclaimed materials, this modern hotel is just steps away from Central Park. It features a three-story living green exterior, organic bed linens, and an electric Audi e-tron vehicle for guests.

The Mercer

MAP N4 ▪ 147 Mercer St, New York, NY 10012 ▪ 212 966 6060 ▪ www.mercerhotel.com ▪ $$$
A hit with Hollywood luminaries, the Mercer is housed in an 1890 structure built for John Jacob Astor II. Making good use of lofty spaces, it has a voguish, shabby-chic look.

Thompson Central Park

MAP H3 ▪ 119 West 56th St, New York, NY 10019 ▪ 212 245 5000 ▪ www.hyatt.com ▪ $$$
This lively hotel boasts soaring public spaces, a gym, a lavish spa, two restaurants, a burger joint, and a coffee bar. The sleek rooms offer views of Central Park or Midtown.

Park Hyatt

MAP H3 ▪ 157 West 57th St, New York, NY 10019 ▪ 646 774 1234 ▪ www.hyatt.com ▪ $$$
Opened in 2014, this hotel offers rooms with floor-to-ceiling windows, beau-

tiful artwork, and designer linens. Everything within its walls is top of the line, from the massive suites to the indoor saltwater swimming pool and eucalyptus steam room.

Peninsula

MAP H3 ▪ 700 5th Ave, New York, NY 10019 ▪ 212 956 2888 ▪ www.peninsula.com ▪ $$$
The Hong Kong hotel group has turned this 1905 classic into modern luxury lodging. Rooms are contemporary with Art Nouveau accents and bedside controls for the many gadgets. The health club with pool is superb.

The Mark

MAP F3 ▪ 25 East 77th St, New York, NY 10021 ▪ 212 744 4300 ▪ www.themarkhotel.com ▪ $$$
This elegant 1927 hotel has been redecorated by the renowned French interior designer Jacques Grange. Perks include treats by Ladurée, chauffeured pedicabs, and an innovative restaurant by Jean-Georges Vongerichten.

Sherry Netherland

MAP H3 ▪ 781 5th Ave, New York, NY 10022 ▪ 212 355 2800 ▪ www.sherrynetherland.com ▪ $$$
Dating from 1927, this ornate hotel features a spectacular marble-and-bronze lobby and a signature clock that marks the 5th Avenue entrance. The rooms are spacious, and most of them have glorious views over Central Park. The location of the hotel, at a short distance from the LaGuardia airport, is also advantageous.

The Plaza

MAP H3 ▪ 768 5th Ave, at Central Park South, New York, NY 1001 ▪ 212 759 3000 ▪ www.theplazany.com ▪ $$$
The grande dame of New York hotels, this 19-story French Renaissance building opened in 1907 as a residence for the wealthy and is now a National Historic Landmark. The hotel boasts a champagne bar and an exclusive Guerlain Spa.

Renaissance New York

MAP J3 ▪ 714 7th Ave, New York, NY 10026 ▪ 212 765 7676 ▪ www.marriott.com ▪ $$
An upscale oasis located in the Theater District, with an elegant lobby, contemporary furnishings, and mosaic tiles in the bathrooms. The restaurant offers a great view of Times Square.

Roxy Hotel

MAP P3 ▪ 2 6th Ave, New York, NY 10013 ▪ 212 519 6600 ▪ www.roxyhotelnyc.com ▪ $$$
Tribeca's first hotel is still a hit. All the neighborhood gathers at the Roxy Bar, the dramatic lobby bar with 70 translucent columns of light. The elegant rooms are a calm counterpoint.

Pierre

MAP H3 ▪ 2 East 61st St, New York, NY 10021 ▪ 212 838 8000 ▪ www.thepierreny.com ▪ $$$
A landmark since the 1930s, the Pierre is a bastion of old-world elegance. With staff outnumbering guests by a ratio of three to one, the first-class service is a hallmark.

Sofitel

MAP J3 ■ 45 West 44th St, New York, NY 10036 ■ 212 354 8844 ■ www. sofitel-new-york.com ■ $$$

Although it only opened its doors in 2000, this hotel features a distinct old-world elegance and charm. Rooms are comfortable, adorned with tasteful art, and soundproofed. The room rate includes morning tea and coffee at Gaby Brasserie Française. There is also a rooftop bar offering gorgeous city views.

Trump International Hotel and Tower

MAP H2 ■ 1 Central Park West, New York, NY 10023 ■ 212 299 1000 ■ www.trump hotels.com ■ $$$

High ceilings and tall windows result in fabulous views of New York city and Central Park at this huge hotel. Room amenities include useful kitchenettes, room service from the two-Michelin-starred Jean-Georges (see p66), and access to the heated indoor pool.

W New York – Union Square

MAP M4 ■ Park Ave South, New York, NY 10003 ■ 212 253 9119 ■ www.marriott. com ■ $$$

Designer David Rockwell has transformed this charming Beaux Arts building into a contemporary showstopper, complete with a floating staircase. Trademark W features include modern rooms decorated in bright colors, a well-equipped fitness area, and a lively glamorous bar.

Boutique Hotels

The Franklin Hotel

MAP F4 ■ 164 East 87th St, New York, NY 10128 ■ 212 369 1000 ■ www. ihg.com/voco/hotels ■ $$

A comfortable lodging on the Upper East Side, The Franklin offers style rather than size, with sleek furnishings and compact rooms. Other features include free breakfast and a 24-hour espresso machine.

Casablanca

MAP J3 ■ 147 West 43rd St, New York, NY 10036 ■ 212 869 1212 ■ www. casablancahotel.com ■ $$

A Moroccan theme, complete with tiles and arches, sets this Theater District hotel apart. Rooms are small but well furnished. Continental breakfast is served in – where else? – Rick's Café.

Hotel Giraffe

MAP L4 ■ 365 Park Ave South, New York, NY 10016 ■ 212 685 7700 ■ www. hotelgiraffe.com ■ $$

A glass-walled lobby leads to this award-winning hotel with Retro decor and a lovely rooftop garden. Most rooms feature French doors and small balconies. Light breakfast and snacks are complimentary, and the Italian restaurant downstairs serves homestyle fare.

Bowery Hotel

MAP N4 ■ 335 Bowery, New York, NY 10003 www.theboweryhotel. com ■ $$$

Hip hotel on the edge of Nolita, with a bohemian-chic theme. Rooms blend antique-style beds and modern amenities giving an old New York feel. The on-site Italian trattoria, Gemma, is the perfect spot for brunch.

Iroquois

MAP J3 ■ 49 West 44th St, New York, NY 10036 ■ 212 840 3080 ■ www. iroquoisny.com ■ $$

One of the suites in this elegant hotel is named after James Dean, who lived here from 1951 to 1953; other Hollywood guests over the years have included Sandra Bullock and Johnny Depp. Rooms are modestly sized, with classic decor and floor-to-ceiling marble in the bathrooms. Packages offer excellent rates.

Muse Hotel

MAP J3 ■ 130 West 46th St, New York, NY 10036 ■ 212 485 2400 ■ www. themusehotel.com ■ $$

A boutique hotel, the Muse inspires with a smart lobby decorated with stunning contemporary art, and good-size rooms, some of which come with their own balcony. The hotel offers a wine reception in the evenings as well as free bike rentals.

Bryant Park

MAP K3 ■ 40 West 40th St, New York, NY 10018 ■ 212 869 0100 ■ www.bryant parkhotel.com ■ $$$

Raymond Hood's 1924 American Radiator Building has become an ultra-contemporary hotel, with giant windows, bold, red-lacquered lobby desks, and lavishly equipped, pale-hued rooms that are the last word in minimalist decor. Koi restaurant serves

Japanese food with a Californian influence.

Ned NoMad

MAP L3 ■ 1170 Broadway, New York, NY 10001 ■ 212 796 1500 ■ www.thened. com/nomad ■ $$$
Relive 1920s elegance at this sister hotel of the London original, with gorgeous rooms plus a members' club, a rooftop terrace, and Cecconi's tempting restaurant.

Pendry Manhattan West

MAP K2 ■ 438 West 33rd St, New York, NY 10001 ■ www.pendry.com/ manhattan-west ■ $$$
Luxurious boutique near the High Line with an eye-catching façade and plush California-inspired theme. Guests stay in bright, contemporary rooms with floor-to-ceiling windows and can also hangout at the hip on-site Bar Pendry or Zou Zou's restaurant.

The Archer

MAP K3 ■ 45 West 38th St, New York, NY 10018 ■ 212 719 4100 ■ www. archerhotel.com ■ $$
This hotel pays homage to the surrounding Garment District by incorporating fabric-inspired design palettes, along with floor-to-ceiling windows, and subway-tile bathrooms. The rooftop bar has views of the Empire State and Chrysler Buildings.

Crosby Street Hotel

MAP N4 ■ 79 Crosby St, New York, NY 10012 ■ 212 226 6400 ■ www. firmdalehotels.com ■ $$$
SoHo's favorite British import offers plush rooms (upper rooms have views

of lower Manhattan), a daily service of proper afternoon tea, and a lively bar and restaurant. There is even a screening room featuring weekly films.

Le Méridien New York

MAP H3 ■ 120 West 57th St, New York, NY 10019 ■ 212 830 8000 ■ www. marriott.com ■ $$$
For some Downtown edge in Uptown, head to this stylish hotel with a distinctive black brick-and-steel facade and a sexy rooftop lounge. Rooms feature floor-to-ceiling windows and Malin+Goetz bath products. The Kingside restaurant, designed by Roman and Williams, serves delicious New American food.

Library Hotel

MAP K4 ■ 299 Madison Ave, New York, NY 10017 ■ 212 983 4500 ■ www. libraryhotel.com ■ $$$
This themed hotel is filled with books. Each of the 10 floors is devoted to a Dewey Decimal System category, such as the Arts or Philosophy, with appropriate volumes in each room. It includes a rooftop sitting room and terrace, and a complimentary wine and cheese reception every evening.

Lowell

MAP H4 ■ 28 East 63rd St, New York, NY 10021 ■ 212 838 1400 ■ www. lowellhotel.com ■ $$$
Luxurious and intimate, the Lowell exudes an old-world charm. Its rooms feature wood-burning fireplaces, libraries, flowers, and marble baths. The decor

is an eclectic and appealing mix of French, Art Deco, and Oriental.

ModernHaus SoHo

MAP P3 ■ 227 Grand St, New York, NY 10013 ■ 212 465 2000 ■ www. modernhaushotel.com ■ $$$
Gaze out on the lights of Manhattan from the rooftop bar and seasonal pool of this trendy hotel. Later, cozy up in the handsome Bauhaus-inspired rooms or grab dinner at the Veranda Restaurant from Chef George Mendes.

Refinery Hotel

MAP K3 ■ 63 West 38th St, New York, NY 10018 ■ 646 664 0310 ■ www. refineryhotelnewyork. com ■ $$$
Celebrate the history of the Garment District at this former hat factory in the Colony Arcade building that has been transformed into a sophisticated hotel. The neighborhood's past is revealed throughout the building, from sewing machine desks to carpets emblazoned with a design of interlocking scissors.

SIXTY SoHo

MAP N3 ■ 60 Thompson St, New York, NY 10012 ■ 877 431 0400 ■ www. sixtyhotels.com ■ $$$
SoHo's 12-story luxurious hotel offers 97 rooms and suites, each elegantly decked out with custom furnishings and enviable marble bathrooms. Guests can enjoy the view from the stylish roof garden lounge or watch the buzzy neighborhood scene from the sidewalk Bistrot Leo, which serves up classic French fare in a casual setting.

For a key to hotel price categories see p172

Business Hotels

Kixby Hotel

MAP K3 ■ 45 West 35th St, New York, NY 10001 ■ 212 947 2500 ■ www.kixby.com ■ $$

Popular with the fashion industry, but also good value, the Kixby has a sophisticated Art Deco feel and offers spacious rooms. Public spaces include a rooftop terrace and bar, a lounge, and an on-site restaurant, Black Tap.

The Manhattan at Times Square

MAP J3 ■ 790 7th Ave, New York, NY 10019 ■ 212 581 3300 ■ www.manhattanhoteltimessquare.com ■ $$

High speed Wi-Fi, a 24-hour fitness center, and large, comfortable rooms with plush furnishings are among the features of this 22-story hotel, built in 1962. The Manhattan is a quieter neighbor of the Sheraton New York, which serves as a major convention venue. The Theater District is just steps away.

Millennium Hilton New York One UN Plaza

MAP J5 ■ U.N. Plaza, 44th St, between 1st & 2nd Ave, New York, NY 10017 ■ 212 758 1234 ■ www.hilton.com ■ $$

Kevin Roche's soaring tower close to the UN Headquarters attracts an international clientele. There are panoramic views from the rooms beginning on the 28th floor, a fitness room with views of the East River, and New York City's only indoor hotel tennis court.

Millennium Hotel Broadway Times Square

MAP J3 ■ 145 West 44th St, New York, NY 10036 ■ www.millenniumhotels.com ■ $$

A postmodern skyscraper, encompassing a theater, the Millennium is sleek and streamlined. The compact rooms have beautiful cityscape views and are well appointed, with high-tech features that include Wi-Fi and a 40-inch Smart TV with streaming capabilities.

Benjamin

MAP J4 ■ 125 East 50th St, New York, NY 10022 ■ 212 715 2500 ■ www.thebenjamin.com ■ $$$

This 1927 building designed by Emery Roth has been converted to a hotel with kitchenettes and all the requisite high-tech amenities. There is also a chic restaurant, the National, which serves bistro dishes with a Modern American influence by celebrity chef Geoffrey Zakarian.

Fifty NYC

MAP J4 ■ 155 East 50th St, New York, NY 10022 ■ www.affinia.com/fifty-hotel-suites ■ $$

This stylish residential hotel situated in the heart of Midtown boasts large suites with full kitchens and separate living areas that are outfitted with comfy sofa beds, making it an ideal choice for families and groups.

Gild Hall

MAP Q4 ■ 15 Gold St, New York, NY 10038 ■ www.hyatt.com ■ $$$

Combining luxury with business in the heart of the Financial District, the Gild Hall offers sleek, well equipped rooms. The hotel also features a library, a lounge, a wine bar, and a warm, wood-paneled restaurant serving authentic Italian food.

New York Hilton Midtown

MAP J3 ■ 1335 6th Ave, New York, NY 10019 ■ 212 586 7000 ■ www.hilton.com ■ $$$

The quintessential business hotel, the Hilton boasts a central location, 1,878 rooms, a ballroom, and extensive meeting facilities. A redesign transformed the lobby, upgraded the guest rooms, and added a fitness club and in-room spa.

Hotel 48LEX

MAP J4 ■ 517 Lexington Ave, at 48th, New York, NY 10017 ■ 212 838 1234 ■ www.hotel48lexnewyork.com ■ $$$

This contemporary hotel is located within walking distance of Grand Central Terminal and Central Park. All rooms and suites are spacious and sleek, styled in the manner of a luxury pied-à-terre.

Club Quarters World Trade Center

MAP Q3 ■ 140 Washington St, New York, NY 10006 ■ 212 344 0800 ■ www.clubquartershotels.com/new-york-city/world-trade-center ■ $$

This is a solid business option from the Club Quarters brand. Rooms are compact but stylish and close to One World Trade Center and the 9/11 Memorial.

There's a small multi-purpose work station, ultra-fast Wi-Fi, and iPhone docking, too.

Mid-Range Hotels

Nesva Hotel
39-12 29th St, Long Island City, NY 11101 ▪ 917 745 1000 ▪ www.nesvahotel.com ▪ $

A boutique hotel just one subway stop from Manhattan, Nesva offers minimalist rooms that feature walnut wood furniture, large windows overlooking the city skyline, and ultra deep soaking tubs. Amenities include complimentary continental breakfast, a business center, and off-site parking.

Arthouse Hotel
MAP F2 ▪ 2178 Broadway, New York, NY 10024 ▪ 212 362 1100 ▪ www.arthousehotelnyc.com ▪ $$

This Upper West Side gem combines vintage charm with contemporary style. Set in a century-old building, the hotel features original artwork, an antique fireplace, and a quirky 1920s French elevator system.

IBEROSTAR 70 Park Avenue
MAP K4 ▪ 70 Park Ave, New York, NY 10016 ▪ 212 973 2400 ▪ www.iberostar.com ▪ $$

A small, sophisticated haven, this centrally located hotel has smart decor of contemporary furnishings and a rich, gold-and-cream color scheme. Other features here include a 24-hour fitness center, valet parking, and a business

center. Pets are welcome to stay too.

Belvedere Hotel
MAP J2 ▪ 319 West 48th St, New York, NY 10036 ▪ 212 245 7000 ▪ www.belvederehotelnyc.com ▪ $$

Built in 1923, Belvedere has retained its classic Art Deco features. The executive rooms are equipped with kitchenettes. The hotel is located close to Times Square and has a Brazilian restaurant, Churrascaria Plataforma, onsite.

Chelsea Savoy
MAP L2 ▪ 204 West 23rd St, New York, NY 10011 ▪ 212 929 9353 ▪ www.chelseasavoynyc.com ▪ $$

This is an excellent neighborhood lodging, close to the shops, cafés, and galleries of Chelsea. Pleasantly furnished rooms are of a decent size, with all the necessary amenities. Choose rooms that face away from 23rd Street.

Dream Midtown
MAP H3 ▪ 210 W 55th St, New York, NY 10019 ▪ 212 247 2000 ▪ www.dreamhotels.com/midtown ▪ $$

Set inside a restored 1895 Beaux-Arts building in the heart of Midtown, this hotel has small rooms and a cool rooftop bar, the PHD Terrace.

The Jane
MAP M2 ▪ 113 Jane St, New York, NY 10014 ▪ 212 924 6700 ▪ www.thejanenyc.com ▪ $

This alternative hotel has rooms modeled after vintage ship cabins, ranging from "captain's

cabins" to "bunk bed cabins". They also provide complimentary bicycles.

Aloft Manhattan Downtown-Financial District
MAP Q4 ▪ 49-53 Ann St, New York, NY 10038 ▪ 212 513 0003 ▪ www.marriott.com ▪ $$

Opened in 2015, this hotel has simple but modern and functional rooms with ergonomic workstations, a grab-and-go café onsite, the WXYZ Bar, and a 24-hour fitness center.

Pod 51
MAP J4 ▪ 230 East 51st St, New York, NY 10022 ▪ 212 355 0300 ▪ www.thepodhotel.com ▪ $$

Clean, cozy rooms, some with bunk beds and shared bathrooms, high-tech features such as free Wi-Fi and iPod connections, a café, a rooftop terrace, and a prime location make Pod 51 a great budget hotel. Low season rates start at $95.

Ravel Hotel Trademark Collection by Wyndham
MAP H6 ▪ 8-08 Queens Plaza South, Long Island City, Queens, NY 11101 ▪ 718 503 4376 ▪ www.wyndhamhotels.com ▪ $

Just across the East River from Midtown, this four-star hotel offers excellent value compared to Manhattan. Rooms are stylishly designed, with pine, Nordic-inspired furnishings, and modern amenities. Some rooms come with balconies and sensational views of the Queensboro Bridge and the city.

The Ridge Hotel
MAP N5 ▪ 151 East Houston St, New York, NY 10002 ▪ 212 777 0012 ▪ www.ridgehotelnyc.com ▪ $

A contemporary boutique hotel, The Ridge offers all the usual amenities supplemented by some quirky extras, which include complimentary access to Brain.fm, a music service designed to "influence your cognitive state".

Belleclaire Hotel
MAP F2 ▪ 250 West 77th St, New York, NY 10024 ▪ 212 362 7700 ▪ www.hotelbelleclaire.com ▪ $$

The rooms in this property are sparse, but well-designed. Bathrooms are small, and some rooms have a shared bath. Ask for a family suite if kids are in tow. Right in the heart of the Upper West Side, it is a great base for exploring.

Lucerne
MAP F2 ▪ 201 West 79th St, New York, NY 10024 ▪ 212 875 1000 ▪ www.thelucernehotel.com ▪ $$

Housed in a 1903 building with a terra cotta trim, Lucerne is the best of the Upper West Side's excellent-value hotels. It has a comfortable lobby, business and fitness centers, a French café, and tasteful rooms.

Off SoHo Suites
MAP N4 ▪ 11 Rivington St, New York, NY 10002 ▪ 212 353 0860 ▪ www.offsoho.com ▪ $

An affordable option in the heart of the Lower East Side, this hotel has spacious rooms. The economy suites come with shared kitchens, while the larger deluxe suites have a living room and a private kitchen. Guests have access to an on-site laundry and a fitness center.

Pod Brooklyn
MAP Q6 ▪ 247 Metropolitan Ave, Brooklyn, NY 11211 ▪ 844 763 7666 ▪ www.thepodhotel.com/pod-brooklyn ▪ $$

This sister hotel to Pod51 offers slightly cheaper rates and close proximity to one of Brooklyn's most fashionable neighborhoods, Williamsburg. The 249 "pods" are simple (bunks or doubles), but chic and cozy, with light dimmers, individual flat-screen TVs, and plenty of ports to connect and charge your devices.

Shoreham
MAP H3 ▪ 33 West 55th St, New York, NY 10019 ▪ 212 247 6700 ▪ www.shorehamhotel.com ▪ $$

A thoroughly modern makeover of the hotel has included creative use of light and textures. The guest rooms feature elegant decor in pale tones and marble bathrooms. The hotel offers free Wi-Fi, and guests can connect up to three devices at a time.

Washington Square Hotel
MAP N3 ▪ 103 Waverly Pl, New York, NY 10011 ▪ 212 777 9515 ▪ www.washingtonsquarehotel.com ▪ $$

A haven in the heart of Greenwich Village, this landmark hotel features small rooms with Art Deco accents, C. O.

Bigelow bath products, and a flat-screen TV. A complimentary continental breakfast is included.

Yotel
MAP K2 ▪ 570 10th Ave, New York, NY 10035 ▪ 646 449 7700 ▪ www.yotel.com ▪ $$

Yotel was inspired by the trendy capsule hotels of Asia. The rooms may be snug but they are ergonomically designed, with comfortable beds that electronically fold into couches, and come with flat-screen TVs.

Budget Accommodations

A & Faye Bed and Breakfast
9 Marlborough Rd, Brooklyn, NY 11226 ▪ 347 406 9143 ▪ www.aandfayebb.com ▪ $

Managed by friendly owners, this B&B is located just south of Prospect Park and offers six cozy rooms.

American Dream
MAP L4 ▪ 168 East 24th St, New York, NY 10010 ▪ 212 260 9779 ▪ www.americandreamhostel.com ▪ $

A great location and complimentary continental breakfast help make this clean hostel a good option for a short-term stay. All rooms come with TVs and shared bathrooms.

Q4 Hotel
MAP H6 ▪ 29-09 Queens Plaza North, Long Island City, NY 11101 ▪ www.q4hotelny.com ▪ $

Conveniently located next to Queens Plaza subway in Queens, this modern budget hotel offers small 3- or 4-bed dorms (mixed or female-only) with shared bathrooms or basic en-suite doubles. There's also a guest kitchen, TV lounge, pool table, and table tennis.

Brooklyn Riviera Hostel

781 Prospect Place, Brooklyn, NY 11216 ■ 212 470 0216 ■ $ Popular hostel in a quiet section of Brooklyn's Crown Heights (just a short walk from Prospect Park). The hostel features a host of simple dorms, plus a small shared kitchen (with free coffee), free baked goods for breakfast, and communal barbecues most Sunday nights in the summer.

Carlton Arms

MAP L4 ■ 160 East 25th St, New York, NY 10010 ■ 212 679 0680 ■ www. carltonarms.com ■ $ There may not be a TV or a phone, but this hostel is popular with young visitors for its hip spirit and funky halls, with walls painted by young artists. Private bathrooms are available in just under half of the hotel's 54 colorful rooms.

Harlem Flophouse

MAP C3 ■ 242 West 123rd St, New York, NY 10027 ■ 212 662 0678 ■ www. harlemflophouse.com ■ $ This characterful 19th-century brownstone features four charming guest rooms each with sinks, and two shared bathrooms with antique clawfoot tubs. The decor and furnishings evoke an old-world vibe.

HI New York City Hostel

MAP D2 ■ 891 Amsterdam Ave, New York, NY 10025 ■ 212 932 2300 ■ www.hiusa.org ■ Most without en-suite bathrooms ■ $ Although run by American Youth Hostels, all ages are welcome to share the clean, safe rooms here. There are 4 to 12 beds per dormitory. This facility offers free Wi-Fi, a coffee bar, cafeteria, and self-service kitchen.

Hotel 31

MAP L4 ■ 120 East 31st St, New York, NY 10016 ■ 212 685 3060 ■ www. hotel31.com ■ $ Built in 1928, this historic property features 60 simple but adequate rooms with air conditioning and cable TV. The cheapest rooms have sinks and shared bathrooms, while the more expensive ones have private bathrooms.

Jazz on Columbus Circle Hostel

MAP H3 ■ 940 8th Ave, New York, NY 10019 ■ 646 876 9282 ■ www. jazzhostels.com ■ $ This hostel is located close to Central Park. It offers clean dorms and private rooms. Amenities include TVs on each floor, washing machines, free storage for luggage before check-in, complimentary breakfast, vending machines, and free in-room lockers.

LIC Hotel

MAP H6 ■ 44-04 21st St, 44th Ave, Long Island City, NY 11101 ■ 718 406 9788 ■ www.lichotelny. com ■ $ A modern motel-like option, this hotel has

small but well-maintained rooms with hardwood floors and flat-screen TVs. The roof deck is a great place to relax in warm weather. The hotel serves a complimentary breakfast buffet.

The Local NYC

MAP H6 ■ 13-02 44th Ave, Long Island City, Queens, NY 11101 ■ 347 738 5251 ■ www. thelocalny.com ■ $ Located just ten minutes away from Grand Central by subway, the chic interiors of this hostel have a white-washed look and feature a convivial bar and kitchen access.

Microtel Inn by Wyndham Long Island City

2912 40th Ave, Queens, NY 11101 ■ 718 606 6850 ■ www.wyndhamhotels. com ■ $ This outpost of the budget motel chain offers some good deals (though it's not as cheap as its sister hotels outside the city). Rooms here are modern and clean, with large beds, and simple, contemporary bathrooms.

NY Moore Hostel

179 Moore St, between Bushwick and White, East Willamsburg, Brooklyn, NY 11206 ■ 347 227 8634 ■ www. nymoorehostel.com ■ $ The friendly NY Moore has spotless rooms with eclectic furnishings that include antique sofas and Modernist bed frames. The hostel is close to the Morgan Avenue subway station and is just a subway ride from Manhattan.

General Index

Acknowledgments

This edition updated by

Contributor Stephen Keeling
Senior Editor Alison McGill
Senior Designer Vinita Venugopal
Project Editor Lucy Sara-Kelly
Assistant Designer Divyanshi Shreyaskar
Picture Researcher Taiyaba Khatoon, Vagisha Pushp
Publishing Assistant Halima Mohammed
Jacket Designer Jordan Lambley
Cartography Manager Suresh Kumar
Cartographer Ashif
Senior Production Editor Jason Little
Production Controller Kariss Ainsworth
Managing Editors Shikha Kulkarni, Hollie Teague
Deputy Editorial Manager Beverly Smart
Senior Managing Art Editor Priyanka Thakur
Art Director Maxine Pedliham
Publishing Director Georgina Dee

DK would like to thank the following for their contribution to the previous editions: Eleanor Berman, AnneLise Sorensen, Sue Lightfoot, Chris Orr & Associates

The publisher would like to thank the following for their kind permission to reproduce their photographs:

(**Key:** a-above; b-below/bottom; c-center; f-far; l-left; r-right; t-top)

Alamy Stock Photo: AA World Travel Library 56br; Tomas Abad 37crb; Tomas Abad/Metropolitan Museum of Art *Petite danseuse de quatorze ans*, executed ca. 1880; cast in 1922, by Edgar Degas 33cra; Mike Booth 21crb; Robert K. Chin 98t, / Storefronts 113br; Richard Cummins 88bc; Randy Duchaine 57cla, 157cl; epa european pressphoto agency b.v. 13cl; Everett Collection Historical 92tl; Alexander Farmer 40-1c; Hemis 106tr; Hemis. fr / Richard Soberka 87bl; Historic Collection 46bl; JLImages 16cla; MediaPunch Inc / Ralph Dominguez 156bl; Patti McConville 92cr, 131br; 138cra; Ellen McKnight 41tl; Wojciech Migda 144tl; Sean Pavone 4cra; Erik Pendzich 29b; PCN Photography 75tr; Prisma Bildagentur AG/Heeb Christian 69br; Radharc Images 13tl; Sergi Reboredo 118bl; Ivo Roospold 80b; Maurice Savage 140tr; Philip Scalia 110cl; Kumar Sriskandan 37tr; Marc Tielemans 73cla; UPI / John Angelillo 43b; Elizabeth Wake 82cra; WENN Ltd 65bl; ZUMA Press, Inc. / Bryan Smith 69tl.

American Museum of Natural History Library: 41br; Denis Finnin 42tr, 42cl.

Artists & Fleas: 120tl.

BeccaPR: Daniel Krieger 66t.

Blake Zidell & Associates: 152tl.

Boulud Sud: 147ca.

Brandy Library: Charles O Steinberg 106clb.

Brooklyn Children's Museum: 159cla.

Corbis: Atlantide Phototravel/Massimo Borchi 144bl; Bain News Service 22bl; Bettmann, 29tl, 47tr; Alex Geana 71crb; imageBROKER/Daniel Kreher 2tr, 44-5; Bob Krist 11bl; Theodore C. Marceau 112ca; Walter McBride 27br; Abraham Nowitz 41tl.

Richard Czapnik: 19cr, 121br.

Daniel Restaurant: Eric Laignel 66clb.

Depositphotos Inc: Felixtm 20–21c.

The Door Idea House/ Lelie Rooftop: 68b.

Dorling Kindersley: Chinatown Ice Cream Factory/Steven Greaves 94br; courtesy of Lincoln Center/Steven Greaves 142bl; New York City Fire Museum/Steven Greaves 103br; Russ and Daughters/Steven Greaves 98bl.

The Drawing Center: 51cl.

Dreamstime.com: Alexpro9500 32br; Andersastphoto 67tr; Matthew Apps 14bl; Zeynep Ayse Kiyas Aslanturk 116bl; Sergio Torres Baus 161tl; Andrey Bayda 13r; Bcbounders 19br; Maciej Bledowski 6tr; Bigapplestock 57tr, 58t, 140bl; Jon Bilous 49tr; Bojan Bokic 16-7c; Breakers 104t; Mike Clegg 11tr, 27tr, 48tr; Jerry Coli 26bl, 63tr; Cpenler

78tl; Giuseppe Crimeni 82bl; Brett Critchley 10c; Cyberfyber 4t; Songquan Deng 30–31ca, 52bl, 74tl; Dibrova 18–19, 80tl; Dragoneye 46ca; Etstock 137tl; Manuel Hurtado Ferrández 35b; F11photo 4cla, 4br, 138bl; Gary718 7tr, 11ca; Gran Turismo 108cr; Joe Grossinger 47bl; Dan Henson 4crb; Laszlo Halasi 17c; Wangkun Jia 115br; Jeremyreds 53bl; Jgaunion 129cl; Jjfarq 71cla, 102bl, 110tr; Julia161 133crc; Vichaya Kiatying-angsulee 127t; Kmiragaya 18bl; Jan Kratochvila 21cra; Kropic 3tr, 162-3b; Lavendertime 91t; Littleny 20clb, 73tr, 108tl; Brian Logan 60tl; Marcorubino 150cr; Ilja Mašík 134-5; mentat 4clb; Luciano Mortula 4bl, 26–7c; Vladimir Mucibabic 17br; Carlos Neto 54crb; Oriol Oliva 58bc; Palinchak 72t; Yooran Park 18cla, 36-37c; Sean Pavone 22cr, 23b, 30crb, 54t, 97b, 122tl, 136b, 136tl; Metropolitan Museum of Art painted gold funerary mask (10th–14th century) from the necropolis of Batán Grande, Peru Gift and Bequest of Alice K. Bache, 1974, 1977 32clb; William Perry 79bl; Prillfoto 52tl; Radekdrewek 26cl, 75c; Rcavalleri 56tl; Sangaku 7cra; Mykhailo Shcherbyna 128br; Shiningcolors 111bl; Marcio Silva 14-bc; Lee Snider 70t; Stockshooter 11tl; Alyaksandr Stzhalkouski 3tl, 76-7; Travnikovstudio 12bl; Tupungato 55tr, 81clb, 146tl; Vacclav 85t; Victorianl 10l, 90tl; Vitalyedush 115t; Gao Wenhao 32–3c; Lei Xu 11cra; Mark Zhu 95cl; Zhukovsky 81tc, 125cl.

The Dutch: Noah Fecks 107cla.

Eataly: Virginia Rollison 119cr.
Economy Candy: 100b.
Freemans/Mediacraft: 101cr.

Getty Images: Andrew Burton 49br; Corbis News / Victor Fraile Rodriguez 38t; Mike Coppola 89cla; Noam Galai 83bl; Kim Grant 61tr; Hulton Archive / Apic 39bl; Siegfried Layda 143tr; Moment / Tony Shi Photography 1; MPI 21tl; Cindy Ord 62t; Stringer/Jason Kempin 65tr; Universal History Archive/ UIG 22tl; Theo Wargo 147bl.

Gramercy Tavern: Daniel Krieger 67clb.

iStockphoto.com: AndreaAstes 93tl; E+/GCShutter 2tl, 8-9, 24–5; JayLazarin 114tl; Joel Carillet 121tl; Heather Shimmin 11crb; Roman Tiraspolsky 129tl.

© Jeff Koons: Tom Powel Imaging 50tl.

Leslie-Lohman Museum of Art: Chitra Ganesh, A city will share her secrets if you know how to ask, 2020, site-specific QUEERPOWER public art installation / Kristine Eudey, 2021 60b.

The Metropolitan Museum of Art: The Harvesters, 1565 by Pieter Bruegel the Elder Rogers Fund, 1919 (19.164) 34cl; Card players (1890) Cezanne, Bequest of Stephen C. Clark, 1960 (61.101.1) 11cl; The Cloisters Collection, 1962 35tl; French silk doublet 1620s The Costume Institute Fund, in memory of Polaire Weissman, 1989 (1989.196) 32–3t; Garden at Sainte–Adresse (1867) by Claude Monet, Purchase, special contributions and funds given or bequeathed by friends of the Museum, 1967 (67.241) 34tr.

New York Philharmonic: Chris Lee 72bl.

Paul Kasmin Gallery: Paul Kasmin Gallery 51br.

The Red Cat: 125cl.

Saks Fifth Avenue: 130bl.

Dorling Kinderlsey 10cb, 16bl, 17tr, 126tl.

Cover

Front and Spine. **Getty Images:** Moment / Tony Shi Photography.

Back: **Alamy Stock Photo:** John Kellerman tr; **Dreamstime.com:** Albachiaraa crb, Ryan Deberardinis tl, Travnikovstudio cla; **Getty Images:** Moment / Tony Shi Photography b.

Pull Out Map Cover
Getty Images: Moment / Tony Shi Photography.

All other images are: © Dorling Kindersley. For further information see www.dkimages.com.

Comissioned Photography: Steven Greaves, Dave King, Tim Knox, Norman McGrath, Michael Moran, Chris Stevens, Rough Guides/Curtis Hamilton, Rough Guides/Nelson Hancock, Rough Guides/Angus Osborn, Rough Guides/Greg Roden, Rough Guides/Susannah Sayler

Penguin
Random
House

First Edition 2002

Published in Great Britain
by Dorling Kindersley Limited,
DK, One Embassy Gardens, 8 Viaduct
Gardens, London SW11 7BW, UK

The authorised representative in the EEA is
Dorling Kindersley Verlag GmbH. Arnulfstr.
124, 80636 Munich, Germany

Published in the United States by
DK Publishing, 1745 Broadway, 20th Floor,
New York, NY 10018, USA

A CIP catalog record is available
from the British Library.

A catalog record for this book is available
from the Library of Congress.

ISSN 1479-344X
ISBN 978-0-2416-2121-9

Printed and bound in Malaysia

www.dk.com

As a guide to abbreviations in visitor information blocks: **Adm** = *admission charge;* **D** = *dinner.*

MIX
Paper | Supporting
responsible forestry
FSC™ C018179

This book was made with Forest
Stewardship Council™ certified
paper – one small step in DK's
commitment to a sustainable future.
**For more information go to
www.dk.com/our-green-pledge**